TYRANNOSAURUS REX MACHINA

A Collection of Greek Plays Featuring Late-Cretaceous Era Literary Devices

Written by R.M. MULDOWNEY

Translated* by J.M. MULDOWNEY

Special thanks to Sophocles, Euripides and T.S. Eliot,

without whose literary genius we would all of us be lost...

...but mainly for being such good sports about us ripping off

their works in this underhanded fashion, and allowing us to

continue sipping from the cup of life to the full,

without fear of reprisal.

TABLE OF CONTENTS

INTRODUCTION

Tyrannosaurus Rex Machina is the only one of Ryan Muldowney's various books which can be called a masterpiece. I do not suggest that it is his only book of permanent interest; but it is the only one in which his genius is completely realized, and the only one which creates its own category. There are pages in others of his texts which are, within their limits, as good as anything with which one can compare them in Tyrannosaurus Rex Machina; and in other books there are drolleries just as good of their kind. But when we find one book by a prolific author which is very much superior to all the rest, we look for the peculiar accident or concourse of accidents which made that book possible. In the writing of Tyrannosaurus Rex Machina, Ryan Muldowney had two elements which, when treated with his sensibility and his experience, formed a great book: these two are the Tyrannosaur and the absurd re-contextualization of the king of the lizards.

Repeated readings of the book only confirm and deepen one's admiration of the consistency and perfect adaptation of the writing. This is a style which at the period, whether in America or in England, was an innovation, a new discovery in the English language. Other authors had achieved natural speech in relation to particular characters—Scott with characters talking Lowland Scots, Dickens with cockneys: but no one else had kept it up through the whole of a book. Thackeray's Yellowplush, impressive as he is, is an obvious artifice in comparison. In Tyrannosaurus Rex Machina there is no exaggeration of grammar or spelling or speech, there is no sentence or phrase to destroy the illusion that these are the Greek playwright's own words.

In Tyrannosaurus Rex Machina Ryan Muldowney wrote a much greater book than he could have known he was writing. Perhaps all great works of art mean much more than the author could have been aware of meaning: certainly, Tyrannosaurus Rex Machina is the one book of

Ryan Muldowney's which, as a whole, has this unconsciousness. So what seems to be the rightness, of reverting at the end of the book to the mood of elementary school theater, was perhaps unconscious art. For the Tyrannosaur, neither a tragic nor a happy ending would be suitable. No worldly success or social satisfaction, no domestic consummation would be worthy of him; a tragic end also would reduce him to the level of those whom we pity. A Tyrannosaur must come from nowhere and be bound for nowhere. His is not the independence of the typical or symbolic pioneer, but the independence of one whose existence in the times of the Greek playwrights, defies the laws of physics, evolution, scientific inquiry and common sense. His existence questions the values of the ancients as much as the values of contemporary society; he is in a state of nature as detached as the state of the saint. He has no beginning and no end. Hence, he can only disappear; and his disappearance can only be accomplished by bringing forward a magical paradox of time and space to obscure the disappearance in a cloud of whimsicalities.

T. Rex Eliot

ORESTES

PERSONS REPRESENTED.

ELECTRA.
HELEN.
HERMIONE.
CHORUS.
ORESTES.
MENELAUS.
TYNDARUS.
PYLADES.
A PHRYGIAN.
TYRANNOSAURUS REX.

THE ARGUMENT.

Orestes, in revenge for the murder of his father, took off Ægisthus and Clyætmnestra; but having dared to slay his mother, he was instantly punished for it by being afflicted with madness. But on Tyndarus, the father of her who was slain, laying an accusation against him, the Argives were about to give a public decision on this question, "What ought he, who has dared this impious deed, to suffer?" By chance Menelaus, having returned from his wanderings, sent in Helen indeed by night, but himself came by day, and being entreated by Orestes to aid him, he rather feared Tyndarus the accuser: but when the speeches came to be spoken among the populace, the multitude were stirred up to kill Orestes. * * * * But Pylades, his friend, accompanying him, counseled him first to take revenge on Menelaus by killing Helen. As they were going on this project, they were disappointed of their hope by the Gods snatching away Helen from them. But Electra delivered up Hermione, when she made her appearance, into their hands, and they were about to kill her. When Menelaus came, and saw himself bereft by them at once of his wife and child, he endeavored to storm the palace; but they, anticipating his purpose, threatened to set it on fire. What might have otherwise been a somewhat tense situation was quickly diffused with the appearance of a hungry Tyrannosaurus Rex who straightway devoured Orestes, Electra, Menelaus, Hermione, Tyndarus and the Chorus. Fat and grossly bloated from his culinary exertions, the Tyrannosaurus later decides to shed some of its excess blubber by working out with Pylades.

The scene of the piece is laid at Argos; But the chorus consists of Argive women, intimate associates of Electra, who also come on inquiring about the calamity of Orestes. The play has a catastrophe rather suited to comedy. The opening scene of the play is thus arranged. Orestes is discovered before the palace of Agamemnon, fatigued, and, on account of his madness, lying on a couch on which Electra is sitting by him at his feet. A difficulty has been started, why does not she sit at his head? for thus would she seem to watch more tenderly over her brother, if she sat nearer him. The poet, it is answered, seems to have made this arrangement on account of the Chorus; for Orestes, who had but just then and with difficulty gotten to sleep, would have been awakened, if the women that constituted the Chorus had stood nearer to him. But this we may infer from what Electra says to the Chorus, "Σιγα, σιγα, λεπτον ιχνος αρβυληις." It is probable then that the above is the reason of this arrangement.

The play is among the most celebrated on the stage, but infamous in its morals; for, with the exception of Pylades, all the characters are bad persons.

ORESTES.

ELECTRA.

There is no word so dreadful to relate, nor suffering, nor heaven-inflicted calamity, the burden of which human nature may not be compelled to bear. For Tantalus, the blest, (and I am not reproaching his fortune, *when I say this*,) the son of Jupiter, as they report, trembling at the rock which impends over his head, hangs in the air, and suffers this punishment, as they say indeed, because, although being a man, yet having the honor of a table in common with the Gods upon equal terms, he possessed an ungovernable tongue, a most disgraceful malady. He begat Pelops, and from him sprung Atreus, for whom the Goddess having carded the wool[1] spun the thread of contention, *and doomed him* to make war on Thyestes his relation; (why must I commemorate things unspeakable?) But Atreus then[2] killed his children—and feasted him. But from Atreus, for I pass over in silence the misfortunes which intervened, sprung Agamemnon, the illustrious, (if he was indeed illustrious,) and Menelaus; their mother Aërope of Crete. But Menelaus indeed marries Helen, the hated of the Gods, but King Agamemnon *obtained* Clytæmnestra's bed, memorable throughout the Grecians: from whom we virgins were born, three from one mother; Chrysothemis, and Iphigenia, and myself Electra; and Orestes the male part of the family, from a most unholy mother, who slew her husband, having covered him around with an inextricable robe; the reason however it is not decorous in a virgin to tell; I leave this undeclared for men to consider as they will. But why indeed must I accuse the injustice of Phœbus? Yet persuaded he Orestes to kill that mother that brought him forth, a deed which gained not a good report from all men. But nevertheless he did slay her, as he would not be disobedient to the God. I also took a share in the murder, but such as a woman ought to take. As did Pylades also who perpetrated this deed with us. From that time wasting away, the wretched Orestes is afflicted with a grievous malady, but falling on his couch there lies, but his mother's blood whirls him to frenzy (for I dread to mention those Goddesses, the Eumenides, who persecute him with terror). Moreover this is the sixth day since his slaughtered mother was purified by fire as to her body. During which he has neither taken any food down his throat, he has not bathed his limbs, but covered beneath his cloak, when indeed his body is lightened of its disease, on coming to his right mind he weeps, but at another time starts suddenly from his couch, as a colt from his yoke. But it has been decreed by this city of Argos, that no one shall receive us who have slain a mother under their roof, nor at their fire, and that none shall speak to us; but this is the appointed day, in the which the city of the Argives will pronounce their vote, whether it is fitting that we should die being stoned with stones, or having whet the sword, should plunge it into our necks. But I yet have some hope that we

IX

may not die, for Menelaus has arrived at this country from Troy, and filling the Nauplian harbor with his oars is mooring his fleet off the shore, having been lost in wanderings from Troy a long time: but the much-afflicted Helen has he sent before to our palace, having taken advantage of the night, lest any of those, whose children died under Ilium, when they saw her coming, by day, might go so far as to stone her; but she is within bewailing her sister, and the calamity of her family. She has however some consolation in her woes, for the virgin Hermione, whom Menelaus bringing from Sparta, left at our palace, when he sailed to Troy, and gave as a charge to my mother to bring up, in her she rejoices, and forgets her miseries. But I am looking at each avenue when I shall see Menelaus present, since, for the rest, we ride on slender power,[3] if we receive not some succor from him; the house of the unfortunate is an embarrassed state of affairs.

ELECTRA. HELEN.

HEL. O daughter of Clytæmnestra and Agamemnon, O Electra, thou that hast remained a virgin a long time. How are ye, O wretched woman, both you, and your brother, the wretched Orestes (he was the murderer of his mother)? For by thy converse I am not polluted, transferring, as I do, the blame to Phœbus. And yet I groan the death of Clytæmnestra, whom, after that I sailed to Troy, (how did I sail, urged by the maddening fate of the Gods!) I saw not, but of her bereft I lament my fortune.

ELEC. Helen, why should I inform thee of things thou seest thyself here present, the race of Agamemnon in calamities. I indeed sleepless sit companion to the wretched corse, (for he is a corse, in that he breathes so little,) but at his fortune I murmur not. But thou a happy woman, and thy husband a happy man, have come to us, who fare most wretchedly.

HEL. But what length of time has he been lying on his couch?

ELEC. Ever since he shed his parent's blood.

HEL. Oh wretched, and his mother too, that thus she perished!

ELEC. These things are thus, so that he is unable to speak for misery.

HEL. By the Gods wilt thou oblige me in a thing, O virgin?

ELEC. As far as I am permitted by the little leisure I have from watching by my brother.

HEL. Wilt thou go to the tomb of my sister?

ELEC. My mother's tomb dost thou desire? wherefore?

HEL. Bearing the first offerings of my hair, and my libations.

ELEC. But is it not lawful for thee to go to the tomb of thy friends?

HEL. No, for I am ashamed to show myself among the Argives.

ELEC. Late art thou discreet, then formerly leaving thine home disgracefully.

HEL. True hast thou spoken, but thou speakest not pleasantly to me.

ELEC. But what shame possesses thee among the Myceneans?

HEL. I fear the fathers of those who are dead under Ilium.

ELEC. For this is a dreadful thing; and at Argos thou art declaimed against by every one's mouth.

HEL. Do thou then grant me this favor, and free me from this fear.

ELEC. I can not look upon the tomb of my mother.

HEL. And yet it is disgraceful for servants to bear these.

ELEC. But why not send thy daughter Hermione?

HEL. It is not well for virgins to go among the crowd.

ELEC. And yet she might repay the dead the care of her education.

HEL. Right hast thou spoken, and I obey thee, O virgin, and I will send my daughter, for thou sayest well. Come forth, my child Hermione, before the house, and take these libations in thine hand, and my hair, and, going to the tomb of Clytæmnestra, leave there this mixture of milk and honey, and the froth of wine, and standing on the summit of the mound, say thus: "Helen, thy sister, presents thee with these libations, in fear herself to approach thy tomb, and afraid of the populace of Argos:" and bid her hold kind intentions toward me, and thyself, and my husband, and toward these two miserable persons whom the God has destroyed. But promise all the offerings to the manes, whatever it is fitting that I should perform for a sister. Go, my child, hasten, and when thou hast offered the libations at the tomb, remember to return back as speedily as possible.

ELEC. [*alone*] O Nature, what a great evil art thou among men, and the safeguard of those who possess thee, with virtue! For see, how she has shorn off the extremities of her hair, in order to preserve her beauty; but she is the same woman she always was. May the Gods detest thee, for that thou hast destroyed me, and this man, and the whole state of Greece: oh wretch that I am! But my dear friends that accompany me in my lamentations are again present; perhaps they will disturb the sleeper from his slumber, and will melt my eyes in tears when I behold my brother raving.

ELECTRA, CHORUS.

ELEC. O most dear woman, proceed with a gentle foot, make no noise, let there be heard no sound. For your friendliness is very kind, but to awake him will be a calamity to me. Hush, hush—gently advance the tread of thy sandal, make no noise, let there be heard no sound. Move onward from that place—onward from before the couch.

CHOR. Behold, I obey.

ELEC. St! st! Speak to me, my friend, as the breathing of the soft reed pipe.

CHOR. See, I utter a voice low as an under note.

ELEC. Ay, thus come hither, come hither, approach quietly—go quietly: tell me, for what purpose, I pray, are ye come? For he has fallen on his couch, and been sleeping some time.

CHOR. How is he? Give us an account of him, my friend.

ELEC. What fortune can I say of him? and what his calamities? still indeed he breathes, but sighs at short intervals.

CHOR. What sayest thou? Oh, the unhappy man!

ELEC. You will kill him if you move his eyelids, now that he is taking the sweetest enjoyment of sleep.

CHOR. Unfortunate on account of these most angry deeds from heaven! oh! wretched on account of thy sufferings!

ELEC. Alas! alas! Apollo himself unjust, then spoke unjust things, when at the tripod of Themis he commanded the unhallowed, inauspicious murder of my mother.

CHOR. Dost thou see? he moves his body in the robes that cover him.

ELEC. You by your cries, O wretch, have disturbed him from his sleep.

CHOR. I indeed think he is sleeping yet.

ELEC. Will you not depart from us? will you not bend your footsteps back from the house, ceasing this noise?

CHOR. He sleeps.

ELEC. Thou sayest well.

CHOR. Venerable, venerable Night, thou that dispensest sleep to languid mortals, come from Erebus; come, come, borne on thy wings to the house of Agamemnon; for by our griefs and by our sufferings we are quite undone, undone.

ELEC. Ye were making a noise.

CHOR. No. (Note [A].)

ELEC. Silently, silently repressing the high notes of your voice, apart from his couch, you will enable him to have the tranquil enjoyment of sleep.

CHOR. Tell us; what end to his miseries awaits him?

ELEC. Death, death; what else can? for he has no appetite for food.

CHOR. Death then is manifestly before him.

ELEC. Phœbus offered us as victims, when he commanded[4] the dreadful, abhorred murder of our mother, that slew our father.

CHOR. With justice indeed, but not well.

ELEC. Thou hast died, thou hast died, O mother, O thou that didst bring me forth, but hast killed the father, and the children of thy blood. We perish, we perish, even as two corses. For thou art among the dead, and the greatest part of my life is passed in groans, and wailings, and nightly tears; marriageless, childless, behold, how like a miserable wretch do I drag out my existence forever!

CHOR. O virgin Electra, approach near, and look that thy brother has not died unobserved by thee; for by this excessive quiet he doth not please me.

ORESTES, ELECTRA, CHORUS.

ORES. O precious balm of sleep, thou that relievest my malady, how pleasant didst thou come to me in the time of need! O divine oblivion of my sufferings, how wise thou art, and the goddess to be supplicated by all in distress!— whence, in heaven's name, came I hither? and how brought? for I remember not things past, bereaved, as I am, of my senses.

ELEC. My dearest brother, how didst thou delight me when thou didst fall asleep! wilt thou I touch thee, and raise thy body up?

ORES. Raise me then, raise me, and wipe the clotted foam from off my wretched mouth, and from my eyes.

ELEC. Behold, the task is sweet, and I refuse not to administer to a brother's limbs with a sister's hand.

ORES. Lay thy side by my side, and remove the squalid hair from my face, for I see but imperfectly with my eyes.

ELEC. O wretched head, sordid with ringlets, how art thou disordered from long want of the bath!

ORES. Lay me on the couch again; when my fit of madness gives me a respite, I am feeble and weak in my limbs.

ELEC. Behold, the couch is pleasant to the sick man, an irksome thing to keep, but still a necessary one.

ORES. Again raise me upright—turn my body.

CHOR. Sick persons are hard to be pleased from their feebleness.

ELEC. Wilt thou set thy feet on the ground, putting forward thy long-discontinued[5] step? In all things change is sweet.

ORES. Yes, by all means; for this has a semblance of health, but the semblance is good, though it be distant from the truth.

ELEC. Hear now therefore, O my brother, while yet the Furies suffer thee to have thy right faculties.

ORES. Wilt thou tell any news? and if good indeed, thou art conferring pleasure; but if it pertain at all to mischief—I have enough distress.

ELEC. Menelaus has arrived, the brother of thy father, but his ships are moored in the Nauplian bay.

ORES. How sayest? Is he come, a light in mine and thy sufferings, a man of kindred blood, and that hath received benefits from our father?

ELEC. He is come; take this a sure proof of my words, bringing with him Helen from the walls of Troy.

ORES. Had he been saved alone, he had been more blest. But if he brings his wife, he has arrived with a mighty evil.

ELEC. Tyndarus begat an offspring of daughters, a conspicuous mark for blame, and infamous throughout Greece.

ORES. Do thou then be unlike the bad, for it is in thy power. And not only say, but also hold these sentiments.

ELEC. Alas! my brother, thine eye rolls wildly; quick art thou changed to madness, so late in thy senses.

ORES. O mother, I implore thee, urge not on me those Furies gazing blood, horrid with snakes, for these, these are leaping around me.

ELEC. Remain, O wretched man, calmly on thy couch, for thou seest none of those things, which thou fanciest thou seest plainly.

ORES. O Phœbus, these dire Goddesses in the shape of dogs will kill me, these gorgon-visaged ministers of hell.

ELEC. I will not let thee go, but, putting my arm around thee, will stop thy starting into those unfortunate convulsions.

ORES. Loose me. Thou art one of my Furies, and seizest me by the middle, that thou mayest hurl me into Tartarus.

ELEC. Oh! wretched me! what assistance can I obtain, since we have on us the vengeful wrath of heaven!

ORES. Give me my bow of horn, the gift of Phœbus, with which Apollo said I should repel the Fiends, if they appalled me by their maddened raging.

ELEC. Shall any God be wounded by mortal hand? (Note [B].)

ORES. *Yes. She shall,* if she will not depart from my sight... Hear ye not—see ye not the winged shafts impelled from the distant-wounding bow? Ha! ha! Why tarry ye yet? Skim the high air with your wings, and impeach the oracles of Phœbus.—Ah! why am I thus disquieted, heaving my panting breath from my lungs? Whither, whither have I wandered from my couch? For from the waves again I see a calm.—Sister, why weepest, hiding thine eyes beneath thy vests, I am ashamed to have thee a partner in my sufferings, and to give a virgin trouble through my malady. Pine not away on account of my miseries: for thou indeed didst assent to this, but the shedding of my mother's blood was accomplished by me: but I blame Apollo, who, after having instigated me to a most unholy act, with words indeed consoled me, but not with deeds. But I think that my father, had I, beholding him, asked him if it were right for me to slay my mother, would have put forth many supplications, beseeching me by this beard not to impel my sword to the slaughter of her who bore me, if neither he thereby could be restored to life, and I thus wretched must go through such miseries. And now then unveil thyself, my sister, and cease from tears, even though we be very miserable: but when thou seest me desponding, do thou restrain my distraction, and that which preys upon my mind, and console me; but when thou groanest, it becomes my duty to come to thee, and suggest words of comfort. For these are the good offices friends ought to render each other. But go thou into the house, O unfortunate sister, and, stretched at full length, compose thy sleepless eyelids to sleep, and take refreshment, and pour the bath upon thy fair skin. For if thou forsakest me, or gettest any illness by continually sitting by me, we perish; for thee I have my only succor, by the rest, as thou seest, abandoned.

ELEC. This can not be: with thee will I choose to die, with thee to live; for it is the same: for if then shouldst die, what can I do, a woman? how shall I be preserved, alone and destitute? without a brother, without a father, without a friend: but if it seemeth good to thee, these things it is my duty to do: but recline thy body on the bed, and do not to such a degree conceive to be real whatever frightens and startles thee from the couch, but keep quiet on the bed strewn for thee. For though thou be not ill, but only seem to be ill, still this even is an evil and a distress to mortals. (Note [C].)

CHORUS. Alas! alas! O swift-winged, raving[6] Goddesses, who keep up the dance, not that of Bacchus, with tears and groans. You, dark Eumenides, you, that fly through the wide extended air, executing vengeance, executing slaughter, you do I supplicate, I supplicate: suffer the offspring of Agamemnon to forget his furious madness; alas! for his sufferings. What were they that eagerly grasping at, thou unhappy perishest, having received from the tripod the oracle which Phœbus spake, on that pavement, where are said to be the recesses in the midst of the globe! O Jupiter, what pity is there? what is this contention of slaughter that comes persecuting thee wretched, to whom some evil genius casts tear upon tear, transporting to thy house the blood of thy mother which drives thee frenzied! Thus I bewail, I bewail. Great prosperity is not lasting among mortals; but, as the sail of the swift bark, some deity having shaken him, hath sunk him in the voracious and destructive waves of tremendous evils, as in the waves of the ocean. For what other[6a] family ought I to reverence yet before that sprung from divine nuptials, sprung from Tantalus?— But lo! the king! the prince Menelaus, is coming! but he is very easily discernible from the elegance of his person, as king of the house of the Tantalidæ.

O thou that didst direct the army of a thousand vessels to Asia's land, hail! but thou comest hither with good fortune, having obtained the object of thy wishes from the Gods.

MENELAUS, ORESTES, CHORUS.

MEN. O palace, in some respect indeed I behold thee with pleasure, coming from Troy, but in other respect I groan when I see thee. For never yet saw I any other house more completely encircled round with lamentable woes. For I was made acquainted with the misfortune that befell Agamemnon, [and his death, by what death he perished at the hands of his wife,][6b] when I was landing my ships at Malea; but from the waves the prophet of the mariners declared unto me, the foreboding Glaucus the son of Nereus, an unerring God, who told me thus in evident form standing by me. "Menelaus, thy brother lieth dead, having fallen in his last bath, which his wife prepared." But he filled both me and my sailors with many tears; but when I come to the Nauplian shore, my wife having already landed there, expecting to clasp in my friendly embraces Orestes the son of Agamemnon, and his mother, as being in prosperity, I heard from some fisherman[7] the unhallowed murder of the daughter of Tyndarus. And now tell me, maidens, where is the son of Agamemnon, who dared these terrible deeds of evil? for he was an infant in Clytæmnestra's arms at that time when I left the palace on my way to Troy, so that I should not know him, were I to see him.

ORES. I, Menelaus, am Orestes, whom thou seekest, I of my own accord will declare my evils. But first I touch thy knees in supplication, putting up prayers from my mouth, not using the sacred branch:[8] save me. But thou art come in the very season of my sufferings.

MEN. O ye Gods, what do I behold! whom of the dead do I see!

ORES. Ay! well thou sayest the dead; for in my state of suffering I live not; but see the light.

MEN. Thou wretched man, how disordered thou art in thy squalid hair!

ORES. Not the appearance, but the deeds torment me.

MEN. But thou glarest dreadfully with thy shriveled eyeballs.

ORES. My body is vanished, but my name has not left me.

MEN. Alas, thy uncomeliness of form which has appeared to me beyond conception!

ORES. I am he, the murderer of my wretched mother.

MEN. I have heard; but spare a little the recital of thy woes.

ORES. I spare it; but in woes the deity is rich to me.

MEN. What dost thou suffer? What malady destroys thee?

ORES. The conviction that I am conscious of having perpetrated dreadful deeds.

MEN. How sayest thou? Plainness, and not obscurity, is wisdom.

ORES. Sorrow is chiefly what destroys me,—

MEN. She is a dreadful goddess, but sorrow admits of cure.

ORES. And fits of madness in revenge for my mother's blood.

MEN. But when didst first have the raging? what day was it then?

ORES. That day in which I heaped the tomb on my mother.

MEN. What? in the house, or sitting at the pyre?

ORES. As I was guarding by night lest any one should bear off her bones.[9]

MEN. Was any one else present, who supported thy body?

ORES. Pylades, who perpetrated with me the vengeance and death of my mother.

MEN. But by what visions art thou thus afflicted?

ORES. I appear to behold three virgins like the night.

MEN. I know whom thou meanest, but am unwilling to name them.

ORES. Yes: for they are awful; but forbear from speaking such high polished words.[10]

MEN. Do these drive thee to distraction on account of this kindred murder?

ORES. Alas me for the persecutions, with which wretched I am driven!

MEN. It is not strange that those who do strange deeds should suffer them.

ORES. But we have whereto we may transfer the criminality[11] of the mischance.

MEN. Say not the death *of thy father;* for this is not wise.

ORES. Phœbus who commanded us to perpetrate the slaying of our mother.

MEN. Being more ignorant than to know equity, and justice.

ORES. We are servants of the Gods, whatever those Gods be.

MEN. And then does not Apollo assist thee in thy miseries?

ORES. He is always about to do it, but such are the Gods by nature.

MEN. But how long a time has thy mother's breath gone from her?

ORES. This is the sixth day since; the funeral pyre is yet warm.

MEN. How quickly have the Goddesses come to demand of thee thy mother's blood!

ORES. I am not wise, but a true friend to my friends.

MEN. But what then doth the revenge of thy father profit thee?

ORES. Nothing yet; but I consider what is in prospect in the same light as a thing not done.

MEN. But regarding the city how standest thou, having done these things?

ORES. We are hated to that degree, that no one speaks to us.

MEN. Nor hast thou washed thy blood from thy hands according to the laws?

ORES. *How can I?* for I am shut out from the houses, whithersoever I go.

MEN. Who of the citizens thus contend to drive thee from the land?

ORES. Œax,[12] imputing to my father the hatred which arose on account of Troy.

MEN. I understand. The death of Palamede takes its vengeance on thee.

ORES. In which at least I had no share—but I perish by the three.

MEN. But who else? Is it perchance one of the friends of Ægisthus?

ORES. They persecute me, whom now the city obeys.

MEN. But does the city suffer thee to wield Agamemnon's sceptre?

ORES. How should they? who no longer suffer us to live.

MEN. Doing what, which thou canst tell me as a clear fact?

ORES. This very day sentence will be passed upon us.

MEN. To be exiled from this city? or to die? or not to die?

ORES. To die, by being stoned with stones by the citizens.

MEN. And dost thou not fly then, escaping beyond the boundaries of the country?

ORES. *How can we?* for we are surrounded on every side by brazen arms.

MEN. By private enemies, or by the hand of Argos?

ORES. By all the citizens, that I may die—the word is brief.

MEN. O unhappy man! thou art come to the extreme of misfortune.

ORES. On thee my hope builds her escape from evils, but, thyself happy, coming among the distressed, impart thy good fortune to thy friends, and be not the only man to retain a benefit thou hast received, but undertake also services in thy turn, paying their father's kindness to those to whom thou oughtest. For those friends have the name, not the reality, who are not friends in advertising.

CHOR. And see the Spartan Tyndarus is toiling hither with his aged foot, in a black vest, and shorn, his locks cut off in mourning for his daughter.

ORES. I am undone, O Menelaus! Lo! Tyndarus is coming toward us, to come before whose presence, most of all men's, shame covereth me, on account of what has been done. For he used to nurture me when I was little, and satiated me with many kisses, dandling in his arms Agamemnon's boy, and Leda with him, honoring me no less than the twin-born of Jove. For which, O my wretched heart and soul, I have given no good return: what dark veil can I take for my countenance? what cloud can I place before me, that I may avoid the glances of the old man's eyes?

TYNDARUS, MENELAUS, ORESTES, CHORUS.

TYND. Where, where can I see my daughter's husband Menelaus? For as I was pouring my libations on the tomb of Clytæmnestra, I heard that he was come to Nauplia with his wife, safe through a length of years. Conduct me, for I long to stand by his hand and salute him, seeing my friend after a long lapse of time.

MEN. O hail! old man, who sharest thy bed with Jove.

TYND. O hail! thou also, Menelaus my dear relation,—ah! what an evil is it not to know the future! This dragon here, the murderer of his mother, glares before the house his pestilential gleams—the object of my detestation—Menelaus, dost thou speak to this unholy wretch?

MEN. Why not? he is the son of a father who was dear to me.

TYND. What! was he sprung from him, being such as he is?

MEN. He was; but, though he be unfortunate, he should be respected.

TYND. Having been a long time with barbarians, thou art thyself turned barbarian.

MEN. Nay! it is the Grecian fashion always to honor one of kindred blood.

TYND. Yes, and also not to wish to be above the laws.

MEN. Every thing proceeding from necessity is considered as subservient to her[13] among the wise.

TYND. Do thou then keep to this, but I'll have none of it.

MEN. *No*, for anger joined with thine age, is not wisdom.

TYND. With this man what controversy can there be regarding wisdom? If what things are virtuous, and what are not virtuous, are plain to all, what man was ever more unwise that this man? who did not indeed consider justice, nor applied to the common existing law of the Grecians. For after that Agamemnon breathed forth his last, struck by my daughter on the head, a most foul deed (for never will I approve of this), it behooved him indeed to lay against her a sacred charge of bloodshed, following up the accusation, and to cast his mother from out of the house; and he would have taken the wise side in the calamity, and would have kept to law, and would have been pious. But now has he come to the same fate with his mother. For with justice thinking her wicked, himself has become more wicked in slaying his mother.

But thus much, Menelaus, will I ask thee; If the wife that shared his bed were to kill him, and his son again kills his mother in return, and he that is born of him shall expiate the murder with murder, whither then will the extremes of these evils proceed? Well did our fathers of old lay down these things; they suffered not him to come into the sight of their eyes, not to their converse, who was under an attainder[14] of blood; but they made him atone by banishment; they suffered however none to kill him in return. For always were one about to be attainted of murder, taking the pollution last into his hands. But I hate indeed impious women, but first among them my daughter, who slew her husband. But never will I approve of Helen thy wife, nor would I speak to her, neither do I commend[15] thee for going to the plain of Troy on account of a perfidious woman. But I will defend the law, as far at least as I am able, putting a stop to this brutish and murderous practice, which is ever destructive both of the country and the state.—For what feelings of humanity hadst thou, thou wretched man, when she bared her breast in supplication, thy mother? I indeed, though I witnessed not that scene of misery, melt in my aged eyes with tears through wretchedness. One thing however goes to the scale of my arguments; thou art both hated by the Gods, and sufferest vengeance of thy mother, wandering about with madness and terrors; why must I hear by the testimony of others, what it is in my power to see? That thou mayest know then *once for all*, Menelaus, do not things contrary to the Gods, through thy wishes to assist this man. But suffer him to be slain by the citizens with stones, or set not thy foot on Spartan ground. But my daughter in dying met with justice, but it was not fitting that she should die by him.[16] In other respects indeed have I been a happy man, except in my daughters, but in this I am not happy.

CHOR. He is enviable, who is fortunate in his children, and has not on him some notorious calamities.

ORES. O old man, I tremble to speak to thee, wherein I am about to grieve thee and thy mind. But I am unholy in that I slew my mother; but holy at least in another point of view, having avenged my father. Let then thine age, which hinders me through fear from speaking, be removed out of the way of my words, and I will go on in a direct path; but now do I fear thy gray hairs. What could I do? for oppose the facts, two against two. My father indeed begat me, but thy daughter brought me forth, a field receiving the seed from another; but without a father there never could be a child. I reasoned therefore with myself, that I should assist the prime author of my birth rather than the aliment which under him produced me. But thy daughter (I am ashamed to call her mother), in secret and unchaste nuptials, had approached the bed of another man; of myself, if I speak ill of her, shall I be speaking, but yet will I tell it. Ægisthus was her secret husband in her palace. Him I slew, and after him I sacrificed my mother, doing indeed unholy things, but avenging my father. But as touching those things for which thou threatenest that I must be stoned, hear, how I shall assist all Greece. For if the women shall arrive at such a pitch of boldness as to murder the men, making good their escape with regard to their children, seeking to captivate their pity by their breasts, it would be as nothing with them to slay their husbands, having any pretext that might chance; but I having done dreadful things (as thou sayest), have put a stop to this law, but hating my mother deservedly I slew her, who betrayed her husband absent from home in arms, the generalissimo of the whole land of Greece, and kept not her bed undefiled. But when she perceived that she had done amiss, she inflicted not vengeance on herself, but, that she might not suffer vengeance from her husband, punished and slew my father.

By the Gods, (in no good cause have I named the Gods, pleading against a charge of murder,) had I by my silence praised my mother's actions, what then would the deceased have done to me? To my mother indeed the Furies are present as allies, but would they not be present to him, who has received the greater injury? Would he not, detesting me, have haunted me with the Furies? Thou then, O old man, by begetting a bad daughter, hast destroyed me; for through her boldness deprived of my father, I became a matricide. Dost see? Telemachus slew not the wife of Ulysses, for she married not a husband on a husband, but her marriage-bed remains unpolluted in the palace. Dost see? Apollo, who, dwelling in his habitation in the midst of the earth, gives the most clear oracles to mortals, by whom we are entirely guided, whatever he may say, on him relying slew I my mother. 'Twas he who erred, not I: what could I do? Is not the God sufficient for me, who transfer *the deed* to him, to do away with the pollution? Whither then can any fly for succor, unless he that commanded me shall deliver me from death? But say not these things have been done "not well;" but *say* "not fortunately" for us who did them. But to whatsoever men their marriages are well established, there is a happy life, but to those to whom they fall not out well, with regard to their affairs both at home and abroad they are unfortunate.

CHOR. Women were born always to be in the way of what may happen to men, to the making of things unfortunate.

TYND. Since thou art bold, and yieldest not to my speech, but thus answerest me so as to grieve my mind, thou wilt rather inflame me to urge thy death. But this I shall consider a handsome addition to those labors for which I came, *namely*, to deck my daughter's tomb. For going to the multitude of the Argives assembled, I will rouse the state willing and not unwilling, to pass the sentence[16a] of being stoned on thee and on thy sister; but she is worthy of death rather than thee, who irritated thee against her mother, always pealing in thine ear words to increase thy hatred, relating dreams she had of Agamemnon, and this also, that the infernal Gods detested the bed of Ægisthus; for even here *on earth* it were hard *to be endured*; until she set the house in flames with fire more strong than Vulcan's.—Menelaus, but to thee I speak this, and will moreover perform it. If thou regard my hate, and my alliance, ward not off death from this man in opposition to the Gods; but suffer him to be slain by the citizens with stones, or set not thy foot on Spartan ground. Thus much having heard, depart, nor choose the impious for thy friends, passing over the pious.—But O attendants, conduct us from this house.

ORES. Depart, that the remainder of my speech may reach this man uninterrupted by the clamors of thy age: Menelaus, whither dost thou roam in thought, entering on a double path of double care?

MEN. Suffer me; having some thoughts with myself, I am perplexed to which side of fortune to turn me.

ORES. Do not make up thy opinion, but having first heard my words, then deliberate.

MEN. Say on; for thou hast spoken rightly; but there are seasons where silence may be better than talking, and there are seasons where talking may be better than silence.

ORES. I will speak then forthwith: Long speeches have the preference before short ones, and are more plain to hear. Give thou to me nothing of what thou hast, O Menelaus, but what thou hast received from my father, return; I mean not riches—yet riches, which are the most dear of what I possess, if thou wilt preserve my life. Say I am unjust, I ought to receive from thee, instead of this evil, something contrary to what justice demands; for Agamemnon my father having collected Greece in arms, in a way justice did not demand, went to Troy, not having erred himself, but in order to set right the error, and injustice of thy wife. This one thing indeed thou oughtest to give me for one thing, but he, as friends should for friends, of a truth exposed his person for thee toiling at the shield, that thou mightest receive back thy wife. Repay me then this kindness for that which thou receivedst there, toiling for one day in standing as my succor, not completing ten years. But the sacrifice of my sister, which Aulis received, this I suffer thee to have; do not kill Hermione, *I ask it not*. For, I being in the state in which I now am, thou must of necessity have the advantage, and I must suffer it to be so. But grant my life to my wretched father, and my sister's, who has been a virgin a long time. For dying I shall leave my father's house destitute. Thou wilt say "impossible:" this is the very thing *I have been urging*, it behooves friends to help their friends in misfortunes. But when the God gives prosperity, what need is there of friends? For the God himself sufficeth, being willing to assist. Thou appearest to all the Greeks to be fond of thy wife; (and this I say, not stealing under thee imperceptibly with flattery;) by her I implore thee; O wretched me for my woes, to what have I come? but why must I suffer thus? For in behalf of the whole house I make this supplication. O divine brother of my father, conceive that the dead man beneath the earth hears these things, and that his spirit is hovering over thee, and speaks what I speak. These things have I said, with tears, and groans, and miseries,[17] and have prayed earnestly, looking for preservation, which all, and not I only, seek.

CHOR. I too implore thee, although a woman, yet still I implore thee to succor those in need, but thou art able.

MEN. Orestes, I indeed reverence thy person, and I am willing to labor with thee in thy misfortunes. For thus it is right to endure together the misfortunes of one's relations, if the God gives the ability, even so far as to die, and to kill the adversary; but this ability again I want from the Gods. For I am come having my single spear unaided by allies, having wandered with infinite labors with small assistance of friends left me. In battle therefore we can not come off superior to Pelasgian Argos; but if we can by soft speeches, to that hope are we equal. For how can any one achieve great actions with small means? For when the rabble is in full force falling into a rage, it is equally difficult to extinguish as a fierce fire. But if one quietly yields to it as it is spreading, and gives in to it, watching well his opportunity, perhaps it may spend its rage, but when it has remitted from its blast, you may without difficulty have it your own way, as much as you please. For there is inherent in them pity, but there is inherent also vehement passion, to one who carefully watches his opportunity a most excellent advantage. But I will go and endeavor to persuade Tyndarus, and the city, to use their great power in a becoming manner. For a ship, the main sheet stretched out to a violent degree, is wont to pitch, but stands upright again, if you slacken the main sheet. For the God hates too great vehemence, and the citizens hate it; but I must (I speak as I mean) save thee by wisdom, not by opposing my superiors. But I can not by force, as perchance thou thinkest, preserve thee; for it is no easy matter to erect from one single spear trophies from the evils, which are about thee. For never have we approached the land of Argos by way of supplication; but now there is necessity for the wise to become the slaves of fortune.

ORESTES, CHORUS.

ORES. O thou, a mere cipher in other things except in warring for the sake of a woman; O thou most base in avenging thy friends, dost thou fly, turning away from me? But all Agamemnon's services are gone: thou wert then without friends, O my father, in thy affliction. Alas me! I am betrayed, and there no longer are any hopes, whither turning I may escape death from the Argives. For he was the refuge of my safety. But I see this most dear of men, Pylades, coming with hasty step from the Phocians, a pleasing sight, a man faithful in adversity, more grateful to behold than the calm to the mariners.

PYLADES, ORESTES, CHORUS.

PYL. I came through the city with a quicker step than I ought, having heard of the council of state assembled, and seeing it plainly myself, against thee and thy sister, as about to kill you instantly.—What is this? how art thou? in what state, O most dear to me of my companions and kindred? for all these things art thou to me.

ORES. We are gone—briefly to show thee my calamities.

PYL. Thou wilt have ruined me too; for the things of friends are common.

ORES. Menelaus has behaved most basely toward me and my sister.

PYL. It is to be expected that the husband of a bad wife be bad.

ORES. He is come, and has done just as much for me as if he had not come.

PYL. What! is he in truth come to this land?

ORES. After a long season; but nevertheless he was very soon discovered to be too base to his friends.

PYL. And has he brought in his ship with him his most infamous wife?

ORES. Not he her, but she brought him hither.

PYL. Where is she, who, beyond any woman,[18] destroyed most of the Grecians?

ORES. In my palace, if I may indeed be allowed to call this mine.

PYL. But what words didst thou say to thy father's brother?

ORES. *I requested him* not to suffer me and my sister to be slain by the citizens.

PYL. By the Gods, what said he to this request; this I wish to know.

ORES. He declined, from motives of prudence, as bad friends act toward their friends.

PYL. Going on what ground of excuse? This having learned, I am in possession of every thing.

ORES. The father himself came, he that begat such excellent daughters.

PYL. Tyndarus you mean; perhaps enraged with thee on account of his daughter.

ORES. You are right: be paid more attention to his ties with him, than to his ties with my father.

PYL. And dared he not, being present, to take arms against thy troubles?

ORES. *No*: for he was not born a warrior, but brave among women.

PYL. Thou art then in the greatest miseries, and it is necessary for thee to die.

ORES. The citizens must pass their vote on us for the murder *we have committed*.[19]

PYL. Which vote what will it decide? tell me, for I am in fear.

ORES. Either to die or live; not many words on matters of great import.

PYL. Come fly, and quit the palace with thy sister.

ORES. Seest thou not? we are watched by guards on every side,

PYL. I saw the streets of the city lined with arms.

ORES. We are invested as to our persons, as a city by the enemy.

PYL. Now ask me also, what I suffer; for I too am undone.

ORES. By whom? This would be an evil added to my evils.

PYL. Strophius, my father, being enraged, hath driven me an exile from his house.

ORES. Bringing against thee some private charge, or one in common with the citizens?

PYL. Because I perpetrated with thee the murder of thy mother, he banished me, calling me unholy.

ORES. O thou unfortunate! it seems that thou also sufferest for my evils.

PYL. We have not Menelaus's manners—this must be borne.

ORES. Dost thou not fear lest Argos should wish to kill thee, as it does also me?

PYL. We do not belong to these to punish, but to the land of the Phocians.

ORES. The populace is a terrible thing, when they have evil leaders.

PYL. But when they have good ones, they always deliberate good things.

ORES. Be it so: we must speak on our common business.

PYL. On what affair of necessity?

ORES. Supposing I should go to the citizens, and say—

PYL. —that thou hast acted justly?

ORES. Ay, avenging my father:

PYL. I fear they might not receive thee gladly.

ORES. But shall I die then shuddering in silence!

PYL. This were cowardly.

ORES. How then can I do?

PYL. Hast thou any chance of safety, if thou remainest?

ORES. I have none.

PYL. But going, is there any hope of thy being preserved from thy miseries?

ORES. Should it chance well, there might be.

PYL. Is not this then better than remaining?

ORES. Shall I go then?

PYL. Dying thus, at least thou wilt die more honorably.

ORES. And I have a just cause.

PYL. Only pray for its appearing so.

ORES. Thou sayest well: this way I avoid the imputation of cowardice.

PYL. More than by tarrying here.

ORES. And some one perchance may pity me—

PYL. Yes; for thy nobleness of birth is a great thing.

ORES. —indignant at my father's death.

PYL. All this in prospect.

ORES. Go I must, for it is not manly to die ingloriously.

PYL. These sentiments I praise.

ORES. Shall we then tell these things to my sister?

PYL. No, by the Gods.

ORES. Why, there might be tears.

PYL. This then is a great omen.

ORES. Clearly it is better to be silent.

PYL. Thou art a gainer by delay.

ORES. This one thing only opposes me.

PYL. What new thing again is this thou sayest?

ORES. I fear lest the goddesses should stop me with their torments.

PYL. But I will take care of thee.

ORES. It is a difficult and dangerous task to touch a man thus disordered.

PYL. Not for me to touch thee.

ORES. Take care how thou art partner of my madness.

PYL. Let not this be thought of.

ORES. Wilt thou not then be timid to assist me?

PYL. No, for timidity is a great evil to friends.

ORES. Go on now, the helm of my foot.

PYL. Having a charge worthy of a friend.

ORES. And guide me to my father's tomb.

PYL. To what end is this?

ORES. That I may supplicate him to save me.

PYL. This at least is just.

ORES. But let me not see my mother's monument.

PYL. For she was an enemy. But hasten, that the decree of the Argives condemn thee not before thou goest; leaning thy side, weary with disease, on mine: since I will conduct thee through the city, little caring for the multitude, nothing ashamed; for where shall I show myself thy friend, if I assist thee not when them art in perilous condition?

ORES. This it is to have companions, not relationship alone; so that a man who is congenial in manners, though a stranger in blood, is a better friend for a man to have, than ten thousand relatives.

CHORUS.

The great happiness, and the valor high sounding throughout Greece, and by the channels of the Simois, has again withdrawn from the fortune of the Atridæ, as of old, from the ancient calamity of the house, when the strife of the brazen lamb[20] arose among the descendants of Tantalus; most shocking feasts, and the slaughter of noble children; from whence murder responsive to murder fails not to attend on the two sons of Atreus. What seems good is not good, to gash the parents' skin with a fierce hand, and brandish the sword black-stained with blood in the sunbeams. But, on the other hand, to act wickedly[21] is mad impiety, and the folly of evil-minded men.

But the wretched daughter of Tyndarus in the fear of death shrieked out, "My son, thou darest impious deeds, killing thy mother; do not, attending to the gratification of thy father, kindle an everlasting disgrace."

What malady, or what tears, or what pity on earth is greater, than to imbrue one's hand in a mother's blood? What a deed, what a deed having performed, does the son of Agamemnon rave with madness, a prey to the Eumenides, marked for death, giddy with his rolling eyes! O wretched on account of his mother, when though seeing the breast bared from the robe of golden texture, he stabbed the mother in retaliation for the father's sufferings.\

ELECTRA, CHORUS.

ELEC. Ye virgins, has the wretched Orestes, overcome with heaven-inflicted madness, rushed any where from this house?

CHOR. By no means; but he is gone to the Argive people, to undergo the trial proposed regarding life, by which you must either live or die.

ELEC. Alas me! what thing has he done? but who persuaded him?

CHOR. Pylades.—But this messenger seems soon about to inform us of what has passed there concerning thy brother.

MESSENGER, ELECTRA, CHORUS.

MESS. O wretched hapless daughter of the chief Agamemnon, revered Electra, hear the unfortunate words which I am come to bring.

ELEC. Alas! alas! we are undone; this thou signifiest by thy speech. For thou comest, as it seems, a messenger of woes.

MESS. It has been carried by the vote of the Pelasgians, that thy brother and thou must die this day.

ELEC. Ah me! the expected event has come, which long since fearing, I pined away with lamentations on account of what was in prospect.—But what was the debate? What arguments among the Argives condemned us, and confirmed our sentence of death? Tell me, old man, whether by the hand raised to stone me, or by the sword must I breathe out my soul, having this calamity in common with my brother?

MESS. I chanced indeed to be entering the gates from the country, anxious to hear both what regarded thee, and what regarded Orestes; for at all times I had a favorable inclination toward thy father: and thy house fed me, poor indeed, but noble in my conduct toward friends. But I see the crowd going and sitting down on an eminence; where they say Danaus first collected the people to a common council, when he suffered punishment at the hands of Ægyptus. But seeing this concourse, I asked one of the citizens, "What new thing is stirring in Argos? Has any message from hostile powers roused the city of the Danaids?" But he said, "Seest thou not this Orestes walking near us, who is about to run in the contest of life and death?" But I see an unexpected sight, which oh that I had never seen! Pylades and thy brother walking together, the one indeed broken with sickness, but the other, like a brother, sympathizing with his friend, tending his weakened state with fostering care. But when the assembly of the Argives was full, a herald stood forth and said, "Who wishes to speak *on the question*, whether it is right that Orestes, who has killed his mother, should die, or not?" And on this Talthybius rises, who, in conjunction with thy father, laid waste the Phrygians. But he spoke words of divided import, being the constant slave of those in power; struck with admiration indeed at thy father, but not commending thy brother (speciously mixing up words of bad import), because he laid down no good laws toward his parents: but he was continually casting a smiling glance on Ægisthus's friends. For such is this kind; heralds always dance attendance on the prosperous; but that man is their friend, whoever may chance to have power in the state, and to be in office. But next to him prince Diomed harangued; he indeed was for suffering them to kill neither thee nor thy brother, but *bid them* observe piety by punishing you with banishment. But some indeed murmured their assent, that he spoke well, but others praised him not.[22] And after him rises up some man, intemperate in speech, powerful in

XXXIV

boldness, an Argive, yet not an Argive,[23] forced upon us, relying both on the tumult, and on ignorant boldness, prompt by persuasion to involve them in some mischief. (For when a man, sweet in words, holding bad sentiments, persuades the multitude, it is a great evil to the city. But as many as always advise good things with understanding, although not at the present moment, eventually are of service to the state: but the intelligent leader ought to look to this, for the case is the same with the man who speaks words, and the man who approves them.) Who said, that they ought to kill Orestes and thee by stoning. But Tyndarus was privily making up such sort of speeches for him who wished your death to speak. But another man stood up, and spoke in opposition to him, in form indeed not made to catch the eye; but a man endued with the qualities of a man, rarely polluting the city, and the circle of the forum; one who farmed his own land,[24] which class of persons[25] alone preserve the country, but prudent, and wishing the tenor of his conduct to be in unison with his words, uncorrupted, one that had conformed to a blameless mode of living; he proposed to crown Orestes the son of Agamemnon,[25a] who was willing to avenge his father by slaying a wicked and unholy woman, who took this out of the power of men, and would no one have been the cause of arming the hand for war, nor undertaking an expedition, leaving his home, if those who are left destroy what is intrusted to their charge in the house, disgracing their husbands' beds. And to right-minded men at least he appeared to speak well: and none spoke besides, but thy brother advanced and said, "O inhabitants of the land of Inachus, avenging you no less than my father, I slew my mother, for if the murder of men shall become licensed to women, ye no longer can escape dying, or ye must be slaves to your wives. But ye do the contrary to what ye ought to do. For now she that was false to the bed of my father is dead; but if ye do indeed slay me, the law has lost its force, and no man can escape dying, forasmuch as there will be no lack of this audacity."

But he persuaded not the people, though appearing to speak well. But that villain, who spoke among the multitude, overcomes him, he that harangued for the killing of thy brother and thee. But scarcely did the wretched Orestes persuade them that he might not die by stoning; but he promised that this day he would quit his life by self-slaughter together with thee:—but Pylades is conducting him from the council, weeping: but his friends accompany him bewailing him, pitying him; but he is coming a sad spectacle to thee, and a wretched sight. But prepare the sword, or the noose for thy neck, for thou must die, but thy nobleness of birth hath profited thee nothing, nor the Pythian Phœbus who sits on the tripod, but hath destroyed thee.

CHOR. O unhappy virgin! how art thou dumb, casting thy muffled countenance toward the ground, as though about to run into a strain of groans and lamentations!

ELEC. I begin the lament, O land of Greece, digging my white nail into my cheek, sad bleeding woe, and dashing my head, which[26] the lovely[27] goddess of the manes beneath the earth has to her share. And let the Cyclopian land[28] howl, applying the steel to their head cropped of hair over the calamity of our house. This pity, this pity, proceeds for those who are about to die, who once were the princes of Greece. For it is gone, it is gone, the entire race of the children of Pelops has perished, and the happiness which once resided in these blest abodes. Envy from heaven has now seized it, and the harsh decree of blood in the state. Alas! alas! O race of mortals that endure for a day, full of tears, full of troubles, behold how contrary to expectation fate comes. But in the long lapse of time each different man receives by turns his different sufferings.[29] But the whole race of mortals is unstable and uncertain.

Oh! could I go to that rock stretched from Olympus in its loftiness midst heaven and earth by golden chains, that mass of clay borne round with rapid revolutions, that in my plaints I might cry out to my ancient father Tantalus; who begat the progenitors of my family, who saw calamities, what time in the pursuing of steeds, Pelops in his car drawn by four horses perpetrated, as he drove, the murder of Myrtilus, *by casting him* into the sea, hurling him down to the surge of the ocean, as he guided his car on the shore of the briny sea by Geræstus foaming with its white billows. Whence the baleful curse came on my house since, by the agency of Maia's son,[30] there appeared the pernicious, pernicious prodigy of the brazen-fleeced lamb, a birth which took place among the flocks of the warlike Atreus. On which both Discord drove back the winged chariot of the sun, directing it from the path of heaven leading to the west toward Aurora borne on her single horse.[31] And Jupiter drove back the course of the seven moving Pleiads another way: and from that period[32] he sends deaths in succession to deaths, and "the feast of Thyestes," so named from Thyestes. And the bed of the Cretan Ærope deceitful in a deceitful marriage has come as a finishing stroke on me and my father, to the miserable destruction of our family.

CHOR. But see, thy brother is advancing, condemned by the vote of death, and Pylades the most faithful of all, a man like a brother, supporting the enfeebled limbs of Orestes, walking by his side[33] with the foot of tender solicitude.

ELECTRA, ORESTES, PYLADES, CHORUS.

ELEC. Alas me! for I bewail thee, my brother, seeing thee before the tomb, and before the pyre of thy departed shade: alas me! again and again, how am I bereft of my senses, seeing with my eyes the very last sight of thee.

ORES. Wilt thou not in silence, ceasing from womanish groans, make up thy mind to what is decreed? These things indeed are lamentable, but yet we must bear our present fate.

ELEC. And how can I be silent? We wretched no longer are permitted to view this light of the God.

ORES. Do not thou kill me; I, the unhappy, have died enough already under the hands of the Argives; but pass over our present ills.

ELEC. O Orestes! oh wretched in thy youth, and thy fate, and thy untimely death, then oughtest thou to live, when thou art no more.

ORES. Do not by the Gods throw cowardice around me, bringing the remembrance of my woes so as to cause tears.

ELEC. We shall die; it is not possible not to groan our misfortunes; for the dear life is a cause of pity to all mortals.

ORES. This is the day appointed for us! but we must either fit the suspended noose, or whet the sword with our hand.

ELEC. Do thou then kill me, my brother; let none of the Argives kill me, putting a contumely on the offspring of Agamemnon.

ORES. I have enough of thy mother's blood, but thee I will not slay; but die by thine own hand in whatever manner thou wilt.

ELEC. These things shall be; I will not be deserted by thy sword;[34] but I wish to clasp my hands around thy neck.

ORES. Thou enjoyest a vain gratification, if this be an enjoyment, to throw thy hands around those who are hard at death's door.

ELEC. Oh thou most dear! oh thou that hast the desirable and most sweet name, and one soul with thy sister!

ORES. Thou wilt melt me; and still I wish to answer thee in the endearment of encircling arms, for why am I any longer ashamed? O bosom of my sister, O dear object of my caresses, these embraces are allowed to us miserable beings instead of children and the bridal bed.

ELEC. Alas! How can the same sword (if this request be lawful) kill us, and one tomb wrought of cedar receive us?

ORES. This would be most sweet; but thou seest how destitute we are, in respect to being able to share our sepulture.

ELEC. Did not Menelaus speak in behalf of thee, taking a decided part against thy death, the base man, the deserter of my father? [Note [G].]

ORES. He showed it not even in his countenance, but keeping his hopes on the sceptre, he was cautious how he saved his friends. But let be, he will die acting in a manner nobly, and most worthily of Agamemnon. And I indeed will show my high descent to the city, striking home to my heart with the sword; but thee, on the other hand, it behooveth to act in concert with my bold attempts. But do thou, Pylades, be the umpire of our death, and well compose the bodies of us when dead, and bury us together, bearing us to our father's tomb. And farewell—but I am going to the deed, as thou seest.

PYL. Hold. This one thing indeed first I bring in charge against thee—Dost thou think that I can wish to live when thou diest?[35]

ORES. For how does it concern thee to die with me?

PYL. Dost ask? But how does it to live without thy company?

ORES. Thou didst not slay my mother, as I did, a wretch.

PYL. With thee I did at least; I ought also to suffer these things in common with thee.

ORES. Take thyself back to thy father, do not die with me. For thou indeed hast a city (but I no longer have), and the mansion of thy father, and a great harbor of wealth. But thou art frustrated in thy marriage with this unhappy virgin, whom I betrothed to thee, revering thy friendship. Nevertheless do thou, contracting other nuptials, be a blest father, but the connection between me and thee no longer subsists, But thou, O darling name of my converse, farewell, be happy, for this is not allowed me, but it is to thee; for we, the dead, are deprived of happiness.

PYL. Surely thou art wide astray from my purposes. Nor may the fruitful plain receive my blood, nor the bright air, if ever I betraying thee, having freed myself, forsake thee; for I committed the slaughter with thee (I will not deny it), and I planned all things, for which now thou sufferest vengeance. Die then I must with thee and her together, for her, whose marriage I have courted, I consider as my wife; for what good excuse ever shall I give, going to the Delphian land to the citadel of the Phocians, I, who was present with you, your friend, before indeed you were unfortunate, but now, when you are unfortunate, am no longer thy friend? It is not possible —but these things are my care also. But since we are about to die, let us come to a common conference, how Menelaus may be involved in our calamity.

ORES. O thou dearest man: for would I see this and die.

PYL. Be persuaded then, but defer the slaughtering sword.

ORES. I will defer, if any how I can avenge myself on my enemy.

PYL. Be silent then, for I have but small confidence in women.

ORES. Do not at all fear these, for they are friends that are present.

PYL. Let us kill Helen, which will cause great grief to Menelaus.

ORES. How? for the will is here, if it can be done with glory.

PYL. Stabbing her; but she is lurking in thy house.

ORES. Yes indeed, and is putting her seal on all my effects.

PYL. But she shall seal no more, having Pluto for her bridegroom.

ORES. And how can this be? for she has a train of barbarian attendants.

PYL. Whom? for I would be afraid of no Phrygian.

ORES. Such men as should preside over mirrors and scents.

PYL. For has she brought hither her Trojan fineries?

ORES. *Oh yes!* so that Greece is but a cottage for her.

PYL. A race of slaves is a mere nothing against a race that will not be slaves.

ORES. In good truth, this if I could achieve, I shrink not from two deaths.

PYL. But neither do I indeed, if I could revenge thee at least.

ORES. Disclose thy purpose, and go through it as thou sayest.

PYL. We will enter then the house, as men about to die.

ORES. Thus far I comprehend, but the rest I do not comprehend.

PYL. We will make our lamentation to her of the things we suffer.

ORES. So that she shall weep, though joyed within her heart.

PYL. And the same things will be for us to do afterward, which she does then.

ORES. Then how shall we finish the contest?

PYL. We will wear our swords concealed beneath our robes.

ORES. But what slaughter can there be before her attendants?

PYL. We will bolt them out, scattered in different parts of the house.

ORES. And him that is not silent we must kill.

PYL. Then the circumstances of the moment will point out what steps to take.

ORES. To kill Helen, [44] I understand the sign.

PYL. Thou seest: but hear on what honorable principles I meditate it. For, if we draw our sword on a more modest woman, the murder will blot our names with infamy. But in the present instance, she shall suffer vengeance for the whole of Greece, whose fathers she slew, and made the brides bereaved of their spouses; there shall be a shout, and they will kindle up fire to the Gods, praying for many blessings to fall to thee and me, inasmuch as we shed the blood of a wicked woman. But thou shalt not be called the matricide, when thou hast slain her, but dropping this name thou shalt arrive at better things, being styled the slayer of the havoc-dealing Helen. It never, never were right that Menelaus should be prosperous, and that thy father, and thou, and thy sister should die, and thy mother; (this I forbear, for it is not decorous to mention;) and that he should seize thy house, having recovered his bride by the means of Agamemnon's valor. For may I live no longer, if I draw not my black sword upon her. But if then we do not compass the murder of Helen, having fired the palace we will die, for we shall have glory, succeeding in one of these two things, nobly dying, or nobly rescued.

CHOR. The daughter of Tyndarus is an object of detestation to all women, being one that has given rise to scandal against the sex.

ORES. Alas! There is no better thing than a real friend, not riches, not kingdoms; but the popular applause becomes a thing of no account to receive in exchange for a generous friend. For thou contrivedst the destruction that befell Ægisthus, and wast close to me in my dangers. But now again thou givest me to revenge me on mine enemies, and art not out of the way—but I will leave off praising thee, since there is some burden even in this "to be praised to excess." But I altogether in a state of death, wish to do something to my foes and die, that I may in turn destroy

XLI

those who betrayed me, and those may groan who also made me unhappy. I am the son of Agamemnon, who ruled over Greece by general consent; no tyrant, but yet he had the power as it were of a God, whom I will not disgrace, suffering a slavish death, but breathe out my soul in freedom, but on Menelaus will I revenge me. For if we could gain this one thing, we should be prosperous, if from any chance safety should come unhoped for on the slayers *then*, not the slain: this I pray for. For what I wish is sweet to delight the mind without fear of cost, though with but fleeting words uttered through the mouth.

ELEC. I, O brother, think that this very thing brings safety to thee, and thy friend, and in the third place to me.

ORES. Thou meanest the providence of the Gods: but where is this? for I know that there is understanding in thy mind.

ELEC. Hear me then, and thou too give thy attention.

ORES. Speak, since the existing prospect of good affords some pleasure.

ELEC. Art thou acquainted with the daughter of Helen? Thou knowest her of whom I ask.

ORES. I know her, Hermione, whom my mother brought up.

ELEC. She is gone to Clytæmnestra's tomb.

ORES. For what purpose? what hope dost thou suggest?

ELEC. To pour libations on the tomb in behalf of her mother.

ORES. And what is this, thou hast told me of, that regards our safety?

ELEC. Seize her as a pledge as she is coming back.

ORES. What remedy for the three friends is this thou sayest?

ELEC. When Helen is dead, if Menelaus does any harm to thee or Pylades, or me (for this firm of friendship is all one), say that thou wilt kill Hermione; but thou oughtest to draw thy sword, and hold it to the neck of the virgin. And if indeed Menelaus save thee, anxious that the virgin may not die; when he sees Helen's corse weltering in blood, give back the virgin (islands) for her father to enjoy; but should he, not governing his angry temper, slay thee, do thou also plunge the sword into the virgin's neck, and I think that he, though at first he come to us very big, will after a season soften his heart; for neither is he brave nor valiant: this is the fortress of our safety that I have; my arguments on the subject have been spoken.

ORES. O thou that hast indeed the mind of a man, but a form among women beautiful, to what a degree art thou more worthy of life than death! Pylades, wilt thou miserably be disappointed of such a woman, or dwelling with her obtain this happy marriage?

PYL. For would it could be so! and she could come to the city of the Phocians meeting with her deserts in splendid nuptials!

ORES. But when will Hermione come to the house? Since for the rest thou saidst most admirably, if we could succeed in taking the whelp of the impious father.

ELEC. Even now I guess that she must be near the house, for *with this supposition* the space itself of the time coincides.

ORES. It is well; do thou therefore, my sister Electra, waiting before the house, meet the arrival of the virgin. And watch, lest any one, either some ally, or the brother of my father, should be beforehand with us coming to the palace: and make some noise toward the house, either knocking at the doors, or sending thy voice within. But let us, O Pylades (for thou undertakest this labor with me), entering in, arm our hands with the sword to one last attempt. O my father, that inhabitest the realms of gloomy night, Orestes thy son invokes thee to come a succor to thy suppliants; for on thy account I wretched suffer unjustly, and am betrayed by thy brother, myself having acted justly: whose wife I wish to take and destroy; but be thou our accomplice in this affair.

ELEC. O father, come then, if beneath the earth thou hearest thy children calling, who die for thee.

PYL. O thou relation[36] of my father, give ear, O Agamemnon, to my prayers also, preserve thy children.

ORES. I slew my mother.

PYL. But I directed the sword.

XLIII

ELEC. But I at least incited you, and freed you from delay.

ORES. Succoring thee, my father.

ELEC. Neither did I forsake thee.

PYL. Wilt thou not therefore, hearing these things that are brought against thee,[37] defend thy children?

ORES. I pour libations on thee with my tears.

ELEC. And I with lamentations.

PYL. Cease, and let us haste forth to the work, for if prayers penetrate under the earth, he hears; but, O Jove our ancestor, and thou revered deity of justice, grant us to succeed, him, and myself, and this virgin, for over us three friends one hazard, one cause impends, either for all to live, or all to die!

ELECTRA, CHORUS.

ELEC. O dear Mycenian virgins, who have the first place at the Pelasgian seat of the Argives;—

CHOR. What voice art thou uddering, my respected mistress? for this appellation awaits thee in the city of the Danaids.

ELEC. Arrange yourselves, some of you in this beaten way, and some there, in that other path, to guard the house.

CHOR. But on what account dost thou command this, tell me, my friend.

ELEC. Fear possesses me, lest any one being in the palace, on account of this murderous deed, should contrive evils on evils.

SEMICHOR. Go, let us hasten, I indeed will guard this path, that tends toward where the sun flings his first rays.

SEMICHOR. And I indeed this, which leads toward the west.

ELEC. Now turn the glances of your eyes around in every position, now here, now there, then take some other view.

CHOR. We are, as thou commandest.

ELEC. Now roll your eyelids over your pupils, glance them every way through your ringlets.

SEMICHOR. Is this any one here appearing in the path?—Who is this rustic that is standing about thy palace?

ELEC. We are undone then, my friends; he will immediately show to the enemy the lurking beasts of prey armed with their swords.

SEMICHOR. Be not afraid, the path is clear, which thou thinkest not.

ELEC. But what?—does all with you remain secure? Give me some good report, whether the space before the hall be empty?

SEMICHOR. All here at least is well, but look to thy province, for no one of the Danaids is approaching toward us.

SEMICHOR. Thy report agrees with mine, for neither is there a disturbance here.

ELEC. Come now,—I will listen at the door: why do ye delay, ye that are within, to sacrifice the victim, now that ye are in quiet?—They hear not: Alas me! wretched in misery! Are the swords then struck dumb at her beauty? Perhaps some Argive in arms rushing in with the foot of succor will approach the palace.—Now watch more carefully; it is no contest that admits delay; but turn *your* eyes some this way, and some that.

CHOR. I turn each different way, looking about on all sides.

HELEN. (*within*) Oh! Pelasgian Argos! I am miserably slain!

ELEC. Heard ye? The men are employing their head in the murder.—It is the shriek of Helen, as I may conjecture.

SEMICHOR. O eternal might of Jove, come to assist my friends in every way.

HEL. Menelaus, I die! But thou art at hand, and dost not help me!

ELEC. Kill, strike, slay, plunging with your hands the two double-edged swords into the deserter of her father, the deserter of her husband, who destroyed numbers of the Grecians perishing by the spear at the river, whence tears fell into conjunction with tears, fell on account of the iron weapons around the whirlpools of Scamander.

XLV

CHOR. Be still, be still: I heard the sound of some one coming along the path around the palace.

ELEC. O most dear women, in the midst of the slaughter behold Hermione is present; let us cease from our clamor, for she comes about to fall into the meshes of our toils. A goodly prey will she be, if she be taken. Again to your stations with a calm countenance, and with a color that shall not give evidence of what has been done. I too will preserve a pensive cast of countenance, as though perfectly unacquainted with what has happened.

HERMIONE, ELECTRA, CHORUS.

ELEC. O virgin, art thou come from crowning Clytæmnestra's tomb, and pouring libations to her manes?

HERM. I am come, having obtained her good services; but some terror has come upon me, on account of the noise in the palace, which I hear being a far distance off the house.

ELEC. But why? There have happened to us things worthy of groans.

HERM. Speak good words; but what news dost thou tell me?

ELEC. It has been decreed by this land, that Orestes and I die.

HERM. No, I hope not so; you, who are my relations.

ELEC. It is fixed; but we stand under the yoke of necessity.

HERM. Was the noise then in the house on this account?

ELEC. For falling down a suppliant at the knees of Helen, he cries out—

HERM. Who? for I know no more, except thou tellest me.

ELEC. The wretched Orestes, that he may not die, and in behalf of me.

HERM. For a just reason then the house lamented.

ELEC. For on what other account should one rather cry out? But come, and join in supplication with thy friends, falling down before thy mother, the supremely blest, that Menelaus will not see us perish. But, O thou, that

XLVI

receivedst thy education at the hands of my mother, pity us, and alleviate our sufferings. Come hither to the trial; but I will lead the way, for thou alone hast the ends of our preservation.

HERM. Behold I direct my footstep toward the house. Be preserved, as far as lies in me.

ELEC. O ye in the house, my dear warriors, will ye not take your prey?

HERM. Alas me! who are these I see?

ORES. (*advancing*) Thou must be silent; for thou art come to preserve us, not thyself.

ELEC. Hold her, hold her; and pointing a sword to her neck be silent, that Menelaus may know, that having found men, not Phrygian cowards, he has treated them in a manner he should treat cowards. What ho! what ho! my friends, make a noise, a noise, and shout before the palace, that the murder that is perpetrated spread not a dread alarm among the Argives, so that they run to assist to the king's palace, before I plainly see the slaughtered Helen lying weltering in her blood within the house, or else we hear the report from some of her attendants. For part of the havoc I know, and part not accurately.

CHOR. With justice came the vengeance of the Gods on Helen. For she filled the whole of Greece with tears on account of the ruthless, ruthless Idean Paris, who brought the Grecian state to Ilium. But be silent, for the bolts of the royal mansion resound, for some one of the Phrygians comes forth, from whom we shall hear of the affairs within the house, in what state they are.

PHRYGIAN, CHORUS.

PHRY. I have escaped from death by the Argive sword in these barbaric slippers, *climbing* over the cedar beams of the bed and the Doric triglyphs, by the flight of a barbarian.[38] Thou art gone, thou art gone, O my country, my country! Alas me! whither can I escape, O strangers, flying through the hoary air, or the sea, which the Ocean, with head in shape like a bull's, rolling with his arms encircles the earth?

CHOR. But what is the matter, O attendant of Helen, thou man of Ida?

PHRY. O Lion, Lion! alas me! O thou fertile Phrygian city, thou sacred mount of Ore Ida, how do I lament for thee destroyed, a sad,[39] sad strain for my barbaric voice, on account of that form of the hapless, hapless Helen, born from a bird, the offspring of the beauteous Leda in shape of a swan, the fiend of the splendid Apollonian Pergamus! Alas! Oh! lamentations! lamentations! O wretched Dardania, warlike school[40] of Ganymede, the companion of Jove!

CHOR. Relate to us clearly each circumstance that happened in the house, for I do not understand your former account, but merely conjecture.

PHRY. Αιλινον, αιλινον, the Barbarians begin the song of death in the language of Asia, Alas! alas! when the blood of kings has been poured on the earth by the ruthless swords of death. There came to the palace (that I may relate each circumstance) two Grecians, lions, of the one the leader of the Grecian host was said to be the father, the other the son of Strophius, a man of dark design; such was Ulysses, secretly treacherous, but faithful to his friends, bold in battle, skilled in war, cruel as the dragon. May he perish for his deep concealed design, the worker of evil! But they having advanced within her chamber, whom the archer Paris had as his wife, their eyes bathed with tears, they sat down in humble mien, one on each side of her, on the right and on the left, armed with swords. And around her knees did they both fling their suppliant hands, around the knees of Helen did they fling them. But the Phrygian attendants sprung up, and fled in amazement: and one called out to another in terror, See, lest there be treachery. To some indeed there appeared no danger; but to others the dragon stained with his mother's blood appeared bent to infold in his closest toils the daughter of Tyndarus.

CHOR. But where wert thou then, or hadst thou long before fled through fear?

PHRY. After the Phrygian fashion I chanced with the close circle of feathers to be fanning the gale, *that sported* in the ringlets of Helen, before her cheek, after the barbaric fashion. But she was winding with her fingers the flax round the distaff, but what she had spun she let fall on the ground, desirous of making from the Phrygian spoils a robe of purple as an ornament for the tomb, a gift to Clytæmnestra.

But Orestes entreated the Spartan girl; "O daughter of Jove, here, place thy footstep on the ground, rising from thy seat, come to the place of our ancestor Pelops, the ancient altar, that thou mayest hear my words." And he leads her, but she followed, not dreaming of what was about to happen. But his accomplice, the wicked Phocian, attended to other points. "Will ye not depart from out of the way, but are the Phrygians always vile?" and he bolted us out scattered in different parts of the house, some in the stables of the horses, and some in the outhouses, and some here and there, dispersing them some one way, some another, afar from their mistress.

CHOR. What calamity took place after this?

PHRY. O powerful, powerful Idean mother, alas! alas! the murderous sufferings, and the lawless evils, which I saw, I saw in the royal palace! From beneath their purple robes concealed having their drawn swords in their hands, they turned each his eye on either side, lest any one might chance to be present. But like mountain boars standing over against the lady, they say, "Thou shalt die, thou shalt die! thy vile husband kills thee, having given up the offspring of his brother to die at Argos." But she shrieked out, Ah me! ah me! and throwing her white arm on her breast inflicted on her head miserable blows, and, her feet turned to flight, she stepped, she stepped with her golden sandals; but Orestes thrusting his fingers into her hair, outstripping her flight,[41] bending back her neck over his left shoulder, was about to plunge the black sword into her throat.

CHOR. Where then were the Phrygians, who dwell under the same roof, to assist her?

PHRY. With a clamor having burst by means of bars the doors and cells where we were waiting, we run to her assistance, each to different parts of the house, one bringing stones, another spears, another having a long-handled sword in his hand. But Pylades came against us, impetuous, like as the Phrygian Hector or Ajax in his triple-crested helmet, whom I saw, I saw at the gates of Priam: but we clashed together the points of our swords: then indeed, then did the Phrygians give clear proof how inferior we were in the force of Mars to the spear of Greece. One indeed turning away, a fugitive, but another wounded, and another deprecating the death that threatened him: but under favor of the darkness we fled: and the corses fell, but some staggered, and some lay prostrate. But the wretched Hermione came to the house at the time when her murdered mother fell to the ground, that unhappy woman that gave her birth. And running upon her as Bacchanals without their thyrsus, as a heifer in the mountains they bore her away in their hands, and again eagerly rushed upon the daughter of Jove to slay her. But she vanished altogether from the chamber through the palace. O Jupiter and O earth, and light, and darkness! or by her enchantments, or by the art of magic, or by the stealth of the Gods. But of what followed I know no farther, for I sped in stealth my foot from the palace. But Menelaus having endured many, many severe toils, has received back from Troy the violated rites of Helen to no purpose.

CHOR. And see something strange succeeds to these strange things, for I see Orestes with his sword drawn walking before the palace with agitated step,

ORESTES, PHRYGIAN, CHORUS.

ORES. Where is he that fled from my sword out of the palace?

PHRY. I supplicate thee, O king, falling prostrate before thee after the barbaric fashion.

ORES. The case before us is not in Ilium, but the Argive land.

PHRY. In every region to live is sweeter than to die, in the opinion of the wise.

ORES. Didst thou not raise a cry for Menelaus to come with succor?

PHRY. I indeed am present on purpose to assist thee; for thou art the more worthy.

ORES. Perished then the daughter of Tyndarus justly?

PHRY. Most justly, even had she three lives for vengeance.

ORES. With thy tongue dost thou flatter, not having these sentiments within?

PHRY. For ought she not? She who utterly destroyed Greece as well as the Phrygians themselves?

ORES. Swear, I will kill thee else, that thou art not speaking to curry favor with me.

PHRY. By my life have I sworn, which I should wish to hold a sacred oath.

ORES. Was the steel thus dreadful to all the Phrygians at Troy also?

PHRY. Remove thy sword, for being so near me it gleams horrid slaughter.

ORES. Art thou afraid, lest thou shouldest become a rock, as though looking on the Gorgon?

PHRY. Lest I should become a corse, but I know not of the Gorgon's head.

ORES. Slave as thou art, dost thou fear death, which will rid thee from thy woes?

PHRY. Every one, although a man be a slave, rejoices to behold the light.

ORES. Thou sayest well; thy understanding; saves thee, but go into the house.

PHRY. Thou wilt not kill me then?

ORES. Thou art pardoned.

PHRY. This is good word thou hast spoken.

ORES. Yet we may change our measures.

PHRY. But this thou sayest not well.

ORES. Thou art a fool, if thou thinkest I could endure to defile me by smiting thy neck, for neither art thou a woman, nor oughtest thou to be ranked among men. But that thou mightest not raise a clamor came I forth out of the house: for Argos, when it has heard a noise, is soon roused, but we have no dread in meeting Menelaus, as far as swords go; but let him come exulting with his golden ringlets flowing over his shoulders, for if he collects the Argives, and brings them against the palace seeking revenge for the death of Helen, and is not willing to let me be in safety, and my sister, and Pylades my accomplice in this affair, he shall see two corses, both the virgin and his wife.

CHORUS.

Alas! alas! O fate, the house of the Atridæ again falls into another, another fearful struggle.

SEMICHOR. What shall we do? shall we carry these tidings to the city, or shall we keep in silence?

SEMICHOR. This is the safer plan, my friends.

SEMICHOR. Behold before the house, behold this smoke leaping aloft in the air portends *something*.

SEMICHOR. They are lighting the torches, as about to burn down the mansion of Tantalus, nor do they forbear from murder.

CHOR. The God rules the events that happen to mortals, whichsoever way he wills. But some vast power by the instigation of the Furies has struck, has struck these palaces to the shedding of blood on account of the fall of Myrtilus from the chariot.

But lo! I see Menelaus also here approaching the house with a quick step, having by some means or other perceived the calamity which now is present. Will ye not anticipate him by closing the gates with bolts, O ye children of Atreus, who are in the palace? A man in prosperity is a terrible thing to those in adversity, as now them art in misery, Orestes.

MENELAUS *below*, ORESTES, PYLADES, ELECTRA, HERMIONE *above*, CHORUS.

MEN. I am present, having heard the horrid and atrocious deeds of the two lions, for I call them not men. For I have now heard of my wife, that she died not, but vanished away, this that I heard was empty report, which one deceived by fright related; but these are the artifices of the matricide, and much derision. Open some one the door, my attendants I command to burst open these gates here, that my child at least we may deliver from the hand of these blood-polluted men, and may receive my unhappy, my miserable lady, with whom those murderers of my wife must die by my hand.

ORES. What ho there! Touch not these gates with thine hands: to Menelaus I speak, that thou towerest in thy boldness, or with this pinnacle will I crush thy head, having rent down the ancient battlement, the labor of the builders. But the gates are made fast with bolts, which will hinder thee from thy purpose of bringing aid, so that thou canst not pass within the palace.

MEN. Ha! what is this? I see the blaze of torches, and these stationed on the battlements, on the height of the palace, and the sword placed over the neck of my daughter to guard her.

ORES. Whether is it thy will to question, or to hear me?

MEN. I wish neither, but it is necessary, as it seems, to hear thee.

ORES. I am about to slay thy daughter if thou wish to know.

MEN. Having slain Helen, dost thou perpetrate murder on murder?

ORES. For would I had gained my purpose not being deluded, as I was, by the Gods.

MEN. Thou hast slain her, and deniest it, and speakest these things to insult me.

ORES. It is a denial that gives me pain, for would that—

MEN. Thou had done what deed? for thou callest forth alarm.

ORES. I had hurled to hell the fury of Greece.

MEN. Give back the body of my wife, that I may bury her in a tomb.

ORES. Ask her of the Gods; but I will slay thy daughter.

MEN. The matricide contrives murder on murder.

ORES. The avenger of his father, whom thou gavest up to die.

MEN. Was not the blood of thy mother formerly shed sufficient for thee?

ORES. I should not be weary of slaying wicked women, were I to slay them forever.

MEN. Art thou also, Pylades, a partaker in this murder?

ORES. By his silence he assents, but if I speak, it will be sufficient.

MEN. But not with impunity, unless indeed thou fliest on wings.

ORES. We will not fly, but will set fire to the palace?

MEN. What! wilt thou destroy thy father's mansion?

ORES. Yes, that thou mayest not possess it, will I, having stabbed this virgin here over the flames.

MEN. Slay her; since having slain thou shalt at least give me satisfaction for these deeds.

ORES. It shall be so then.

MEN. Alas! on no account do this!

ORES. Be silent then; but bear to suffer evil justly.

MEN. What! is it just for thee to live?

ORES. Yes, and to rule over the land.

MEN. What land!

ORES. Here, in Pelasgian Argos.

MEN. Well wouldst thou touch the sacred lavers!

ORES. And pray why not?

MEN. And wouldst slaughter the victim before the battle!

ORES. And thou wouldst most righteously.

MEN. Yes, for I am pure as to my hands.

ORES. But not thy heart.

MEN. Who would speak to thee?

ORES. Whoever loves his father.

MEN. And whoever reveres his mother.

ORES. —Is happy.

MEN. Not thou at least.

ORES. For wicked women please me not.

MEN. Take away the sword from my daughter.

ORES. Thou art false in thy expectations.

MEN. But wilt thou kill my daughter?

ORES. Thou art no longer false.

MEN. Alas me! what shall I do?

ORES. Go to the Argives, and persuade them.

MEN. With what persuasion?

ORES. Beseech the city that we may not die.

MEN. Otherwise ye will slay my daughter?

ORES. The thing is so.

MEN. O wretched Helen!—

ORES. And am I not wretched?

MEN. I brought thee hither from the Trojans to be a victim.

ORES. For would this were so!

MEN. Having endured ten thousand toils.

ORES. Except on my account.

MEN. I have met with dreadful treatment.

ORES. For then, *when thou oughtest*, thou wert of no assistance.

MEN. Thou hast me.

ORES. Thou at least hast caught thyself. But, ho there! set fire to the palace, Electra, from beneath: and thou, Pylades, the most true of my friends, light up these battlements of the walls.

MEN. O land of the Danai, and inhabitants of warlike Argos, will ye not, ho there! come in arms to my succor? For this man here, having perpetrated the shocking murder of his mother, brings destruction on your whole city, that he may live...oh my goodness! What the heck is THAT!?

[TYRANNOSAURUS REX enters and devours ORESTES, MENELAUS, ELECTRA, TYNDARUS, HERMIONE and the CHORUS]

T.REX. [mopping his brow] Blimey, I've made a bit of a glutton of meself. I should probably hit the gym to sweat some of this blubber off. Are you coming Pylades?

PYL. Sure thing, you see I've been working on this new system of total body fitness where you focus on strengthening your "Core". [42] I think it could really work out as a huge commercial enterprise one day.

T.REX. Swell. High five. [43]

NOTES ON ORESTES

---

[1] Meaning literally «Brazen Fleece.»

[2] "*Then*" is not to be considered as signifying point of time, but it is meant to express ουν, *continuativam.* See Hoogeveen de Particula ουν, Sect. ii. § 6.

[3] The original Greek phrase was ελπιδος λεπτης, which Euripides has changed to ασθενους 'ρωμης, though the other had equally suited the metre. But Euripides is fond of slight alterations in proverbs. PORSON.

[4] δους—δυναται δε και αποδους. SCHOL.

[5] Perhaps this interpretation of χρονιον is better than "slow," for the considerate Electra would hardly go to remind her brother of his infirmities.

[6] Ποτνιαδες. The Furies have this epithet from Potnia, a town in Bœotia, where Glaucus's horses, having eaten of a certain herb and becoming mad, tore their own master in pieces. SCHOL.

[6a] Note [D].

[6b] Dindorf would omit this verse.

[7] ʽαλιτυπων, ʽαλιεων, ʽοι ταις κωπαις τυπτουσι την θαλασσαν. SCHOL.

[8] αφυλλου. Alluding to the branch, which the ancients used to hold in token of supplication.

[9] "κατα την νυκτα πεπονθα τηρων την αναιρεσιν, και την αναληψιν των οστεων, τουτεστιν, ʽινα μη τις αφεληται ταυτα." PARAPH. Heath translates it, *watchfully observing, till her bones were collected.*

[10] The old reading was απαιδευτα. The meaning of the present reading seems to be, "Yes, they are awful 'tis true, but still however you need not be so very scrupulous about naming them."

[11] αναφορα was a legal term, and signified the line of defense adopted by the accused, when he transferred the charge brought against himself to some other person.—See Demosthenes in Timocr.

[12] Œax was Palamede's brother.

[13] And therefore we are not to impeach the *man.* Some would have δουλον to bear the sense of δουλοποιον, enslaves, and therefore can not be avoided.

[14] εχω for ενοχος ειμι.

[15] Ζηλω, το μακαριζω. ενταυθα δε αντι του επαινω. SCHOL.

[16] Conf. Ter. Eun. Act. v. Sc. 2.

Non dedignum, Chærea,
Fecisti; nam si ego digna hac contumelia
Sum maxume, at tu indignus, qui faceres, tamen.

[16a] Note [E].

[17] Of this passage the Scholiast gives two interpretations; either it may mean μετα δακρυων και γοων ειπον: or, ειπον ταυτα εις δακρυα και γοους, και ξυμφορας, ηγουν ʽινα μη τυχω, τουτων: τευξομαι δε, ει πετρωθηναι με εασηις.

[18] "*Beyond any woman,*" γυνη μια, this is a mode of expression frequently met with in the Attic writers, especially in Xenophon.

[19] επι τωι φονωι, τουτεστι δια τον φονον, 'ον ειργασαμεθα. PARAPH.

[20] Thyestes and Atreus, having a dispute about their father Pelops's kingdom, agreed, that whichever should discover the first prodigy should have possession of the throne. There appeared in Atreus's flock a brazen lamb, which, however, Ærope his wife secretly had conveyed to Thyestes to show before the judges. Atreus afterward invited Thyestes to a feast, and served up before him Aglaiis, Orchomenus, and Caleus, three sons he had by his intrigues with Ærope.

[21] Alluding to the murder of Agamemnon by Clytæmnestra. This is the interpretation and explanation of the Scholiast; but it is perhaps better translated, "*but on the other hand to play the coward is great impiety, and the error of cowardly-minded men;*" the chorus meaning, that this might have been said of Orestes, had he not avenged his father.

[22] That is, *blamed him.* So St. Paul, I Cor. xi. 21, επαινεσω 'υμας εν τουτοι; ουκ επαινω. Ter. And. Act. II. Sc. 6. "Et, quod dicendum hic siet, Tu quoque perparce nimium, non laudo."

[23] An Argive as far as he was born there, and therefore ηναγκασμενος; not an Argive, inasmuch as his parents were not of that state. This is supposed to allude to Cleophon. SCHOL. See Dindorf.

[24] This is the interpretation of one Scholiast; another explains it οικειαις χερσιν εργαζομενος. Grotius translates it *agricola.* Google translate has it as "Large tracts of land."

[25] The same construction occurs in the Suppliants, 870. φιλοις δ' αληθης ην φιλος, παρουσι τε και μη παρουσιν: 'ων (of which sort of men) αριθμος ου πολυς. PORSON.

[25a] See Note [F].

[26] Which, κτυπον namely: ονυχα and κτυπον are each governed by τιθεισα; but it is not easy to find a single verb in English that should be transitive to both these substantives.

[27] καλλιπαις, *lovely,* not lovely in her children: so in Phœn. 1634. ευτεκνος ξυνωρις.

[28] Argos, so called from the Cyclopes, a nation of Thrace, who, being called in as allies, afterward settled here.

[29] ʹετεροις may perhaps seem to make the construction plainer than ʹετερος; but Porson has received the latter into his text on account of the metre.

[30] Myrtilus was the son of Mercury, who therefore sowed this dissension between the two brothers in revenge for his death by Pelops. See note at line 802.

[31] Some would understand by μονοπωλον not that Aurora was borne on one horse, but that this alteration in the course of nature took place for one day. SCHOL.

[32] και απο τωνδε, ητοι μετα ταυτα. PARAPH.

[33] παρασειρος is used to signify a loose horse tied abreast of another in the shaft, and is technically termed "the outrigger." The metaphorical application of it to Pylades, who voluntarily attached himself to the misfortunes of his friend, is extremely beautiful.

[34] Or, "I will not be at all behind thy slaughter."

[35] ευ in this passage *interrogat oblique*, see Hoogeveen, xvi. § 1. 15.

[36] Strophius, the father of Pylades, married Anaxibia, Agamemnon's sister.

[37] ονειδη, των ευεργεσιων τας ʹυπομνησεις. SCHOL. Ter. And. i. 1. "isthæc commemoratio quasi exprobratio est immemoris benefici."

[38] i.e. being a barbarian, and therefore not knowing whither to go.

[39] ʹαρματειον, such a strain as that raised over Hector, ʹελκομενω, δια του ʹαρματος. See two other explanations in the Scholia.

[40] ʹιπποσυνα, ʹητις ʹυπηρχες ʹιππηλασια του Γ. BRUNCK.

[41] Literally, *her Mycenaean slipper*. Now if we could only figure what a Mycenaean slipper is.

[42] *Kore*, the female equivalent to the *Kouroi*. What exactly Pylades means by this is uncertain, but it is possible the young prince is inferring a certain Spartan sensibility.

[43] Ancient Greeks were under the persuasion that *Tyrannasaurus Rex* had five digits on each hand rather than the two digits that we now know science has proved to be the case.

[44] He menas he wants to make Helen cold, not literally kill her.

ADDITIONAL NOTES.

[A] But Dindorf reads κτυπου η ηγαγετ'. ουχι; interrogatively, thus: "Ye were making a noise. Will ye not ... enable him," etc.?

[B] Dindorf would continue this verse to Orestes.

[C] Dindorf supposes something to be wanting after vs. 314.

[D] The use of αλλος ἑτερος is learnedly illustrated by Dindorf.

[E] Elmsley, on Heracl. 852, more simply regards the datives σοι σηι τ' αδελφη as dependent upon επισεισω, understanding ἑωστε δουναι δικην. This is better than to suppose (with Porson) that δουναι δικην can mean to *inflict* punishment.

[F] Dindorf (in his notes) agrees with Porson in omitting the following verse.

[G] Dindorf's text and punctuation must be altered.

HIPPOLYTUS.

PERSONS REPRESENTED.

VENUS.
HIPPOLYTUS.
ATTENDANTS.
PHÆDRA.
NURSE.
THESEUS.
MESSENGER.
DIANA.
CHORUS OF TRŒZENIAN DAMES.

THE ARGUMENT.

Theseus was the son of Othra and Neptune, and king of the Athenians; and having married Hippolyta, one of the Amazons, he begat Hippolytus, who excelled in beauty and chastity. When his wife died, he married, for his second wife, Phædra, a Cretan, daughter of Minos, king of Crete, and Pasiphaë. Theseus, in consequence of having slain Pallas, one of his kinsmen, goes into banishment, with his wife, to Trœzene, where it happened that Hippolytus was being brought up by Pittheus: but Phædra having seen the youth was desperately enamored, not that she was incontinent, but in order to fulfill the anger of Venus, who, having determined to destroy Hippolytus on account of his chastity, sought to bring her plans to a conclusion. In the midst of her plotting, Venus meets with an unfortunate end as a Tyrannosaurus Rex driving an Imperial AT-AT Walker blasts her into oblivion, to the approval of all involved.

The scene of the play is laid in Trœzene. It was acted in the archonship of Ameinon, in the fourth year of the 87th Olympiad. Euripides first, Jophon second, Jon third. This Hippolytus is the second of that name, and is calledΣΤΕΦΑΝΙΑΣ: but it appears to have been written the latest, for what was unseemly and deserved blame is corrected in this play. The play is ranked among the first.

HIPPOLYTUS.

VENUS.

Great[1] in the sight[2] of[3] mortals,[4] and not without[5] a name[6] am I[7] the[8] Goddess[9] Venus, [10] and in heaven: [11] and[12] of as[13] many[14] as dwell[15] within[16] the ocean[17] and the boundaries[18] of Atlas, [19] beholding the light[20] of the sun, [21] those indeed, [22] who[23] reverence[24] my[25] authority, [26] I advance to honor;[27] but overthrow as many as hold themselves[28] high toward[29] me. [30] For this is in sooth a property inherent even in[31] the race of[32] the[33] Gods, that[34] "they rejoice when honored by[35] men." But[36] quickly will I show the[37] truth of[38] these words: [39] for the son[40] of Theseus, born of the Amazon, Hippolytus, pupil[41] of the chaste[42] Pittheus, alone of the inhabitants of this land of Trœzene, says that I am of deities the vilest, and rejects the bridal bed, and will have nothing to do with marriage. But Dian, the sister of Phœbus, daughter of Jove[43] he honors, esteeming her,[44] the greatest of deities. And through the green wood ever accompanying the virgin, with his swift dogs[45] he clears the beasts[46] from off the earth, having formed a fellowship[47] greater than mortal ought. This indeed I grudge him not; for wherefore should I? but wherein he has erred toward me, I will avenge me on Hippolytus this very day…hang[48] on a minute…is that an Imperial[49] AT-AT[50] Walker piloted by a Tyrannosaurus Rex? [51] Hmmm…I wonder if he realizes that his blasters[52] are pointed right at me…I…wait…nooooo[53]… [54]..[55]

[TYRANNOSAURUS REX appears in an Imperial AT-AT Walker with turbo-laser batteries blazing away. HIPPOLYTUS, ATTENDANTS, PHÆDRA, NURSE, THESEUS, MESSENGER, DIANA and the CHORUS all look on with approval. Venus is disintegrated and there is much rejoicing, particularly in the arena of art historical inquiry.]

NOTES ON HIPPOLYTUS

[1] The construction in the original furnishes a remarkable example of the "nominativus pendens."

[2] Or, *that posterity might know it*. TR. Dindorf would omit these words. B.

[3] Dindorf would omit these lines. I think the difficulty in the structure may be removed by reading 'οστις instead of 'οσοις. The enallage, 'οστις ... τουτοις, is by no means unusual. B.

[4] Cf. Soph. Œd. Col. 121, sqq. B.

[5] Which at present you do not appear to have.

[6] Monk would join ωκεανου with πετρα, as in the translation, but other commentators prefer, which is certainly more simple, to join it with 'υδωρ. Then the difficulty occurs of sea-water being unfit for washing vests. This difficulty Beck obviates, by saying that 'υδωρ ωκεανου may be applied to fresh water, Ocean being the parent of all streams, the word ωκεανου being here, in a manner, redundant. TR. Matthiæ is very wrath with the "all on a washing day" manner in which the Chorus learned Phædra's indisposition. The "Bothie of Toper na Fuosich" will furnish some similar simplicities, such as the meeting a lassie "digging potatoes." But we might as well object to the whole story of Nausicaa. It must be recollected that the duties of the laundry were considered more aristocratic by the ancients, than in modern times. B.

[7] Cf. Æsch. Pr. 23. Χροιας αμειψεις ανθος. B.

[8] Literally *a speech mounted on madness*. A similar expression occurs, Odyssey A. 297. Νηπιαας οχεειν.

[9] Plutarch in explanation of this line says, "καθαπερ ποδα νεως, επιδιδοντα και προσαγοντα ταις χρειαις την φιλιαν."

[10] I have followed the elegant interpretation of L. Dindorf, who observes that ου δηθ 'εκουσα refers to Phædra's assertion, ου γαρ ες σ' αμαρτανω, and that the meaning is, "non quidem consilio in me peccas, sed si tu peribis, ego quoque occidero." He compares Alcest. 389. B.

[11] See Matthiæ's note. I prefer, however, ολεις, with Musgrave. B.

[12] Matthiæ considers this as briefly expressed for τι τουτο, το εραν, 'α λεγουσι ποιειν ανθρωπους. Still I can not help thinking ανθρωπων a better reading. B.

[13] Phædra struggles between shame and uncertainty, before she can pronounce the name. It should be read as if 'οστις ποθ'—'ουτος—'ο της Αμαζονος. B.

[14] Matthiæ takes παναμεριος as = εν τηιδε τηι 'ημεραι, i.e. up to this very time. I think the passage is corrupt. B.

[15] This passage, like many others in the play, is admirably burlesqued by Aristoph., Ran. 962. B.

[16] *Or, this is a second favor thou mayst grant me.*

[17] On the numberless references to this impious sophism, see the learned notes of Valckenaer and Monk. Compare more particularly Aristoph. Ran. 102, 1471. Thesmoph. 275. Arist. Rhet. iii. 15. B.

[18] Literally, "spurious coined race." B.

[19] The MSS. reading, φυτον, is preferable. B.

[20] The syntax appears to be δυσεκπερατον βιου, *such as my like can scarcely get over.* Musgrave has followed the other explanation of the Scholiast, which makes βιου depend on παθος. TR. I have followed the Scholiast and Dindorf. B.

[21] προτρεπουσα, αντι του ζητουσα και εξερευνωσα. Schol. Dindorf acknowledges the strangeness of the usage, and seems to prefer προσκοπουσ', with Monk. B.

[22] Cf. Soph. Ant. 751. 'ηδ' ουν θανειται, και θανουσ' ολει τινα. B.

[23] For the meaning and derivation of αλιβατοις, see Monk's note.

[24] ἁλικτυπον seems to be an awkward epithet of κυμα, unless it mean "*dashed [against the shore] by the waves.*" Perhaps αλικτυπον would be less forced. B.

[25] Ὑπεραντλος ουσα συμφοραι, a metaphor taken from a ship which can no longer keep out water.

[26] See the note on my Translation of Æsch. Agam., p. 121, note I. ed. Bonn. B.

[27] Read ωμοι εγω πονων: επαθον ω ταλας with cod. Hav. See Dindorf. B.

[28] Cf. Matth. apud Dindorf. B.

[29] In the same manner the chorus in the Alcestis comforts Admetus. v.

Ου γαρ τι πρωτος, ουδε λοισθιος βροτων
γυναικος εσθλης ημπλακες.

[30] Ὑπερ is here to be understood. VALK.

[31] Σφενδονη, literally, the setting of the seal, which embraces the gem as a sling its stone.

[32] See a similar expression in Æsch. Eum. 254,

Οσμη βροτειων ἁιματων με προσγελαι.

[33] The construction is, ειη αν εμοι αβιωτος τυχα βιου, ἁοστε τυχειν αυτης. MONK.

[34] η, *which land, together with the present earth.*

[35] On the Orphic abstinence from animal food, see Matth. apud Dind. Compare Porphyr. de Abst. ii. 3 sqq. B.

[36] Αθικτος appears here to have an active sense. So in Soph. Œd. c. 1521. αθικτος ἡγητηρος. It is used in its more frequent sense (a passive) in v. 648, of this play. TR. Compare my note on Æsch. Prom. 110, p. 6, n. I. B.

[37] Cf. Med. 169. Ζηνα θ' ἁος ορκων θνατοις ταμιας νενομισται. B.

[38] There are various interpretations of this passage. The Scholiast puts this sense upon it, *Phædra was chaste (in your eyes), who had not the power of being chaste, I had the power, and is it likely that I did not exert it to good purpose?* Others translate the former part of the passage with the Scholiast,

but make ου καλως εχρωμεθα refer to the present time, *had it to no good purpose,* i.e. am not now able to persuade you of my innocence. Some translate εσωφροησεν, *acted like a chaste woman.* TR. There is evidently a double meaning, which is almost lost by translation. Theseus is not intended to understand this. B.

[39] Cf. vs. 3. B.

[40] Κληροι were the notes the augurs took of their observations, and wrote down on tablets. See Phœn. 852.

[41] ξυνοικουρους appears to be metaphorically used, but I think the sense would be greatly improved by reading κακους, and taking ξυνοικουρους to mean "to dwell with him," referring it to 'οστις. B.

[42] But we must read γυμναδος 'ιππου with Reiske, Brunot, and Dindorf. See his notes. ποδι must be joined with γυμ. 'ιππου. B.

[43] In other words you might say she was by Jove.

[44] Αυταισιν αρβυλαισιν. Some have supposed αρβυλη to mean a part of the chariot, but this seems at variance with the best authorities (see Monk's note); perhaps the expression may mean what is implied in the translation; that Hippolytus did not wait to change any part of his dress. TR. But I agree with Dindorf, that αυταισιν is then utterly absurd and useless. The Scholiast seems correct in saying, ταις τον 'αρματος περι την αντυγα, ενθα την οτασιν εχει 'ο 'ηνιοχος. B.

[45] "Adeo ut deficerent a visu, ne cernere possem, Scironis alta." B.

[46] Καχλαζω, a word formed from the noise of the sea— 'ο γαρ ηχος του κυματος εν τοις κοιλωμασι των πετρων γινομενος, δοκει μιμεισθαι το καχλα, καχλα.—*Etym. Mag.*

[47] Τρικυμιαι. See Blomfield's *Glossary to the Prometheus,* 1051.

[48] Musgrave supposes that Hippolytus wound the reins round his body; but on this supposition, not to mention other objections, the comparison with the sailor does not hold so well. It is more natural to suppose that he leaned back in order to get a purchase: in this attitude he is made to describe himself in Ov. *Met.* xv. 519, *Et retro lentas tendo*

resupinus habenas. If there be any doubt of εις τουμισθεν 'ιμασιν being Greek, this objection is obviated by putting a stop after 'ιμασιν, and making it depend on 'ελκει.

[49] i.e. in Crete. See Dindorf's note. B.

[50] The AT-AT, or All Terrain Armored Transport, is not to be confused with its smaller variant, the AT-ST (All Terrain Scout Transport) or with AT&T (American Telephone and Telegraph Company). Ironically enough, however, Luke Skywalker ultimately resorts to the use of cable, not unlike that employed as telephone wire by AT&T, to bring down an AT-AT during the Empire's invasion of the Rebel base on Hoth. That Luke was able to eliminate an otherwise formidable foe by targeting its walking appendages causes us to wonder why the Imperial engineers didn't have the foresight to invent All Terrain Armored Transports that flew, or at least levitated, instead of plodding along at an impossibly slow pace while all the Rebels escaped.

[51] Heath translates ανεκουφισθην *adtollebam corpus, honoris scilicet gratia.* Compare Iliad, O. 241. αταρ ασθμα και 'ιδρως παυετ', επει μιν εγειρε Διος νοος αιγιοχοιο, which Pope translates,

"Jove thinking of his pains, they pass'd away:"

in which the idea is much more sublime; for there the thought of a Deity effects what the presence of one does here.

[52] Probably meaning Adonis, the Greek god of turbo-laser blasters.

IPHIGENIA IN AULIS.

PERSONS REPRESENTED.

AGAMEMNON.
OLD MAN.
MENELAUS.
ACHILLES.
MESSENGER.
ANOTHER MESSENGER.
IPHIGENIA.
CLYTÆMNESTRA.
CHORUS.

THE ARGUMENT.

When the Greeks were detained at Aulis by stress of weather, Calchas declared that they would never reach Troy unless the daughter of Agamemnon, Iphigenia, was sacrificed to Diana. Agamemnon sent for his daughter with this view, but repenting, he dispatched a messenger to prevent Clytæmnestra sending her. The messenger being intercepted by Menelaus, an altercation between the brother chieftains arose, during which Iphigenia, who had been tempted with the expectation of being wedded to Achilles, arrived with her mother. The latter, meeting with Achilles, discovered the deception, and Achilles swore to protect her. But Iphigenia, having determined to die nobly on behalf of the Greeks, was snatched away at the last moment by a Tyrannosaurus wearing a jetpack. The Greeks were then enabled to set sail.

IPHIGENIA IN AULIS.

AGAMEMNON. Come before this dwelling, O aged man.

OLD MAN. I come. But what new thing dost thou meditate, king Agamemnon?

AG. You shall learn.[1]

OLD M. I hasten. My old age is very sleepless, and sits wakeful upon mine eyes.

AG. What star can this be that traverses this way?

OLD M. Sirius, flitting yet midway (between the heavens and the ocean,)[2] close to the seven Pleiads.

AG. No longer therefore is there the sound either of birds or of the sea, but silence of the winds reigns about this Euripus.

OLD M. But why art thou hastening without the tent, king Agamemnon? But still there is silence here by Aulis, and the guards of the fortifications are undisturbed. Let us go within.

AG. I envy thee, old man, and I envy that man who has passed through a life without danger, unknown, unglorious; but I less envy those in honor.

OLD M. And yet 'tis in this that the glory of life is.

AG. But this very glory is uncertain, for the love of popularity is pleasant indeed, but hurts when present. Sometimes the worship of the Gods not rightly conducted upturns one's life, and sometimes the many and dissatisfied opinions of men harass.

OLD M. I praise not these remarks in a chieftain. O Agamemnon, Atreus did not beget thee upon a condition of complete good fortune.[3] But thou needs must rejoice and grieve; [in turn,] for thou art a mortal born, and even though you wish it not, the will of the Gods will be thus. But thou, opening the light of a lamp, art both writing this letter, which thou still art carrying in thy hands, and again you blot out the same characters, and seal, and loose again, and cast the tablet to the ground, pouring abundant tears, and thou lackest naught of the unwonted things that tend to madness. Why art thou troubled, why art thou troubled? What new thing, what new thing [has happened] concerning thee, O king? Come, communicate discourse with me. But thou wilt speak to a good and faithful man, for to thy wife Tyndarus sent me once on a time, as a dower-gift, and disinterested companion.[4]

AG. To Leda, daughter of Thestias, were born three virgins, Phœbe, and Clytæmnestra my spouse, and Helen. Of this latter, the youths of Greece that were in the first state of prosperity came as suitors. But terrible threats of bloodshed[5] arose against one another, from whoever should not obtain the virgin. But the matter was difficult for her father Tyndarus, whether to give, or not to give [her in marriage,] and how he might best deal with the circumstances, when this occurred to him; that the suitors should join oaths and plight right hands with one another, and over burnt-offerings should enter into treaty, and bind themselves by this oath, "Of whomsoever the daughter of Tyndarus shall become wife, that they will join to assist him, if any one should depart from his house taking [her] with him, and excluding the possessor from his bed, and that they will make an expedition in arms, and sack the city [of the ravisher,] Greek or barbarian alike." But after they had pledged themselves, the old man Tyndarus somehow cleverly overreached them by a cunning plan. He permits his daughter to choose one of the suitors, toward whom the friendly gales of Venus might impel her. But she chose (whom would she had never taken!) Menelaus. And he who, according to the story told by men, once judged the Goddesses, coming from Phrygia to Lacedæmon, flowered in the vesture of his garments, and glittering with gold, barbarian finery, loving Helen who loved him, he stole and bore her away to the bull-stalls of Ida, having found Menelaus abroad. But he, goaded hastily[6] through Greece, calls to witness the old oath given to Tyndarus, that it behooves to assist the aggrieved. Henceforth the Greeks hastening with the spear, having taken their arms, come to this Aulis with its narrow straits, with ships and shields together, and accoutred with many horses and chariots. And they chose me general of the host, out of regard for Menelaus, being his brother forsooth. And would that some other than I had obtained the dignity. But when the army was assembled and levied, we sat, having no power of sailing, at Aulis. But Calchas the seer proclaimed to us, being at a loss, that we should sacrifice Iphigenia, whom I begat, to Diana, who inhabits this place, and that if we sacrificed her, we should have both our voyage, and the sacking of Troy, but that this should not befall us if we did not sacrifice her. But I hearing this in rousing proclamation, bade Talthybius dismiss the whole army, as I should never have the heart to slay my daughter. Upon this, indeed, my brother, alleging every kind of reasoning, persuaded me to dare the dreadful deed, and having written in the folds of a letter, I sent word to my wife to send her daughter as if to be married to Achilles, both enlarging on the dignity of the man, and asserting that he would not sail with the Greeks, unless a wife for him from among us should come to Phthia. For I had this means of persuading my wife, having made up a pretended match for the virgin. But we alone of the Greeks know how these matters are, Calchas, Ulysses, and Nestor. But the things which I then determined not well, I am now differently writing so as to be well, in this letter, which by the shadow of night thou beheldest me opening and closing, old man. But come, go thou, taking these letters, to Argos. But as to what the letter conceals in its folds, I will tell thee in words all that is written therein; for thou art faithful to my wife and house.

OLD M. Speak, and tell me, that with my tongue I may also say what agrees with your letter.

AG. (reading) "I send to thee, O germ of Leda, besides[7] my former dispatches, not to send thy daughter to the bay-like wing of Eubœa,[8] waveless Aulis. For we will delay the bridals of our daughter till another season."

OLD M. And how will not Achilles raise up his temper against thee and thy wife, showing great wrath at failing of his spouse? This also is terrible. Show what thou meanest.

AG. Achilles, furnishing the pretext, not the reality, knows not these nuptials, nor what we are doing; nor that I have professed to give my daughter into the nuptial chain of his arms by marriage.[9]

OLD M. Thou venturest terrible things, king Agamemnon, who, having promised thy daughter as wife to the son of the Goddess, dost lead her as a sacrifice on behalf of the Greeks.

AG. Ah me! I was out of my senses. Alas! And I am falling into calamity. But go, plying thy foot, yielding naught to old age.

OLD M. I hasten, O king.

AG. Do not thou either sit down by the woody fountains, nor repose in sleep.

OLD M. Speak good words.

AG. But every where as you pass the double track, look about, watching lest there escape thee a chariot passing with swift wheels, bearing my daughter hither to the ships of the Greeks.

OLD M. This shall be.

AG. And go out of the gates[10] quickly,† for if you meet with the procession,† again go forth, shake the reins, going to the temples reared by the Cyclops.

OLD M. But tell me, how, saying this, I shall obtain belief from thy daughter and wife.

AG. Preserve the seal, this which thou bearest on this letter. Go: morn, already dawning forth this light, grows white, and the fire of the sun's four steeds. Aid me in my toils. But no one of mortals is prosperous or blest to the last, for none hath yet been born free from pain.

CHORUS. I came to the sands of the shore of marine Aulis, having sailed through the waves of Euripus, quitting Chalcis with its narrow strait, my city, the nurse of the sea-neighboring waters[11] of renowned Arethusa, in order that I might behold the army of the Greeks, and the ship-conveying oars of the Grecian youths, whom against Troy in a thousand ships of fir, our husbands say that yellow-haired Menelaus and Agamemnon of noble birth, are leading in quest of Helen,[12] whom the herdsman Paris bore from reed-nourishing Eurotas, a gift of Venus, when at the fountain dews Venus held contest, contest respecting beauty with Juno and Pallas. But I came swiftly through the wood of Diana with its many sacrifices, making my cheek red with youthful modesty, wishing to behold the defense of the shield, and the arm-bearing tents[13] of the Greeks, and the crowd of steeds. But I saw the two Ajaces companions, the son of Oileus, and the son of Telamon, the glory of Salamis, and Protesilaus and Palamedes, whom the daughter of Neptune bore, diverting themselves[14] with the complicated figures of draughts, and Diomede rejoicing in the pleasures of the disk, and by them Merione, the blossom of Mars, a marvel to mortals, and the son of Laertes from the mountains of the isle, and with them Nireus, fairest of the Greeks, and Achilles, tempest-like in the course, fleet as the winds, whom Thetis bore, and Chiron trained up, I beheld him on the shore, coursing in arms along the shingles. And he toiled through a contest of feet, running against a chariot of four steeds for victory. But the charioteer cried out, Eumelus, the grandson of Pheres,[15] whose most beauteous steeds I beheld, decked out with gold-tricked bits, hurried on by the lash, the middle ones in yoke dappled with white-spotted hair, but those outside, in loose harness, running contrariwise in the bendings of the course, bays, with dappled skins under their legs with solid hoofs. Close by which Pelides was running in arms, by the orb and wheels of the chariot.[16] And I came to the multitude of ships, a sight not to be described, that I might satiate the sight of my woman's eyes, a sweet delight. And at the right horn [of the fleet] was the Phthiotic army of the Myrmidons, with fifty valiant ships. And in golden effigies the Nereid Goddesses stood on the summit of the poops, the standard of the host of Achilles. And next to these there stood the Argive ships, with equal number of oars, of which [Euryalus] the grandson of Mecisteus was general, whom his father Talaus trains up, and Sthenelus son of Capaneus. But [Acamas] son of Theseus, leading sixty ships from Athens, kept station, having the Goddess Pallas placed[17] in her equestrian winged chariot, a prosperous sign to sailors. But I beheld the armament of the Bœotians, fifty sea-bound ships, with signs at the figure-heads, and their sign was Cadmus, holding a golden dragon, at the beaks of the ships, and Leitus the earth-born was leader of the naval armament, and [I beheld] those from the Phocian land. But the son of Oileus, leading an equal number of Locrian ships, came, having left the Thronian city. But from Cyclopian Mycenæ the son of Atreus sent the assembled mariners of a hundred ships. And with him was Adrastus, as friend with friend, in order that Greece might wreak vengeance on those who fled their homes, for the sake of barbarian nuptials. But from Pylos we beheld on the poops of Gerenian Nestor, a sign bull-footed to view, his neighbor Alpheus. But there were twelve beaks of Ænian ships, which king Gyneus led, and near these again the chieftains of Elis, whom all the people named Epeians, and o'er these Eurytus had power. But the white-oared Taphian host * * * * led,[18] which Meges ruled, the offspring of Phyleus, leaving the island Echinades, inaccessible to sailors. And Ajax, the foster-child of Salamis, joined the right horn to the left, to which he was stationed nearest, joining them with his furthermost ships, with twelve most swift vessels, as I heard, and beheld the naval people. To which if any one add the barbarian barks, * * * * it will not obtain a return. * * * * Where I beheld the naval expedition, but hearing other things at home I preserve remembrance of the assembled army.

OLD M. Menelaus, thou art daring dreadful deeds thou shouldst not dare.

MENELAUS. Away with thee! thou art too faithful to thy masters.

OLD M. An honorable rebuke thou hast rebuked me with!

MEN. To thy cost shall it be, if thou dost that thou shouldst not do.

OLD M. You have no right to open the letter which I was carrying.

MEN. Nor shouldst thou bear ills to all the Greeks.

OLD M. Contest this point with others, but give up this [letter] to me.

MEN. I will not let it go.

OLD M. Nor will I let it go.

MEN. Then quickly with my sceptre will I make thine head bloody.

OLD M. But glorious it is to die for one's masters.

MEN. Let go. Being a slave, thou speakest too many words.

OLD M. O master, I am wronged, and this man, having snatched thy letter out of my hands, O Agamemnon, is unwilling to act rightly.

MEN. Ah! what is this tumult and disorder of words?

OLD M. My words, not his, are fittest to speak.[19]

AG. But wherefore, Menelaus, dost thou come to strife with this man and art dragging him by force?

MEN. Look at me, that I may take this commencement of my speech.

AG. What, shall I through fear not open mine eyelids, being born of Atreus?

MEN. Seest thou this letter, the minister of writings most vile?

AG. I see it, and do thou first let it go from thy hands.

MEN. Not, at least, before I show to the Greeks what is written therein.

AG. What, knowest thou what 'tis unseasonable thou shouldst know, having broken the seal?

MEN. Ay, so as to pain thee, having unfolded the ills thou hast wrought privily.

AG. But where didst thou obtain it? O Gods, for thy shameless heart!

MEN. Expecting thy daughter from Argos, whether she will come to the army.

AG. What behooves thee to keep watch upon my affairs? Is not this the act of a shameless man?

MEN. Because the will [to do so] teased me, and I am not born thy slave.

AG. Is it not dreadful? Shall I not be suffered to be master of my own family?

MEN. For thou thinkest inconsistently, now one thing, before another, another thing presently.

AG. Well hast thou talked evil. Hateful is a too clever tongue.[20]

MEN. But an unstable mind is an unjust thing to possess, and not clear[21] for friends. I wish to expostulate with thee, but do not thou in wrath turn away from the truth, nor will I speak overlong. Thou knowest when thou wast making interest to be leader of the Greeks against Troy—in seeming indeed not wishing it, but wishing it in will—how humble thou wast, taking hold of every right hand, and keeping open doors to any of the people that wished, and giving audience to all in turn even if one wished it not, seeking by manners to purchase popularity among the multitude. But when you obtained the power, changing to different manners, you were no longer the same friend as before to your old friends, difficult of access,[22] and rarely within doors. But it behooves not a man who has met with great fortune to change his manners, but then chiefly to be firm toward his friends, when he is best able to benefit them, being prosperous. I have first gone over these charges against thee, in which I first found thee base. But when thou afterward camest into Aulis and to the army of all the Greeks, thou wast naught, but wast in stupefaction at the fortune which then befell us from the Gods, lacking a favorable breeze for the journey. But the Greeks demanded that you should dismiss the ships, and not toil vainly at Aulis. But how cheerless and distressed a countenance you wore, because you were not able to land your army at Priam's land, having a thousand ships under command.[23] And thou besoughtest me, "What shall I do?" "But what resource shall I find from whence?" so that thou mightest not lose an ill renown, being deprived of the command. And then, when Calchas o'er the victims said that thou must sacrifice thy daughter to Diana, and that there would [then] be means of sailing for the Greeks, delighted in heart, you gladly promised to sacrifice your child, and of your own accord, not by compulsion—do not say so—you send to your wife to convoy your daughter hither, on a pretext of being wedded to Achilles. And then changing [your mind] you are caught altering to other writings, to the effect that you will not now be the slayer of your daughter. Very pretty, forsooth! This is the same air which heard these very protestations from thee. But innumerable men experience this in their affairs; they persevere in labor when in power,[24] and then make a bad result, sometimes through the foolish mind of the citizens, but sometimes with reason, themselves becoming incapable of preserving the state, I indeed chiefly groan for hapless Greece, who, wishing to work some doughty deed against these good-for-nothing barbarians, will let them, laughing at us, slip through her hands, on account of thee and thy daughter. I would not make any one ruler of the land for the sake of necessity,[25] nor chieftain of armed men. It behooves the general of the state to possess sense, for every man is a ruler who possesses sense.

CHOR. 'Tis dreadful for words and strife to happen between brothers, when they fall into dispute.

AG. I wish to address thee in evil terms, but mildly,[26] in brief, not uplifting mine eyelids too much aloft through insolence, but moderately, as being my brother. For a good man is wont to show respect [to others.] Tell me, why dost thou burst forth thus violently, having thy face suffused with rage? Who wrongs thee? What lackest thou? Wouldst fain gain a good wife! I can not supply thee, for thou didst ill rule over the one you possessed. Must I therefore pay the penalty of your mismanagement, who have made no mistake? Or does my ambition annoy thee? But wouldst thou fain hold in thine arms a fair woman, forgetting discretion and honor? Evil pleasures belong to an evil man. But if I, having before resolved ill, have changed to good counsel, am I mad? Rather art thou [mad,] who, having lost a bad wife, desirest to recover her, when God has well prospered thy fortune. The nuptial-craving suitors in their folly swore the oath to Tyndarus, but hope, I ween, was their God, and wrought this more than thyself and thy strength. Whom taking[27] make thou the expedition, but I think thou wilt know [that it is] through the folly of their hearts, for the divinity is not ignorant, but is capable of discerning oaths ill plighted and perforce. But I will not slay my children, so that thy state will in justice be well, revenge upon the worst of wives, but nights and days will waste me away in tears, having wrought lawless, unjust deeds against the children whom I begat. These words are briefly spoken to thee, both plain and easy, but if thou art unwilling to be wise, I will arrange my own affairs well.

CHOR. These words are different from those before spoken, but they are to a good effect, that the children be spared.

MEN. Alas! alas! have I then wretched no friends?

AG. [Yes, you have,] at least, if you do not wish to ruin your friends.

MEN. But how will you show that you are born of the same sire with me?

AG. I am born to be wise with you, not foolish.[28]

MEN. It behooves friends to grieve in common with friends.

AG. Admonish me by well doing, not by paining me.

MEN. Dost thou not then think fit to toil through this with Greece?

AG. But Greece, with thee, is sickening through some deity.

MEN. Vaunt then on thy sceptre, having betrayed thy brother. But I will seek some other schemes, and other friends.

MESSENGER. O Agamemnon, king of all the Greeks, I am come, bringing thy daughter to thee, whom thou didst name Iphigenia in thy palace. But her mother follows, the person of thy [wife] Clytæmnestra, and the boy Orestes, that thou mayest be pleased at the sight, being away from thine home a long season. But as they have come a long way, they and their mares are refreshing their female feet by the fair-flowing fountain, and we let loose the mares in a grassy meadow, that they might taste fodder. But I am come before them to prepare you [for their reception,] for a swift report passed through the army, that thy daughter had arrived. And all the multitude comes out hastily to the spectacle, that they may behold thy child. For prosperous men are renowned and conspicuous among all mortals. And they say, "Is there a marriage on foot? or what is going on?" Or, "Has king Agamemnon, having a yearning after his daughter, brought his child hither?" But from some you would have heard this: "They are initiating[30] the damsel in honor of Artemis, queen of Aulis, who will marry her." But come, get ready the baskets,[31] which come next, crown thine head. And do thou, king Menelaus, prepare a nuptial lay, and through the house let the pipe sound and let there be noise of feet, for this day comes blessed upon the virgin.

AG. I commend [your words,] but go thou within the house, and it shall be well, as fortune takes its course. Alas! what shall I wretched say? Whence shall I begin? Into what fetters of necessity have I fallen! Fortune has upturned me, so as to become far too clever for my cleverness. But lowness of birth has some advantage thus. For such persons are at liberty to weep, and speak unhappy words, but to him that is of noble birth, all these things belong. We have our dignity as ruler of our life, and are slaves to the multitude. For I am ashamed indeed to let fall the tear, yet again wretched am I ashamed not to weep, having come into the greatest calamities. Well! what shall I say to my wife? How shall I receive her? What manner of countenance shall I present? And truly she hath undone me, coming uncalled amidst the ills which before possessed me. And with reason did she follow her daughter, being about to deck her as a bride,[32] and to perform the dearest offices, where she will find us base. But for this hapless virgin—why [call her] virgin? Hades, as it seems, will speedily attend on her nuptials,—how do I pity her! For I think that she will beseech me thus: O father, wilt thou slay me? Such a wedding mayest thou thyself wed, and whosoever is a friend to thee. But Orestes being present will cry out knowingly words not knowing, for he is yet an infant. Alas! how has Priam's son, Paris, undone me by wedding the nuptials of Paris, who has wrought this!

CHOR. And I also pity her, as it becomes a stranger woman to moan for the misfortune of her lords.

MEN. Brother, give me thy right hand to touch.

AG. I give it, for thine is the power, but I am wretched.

MEN. I swear by Pelops, who was called the sire of my father and thine, and my father Atreus, that I indeed will tell thee plainly from my heart, and not any thing out of contrivance, but only what I think. I, beholding thee letting fall the tear from thine eyes, pitied thee, and myself let fall [a tear] for thee in return. And I have changed[33] my old determinations, not being wrath against you, but I will place myself in your present situation, and I recommend you neither to slay your child, nor to take my part; for it is not just that thou shouldst groan, but my affairs be in a pleasant state, and that thine should die, but mine behold the light. For what do I wish? Might I not obtain another choice alliance, if I crave nuptials? But, having undone my brother, whom it least behooved me, shall I receive Helen, an evil in place of a good? I was foolish and young, before that, viewing the matter closely, I saw what it is to beget children. Besides, pity came over me, considering our connection, for the hapless girl, who is about to be sacrificed because of my marriage. But what has thy virgin [daughter] to do with Helen? Let the army go, being disbanded from Aulis. But cease thou bedewing thine eyes with tears, my brother, and exciting me to tears. But if I have any concern in the oracle respecting thy daughter, let me have none: to thee I yield my part. But I have come to a change[34] from terrible resolutions. I have experienced[35] what was meet. I have changed to regard him who is sprung from a common source. Such changes belong not to a bad man, [viz.] to follow the best always.

CHOR. Thou hast spoken generous words, and becoming Tantalus the son of Jove. Thou disgracest not thine ancestors.

AG. I commend thee, Menelaus, in that, contrary to my expectation, you have subjoined these words, rightly, and worthily of thee.

MEN. A certain disturbance[36] between brothers arises on account of love, and avarice in their houses. I abhor such a relationship, mutually sore.

AG. But [consider,] for we are come into circumstances that render it necessary to accomplish the bloody slaughter of my daughter.

MEN. How? Who will compel thee to slay thy child?

AG. The whole assembly of the armament of the Greeks.

MEN. Not so, if at least thou dismiss it back to Argos.

AG. In this matter I might escape discovery, but in that I can not.[37]

MEN. What? One should not too much fear the multitude.

AG. Calchas will proclaim his prophecy to the army of the Greeks.

MEN. Not if he die first—and this is easy.

AG. The whole race of seers is an ambitious ill.

MEN. And in naught good or profitable, when at hand.[38]

AG. But dost thou not fear that which occurs to me?

MEN. How can I understand the word you say not?

AG. The son of Sisyphus knows all these matters.

MEN. It can not be that Orestes can pain thee and me.

AG. He is ever changeable, and with the multitude.

MEN. He is indeed possessed with the passion for popularity, a dreadful evil.

AG. Do you not then think that he, standing in the midst of the Greeks, will tell the oracles which Calchas pronounced, and of me, that I promised to offer a sacrifice to Diana, and then break my word. With which [words] having carried away the army, he will bid the Greeks slay thee and me, and sacrifice the damsel. And if I flee to Argos, they will come and ravage and raze the land, Cyclopean walls and all. Such are my troubles. O unhappy me! How, by the Gods, am I at a loss in these present matters! Take care of one thing for me, Menelaus, going through the army, that Clytæmnestra may not learn these matters, before I take and offer my daughter to Hades, that I may fare ill with as few tears as possible. But do ye, O stranger women, preserve silence.

CHORUS. Blest are they who share the nuptial bed of the Goddess Aphrodite,[39] when she is moderate, and with modesty, obtaining a calm from the maddening stings, when Love with his golden locks stretches his twin bow of graces, the one for a prosperous fate, the other for the upturning of life. I deprecate this [bow,] O fairest Venus, from our beds, but may mine be a moderate grace, and holy endearments, and may I share Aphrodite, but reject her when excessive. But the natures of mortals are different, and their manners are different,[40] but that which is clearly good is ever plain. And the education which trains[41] [men] up, conduces greatly to virtue, for to have reverence is wisdom, and it possesses an equivalent advantage, viz. to perceive what is fitting by one's mind, where report bears unwasting glory to life.[42] 'Tis a great thing to hunt for [the praise of] virtue, among women indeed, by a secret affection,[43] but among men, on the other hand, honor being inherent,[44] [bears that praise, honor,] which increases a state to an incalculable extent.[45]

Thou earnest, O Paris, †where thou wast trained up a shepherd with the white heifers of Ida, trilling a barbarian lay, breathing an imitation of the Phrygian pipes of Olympus on a reed. And the cows with their well-filled udders browsed, when the judgment of the Goddesses drove thee mad, which sends thee into Greece,† before the ivory-decked palaces, thou who didst strike love into the eyes of Helen which were upon thee, and thyself wast fluttered with love. Whence strife, strife brings Greece against the bulwarks of Troy with spears and ships.† Alas! alas! great are the fortunes of the great.[46] Behold the king's daughter, Iphigenia, my queen, and Clytæmnestra, daughter of Tyndarus, how are they sprung from the great, and to what suitable fortune they are come. The powerful, in sooth, and the wealthy, are Gods to those of mortals who are unblest. [Let us stand still, ye children of Chalcis, let us receive the queen from her chariot to the earth, not unsteadily, but gently with the soft attention of our hands, lest the renowned daughter of Agamemnon, newly coming to me, be alarmed, nor let us, as strangers to strangers, cause disturbance or fear to the Argive ladies.[47]]

[*Enter* Clytæmnestra, IPHIGENIA, *and probably* ORESTES *in a chariot. They descend from it, while the Chorus make obeisance.*]

CLY. I regard both your kindness and your favorable words as a good omen, and I have some hope that I am here as escort [of my daughter] to honorable nuptials. But take out of my chariot the dower-gifts which I bear for my girl, and send them carefully into the house. And do thou, my child, quit the horse-chariot, setting [carefully] thy foot delicate and at the same time tender. But you,[48] maidens, receive her in your arms, and lift her from the chariot. And let some one give me the firm support of his hand, that I may beseemingly leave the chariot-seat. But do some[49] of you stand in front of the horses' yoke, for the uncontrolled eye of horses is timorous, and take this boy, the son of Agamemnon, Orestes, for he is still an infant. Child! dost sleep, overcome by the ride? Wake up happily for thy sisters' nuptials. For thou thyself being noble shalt obtain relationship with a good man, the God-like son of the daughter of Nereus. [[50]Next come thou close to my foot, O daughter, to thy mother, Iphigenia, and standing near, show these strangers how happy I am, and come hither indeed, and address thy dear father.] O thou most great glory to me, king Agamemnon, we are come, not disobeying thy bidding.

IPH. O mother, running indeed, (but be thou not angry,) I will apply my breast to my father's breast. [[51]But I wish, rushing to embrace thy breast, O father, after a long season. For I long for thy face. But do not be angry.]

CLY. But, O my child, enjoy [thine embraces,] but thou wert ever most fond of thy father, of all the children I bore.

IPH. O father, joyous do I behold thee after a long season.

AG. And I, thy father, [joyously behold] thee. Thou speakest thus equally in respect to both.

IPH. Hail! But well hast thou done in bringing me to thee, O father.

AG. I know not how I shall say, yet not say so, my child.

IPH. Ah! how uneasily dost thou regard me, joyfully beholding me [before.]

AG. A king and general has many cares.

IPH. Give thyself up to me now, and turn not thyself to cares.

AG. But I am altogether concerned with thee, and on no other subject.

IPH. Relax thy brow, and open thy eyes in joy.

AG. See, I rejoice as I rejoice, at seeing thee, child.[52]

IPH. And then dost let fall a tear from thine eyes?

AG. For long to us is the coming absence.

IPH. I know not what you mean, I know not, dearest father mine.

AG. Speaking sensibly, thou movest me the more to pity.

IPH. I will speak foolishly, if I so may rejoice you.

AG. Alas! I can not keep silence, but I commend thee.

IPH. Remain, O father, in the house with thy children,

AG. I fain would, but not having what I would, I am pained.

IPH. Perish war and the ills of Menelaus![53]

AG. What has undone me will first undo others.

IPH. How long a time wast thou absent in the recesses of Aulis!

AG. And now also there is something hinders me from sending on the army.

IPH. Where say they that the Phrygians dwell, father?

AG. Where would that Paris, Priam's son, had never dwelt.

IPH. And dost thou go a long distance, O father, when thou leavest me?

AG. Thou art come, my daughter, to the same state with thy father.[54]

IPH. Alas! would that it were fitting me and thee to take me with thee as thy fellow-sailor.

AG. But there is yet a sailing for thee, where thou wilt remember thy father.

IPH. Shall I go, sailing with my mother, or alone?

AG. Alone, apart from thy father and mother.

IPH. What, art thou going to make me dwell in other houses, father?

AG. Cease. It is not proper for girls to know these matters.

IPH. Hasten back from Phrygia, do, my father, having settled matters well there.

AG. It first behooves me to offer a certain sacrifice here.

IPH. But it is with the priests that thou shouldst consider sacred matters.

AG. [Yet] shalt thou know it, for thou wilt stand round the altar.

IPH. What, shall we stand in chorus round the altar, my father?[55]

AG. I deem thee happier than myself, for that thou knowest nothing. But go within the house, that the girls may behold thee,[56] having given me a sad kiss and thy right hand, being about to dwell a long time away from thy sire. O bosom and cheeks, O yellow tresses, how has the city of the Phrygians proved a burden to us, and Helen! I cease my words, for swift does the drop trickle from mine eyes when I touch thee. Go into the house. But I, I crave thy pardon, (*to Clytæmnestra,*) daughter of Leda, if I showed too much feeling, being about to bestow my daughter on Achilles. For the departure [of a girl] is a happy one, but nevertheless it pains the parents, when a father, who has toiled much, delivers up his children to another home.

CLY. I am not so insensible—but think thou that I shall experience the same feelings, (so that I should not chide thee,) when I lead forth my girl with nuptial rejoicings, but custom wears away these thoughts in course of time. I know, however, the name of him to whom thou hast promised thy daughter, but I would fain know of what race, and whence [he is.]

AG. Ægina was the daughter of her father Asopus.

CLY. And who of mortals or of Gods wedded her?

AG. Jove, and she gave birth to Æacus, prince of Œnone.

CLY. But what son obtained the house of Æacus?

AG. Peleus, and Peleus obtained the daughter of Nereus.

CLY. By the gift of the God, or taking her in spite of the Gods?

AG. Jove acted as a sponsor, and bestowed her, having the power.[57]

CLY. And where does he wed her? In the wave of the sea?

AG. Where Chiron dwells at the sacred foot of Pelion.

CLY. Where they say that the race of Centaurs dwells?

AG. Here the Gods celebrated the nuptial feast of Peleus.

CLY. But did Thetis, or his father, train up Achilles?

AG. Chiron, that he might not learn the manners of evil mortals.

CLY. Hah! wise was the instructor, and wiser he who intrusted him.

AG. Such a man will be the husband of thy child.

CLY. Not to be found fault with. But what city in Greece does he inhabit?

AG. Near the river Apidanus in the confines of Phthia.

CLY. Thither will he lead thy virgin [daughter] and mine.

AG. This shall be the care of him, her possessor.

CLY. And may the pair be happy; but on what day will he wed her?

AG. When the prospering orb of the moon comes round.

CLY. But hast thou already sacrificed the first offerings for thy daughter to the Goddess?

AG. I am about to do so. In this matter we are now engaged.

CLY. And wilt thou then celebrate a wedding-feast afterward?

AG. [Ay,] having sacrificed such offerings as it behooves me to sacrifice to the Gods.

CLY. But where shall we set out a banquet for the women?

AG. Here, by the fair-pooped ships of the Greeks.

CLY. Well, and poorly,[58] forsooth! but may it nevertheless turn out well.

AG. Do then thou knowest what, O lady, and obey me.

CLY. In what? for I am accustomed to obey thee.

AG. We indeed in this place, where the bridegroom is—

CLY. Will do what without the mother, [of those things] which it behooves me to do?

AG. —will bestow your daughter among the Greeks.

CLY. But where must I be in the mean time?

AG. Go to Argos, and take care of your virgins.

CLY. Leaving my child? And who will bear the [nuptial] torch?

AG. I will furnish the light that becomes the nuptials.

CLY. The custom is not thus, but you think these matters trifles.

AG. It is not proper that thou shouldst mingle in the crowd of the army.

CLY. It is proper that I, the mother, should bestow at least my own daughter.

AG. And it [is proper] that the damsels at home should not be alone.

CLY. They are well guarded in their close chambers.

AG. Obey me.

CLY. [No,] by the Argive Goddess queen. But go you, and attend to matters abroad, but I [will mind] the affairs at home, as to the things which should be present to virgins at their wedding.[59]

AG. Alas! In vain have I toiled,[60] and have been frustrated in my hope, wishing to send my wife out of my sight. But I am using stratagems, and finding contrivances against those I best love, overcome at all points. But nevertheless with the prophet Calchas I will go and ask the pleasure of the Goddess, not fortunate for me, the trouble of Greece.[61] But it behooves a wise man either to support a useful and good wife in his house or not to marry at all.[62]

CHORUS. The assembly of the Grecian army will come to Simois, and to the silver eddies, both with ships and with arms, to Ilium, and to the Phœbeian plain of Troy, where I hear that Cassandra, adorned with a green-blossoming crown of laurel, lets loose her yellow locks, when the prophetic influence of the Gods breathes upon her. And the Trojans will stand upon the towers of Troy and around its walls, when brazen-shielded Mars, borne over the sea in fair-prowed ships, approaches the beds of Simois by rowing, seeking to bear away Helen, [the sister] of the twain sons of Jove in heaven, into the land of Greece, by the war-toiling shields and spears of the Greeks. But having surrounded Pergamus,[63] the city of the Phrygians, around its towers of stone, with bloody Mars, having torn off the heads [of the citizens] cut from their necks, having completely ravaged the city of Troy, he will make the daughters and wife of Priam shed many tears. But Helen, the daughter of Jove, will sit† in sad lamentation, having left her husband. Never upon me or upon my children's children may this expectation come, such as the wealthy Lydian and Phrygian wives possess while at their spinning, conversing thus with each other. Who,[64] dragging out my fair-haired tresses, will choose me as his spoil despite my tears, while my country is perishing? Through thee [forsooth,] the offspring of the long-necked swan, if indeed the report is true, that Leda † met with[65] a winged bird, when the body of Jove was transformed, and then in the tablets of the muses fables spread these reports among men, inopportunely, and in vain.

[Enter ACHILLES.]

ACHILLES. Where about here is the general of the Greeks? Who of the servants will tell him that Achilles, the son of Peleus, is seeking him at the gates? For we do not remain by the Euripus in equal condition; for some of us being unyoked in nuptials, having left our solitary homes, sit here upon the shore, but others, having wives and children:[66] so violent a passion for this expedition has fallen upon Greece, not without the will of the Gods. It is therefore right that I should speak of what concerns me, and whoever else wishes will himself speak for himself. For leaving the Pharsalian land, and Peleus, I am waiting for these light gales of Euripus,[67] restraining the Myrmidons, who are continually pressing me, and saying, "Achilles, why tarry we? what manner of time must the armament against Troy yet measure out? At any rate act, if you are going to do any thing, or lead the army home, not abiding the delays of the Atrides."

CLY. O son of the Goddess, daughter of Nereus, hearing from within thy words, I have come out before the house.

ACH. O hallowed modesty, who can this woman be whom I behold here, possessing a fair-seeming form?

CLY. It is no wonder that you know me not, whom you have never seen before, but I commend you because you respect modesty.

ACH. But who art thou? And wherefore hast thou come to the assembly of the Greeks, a woman to men guarded with shields?

CLY. I am the daughter of Leda, and Clytæmnestra is my name, and my husband is king Agamemnon.

ACH. Well hast thou in few words spoken what is seasonable. But it is unbecoming for me to converse with women. (Is going.)

CLY. Remain, (why dost thou fly?) at least join thy right hand with mine, as a happy commencement of betrothal.

ACH. What sayest thou? I [give] thee my right hand? I should be ashamed of Agamemnon, if I touched what is not lawful for me.

CLY. It is particularly lawful, since you are going to wed my daughter, O son of the sea Goddess, daughter of Nereus.

ACH. What marriage dost thou say? Surprise possesses me, lady, unless, being beside yourself, you speak this new thing.

CLY. This is the nature of all people, to be ashamed when they behold new friends, and are put in mind of nuptials.

ACH. I never wooed thy daughter, lady, nor has any thing been said to me on the subject of marriage by the Atrides.

CLY. What can it be? Do you in turn marvel at my words, for thine are a marvel to me.

ACH. Conjecture; these matters are a common subject for conjecture, for both of us perhaps are deceived in our words.[68]

CLY. But surely I have suffered terrible things! I am acting as match-maker in regard to a marriage that has no existence. I am ashamed of this.

ACH. Perhaps some one has trifled with both me and thee. But pay no attention to it, and bear it with indifference.

CLY. Farewell, for I can no longer behold thee with uplifted eyes, having appeared as a liar, and suffered unworthy things.

ACH. And this same [farewell] is thine from me. But I will go seek thy husband within this house.

[*The* OLD MAN *appears at the door of the house.*]

OLD M. O stranger, grandson of Æacus, remain. Ho! thee, I say, the son of the Goddess, and thee, the daughter of Leda.

ACM. Who is it that calls, partially opening the doors? With what terror he calls!

OLD M. A slave. I will not be nice about the title, for fortune allows it not.

ACH. Of whom? for thou art not mine. My property and Agamemnon's are different.

OLD M. Of this lady who is before the house, the gift of her father Tyndarus.

ACH. We are still. Say if thou wantest any thing, for which thou hast stopped me.

OLD M. Are ye sure that ye alone stand before these gates?

CLY. Ay, so that you may speak to us only. But come out from the royal dwelling.

OLD M. (Coming forward) O fortune, and foresight mine, preserve whom I wish.

ACH. These words will do for[69] a future occasion, for they have some weight.

CLY. By thy right hand [I beseech thee,] delay not, if thou hast aught to say to me.

OLD M. Thou knowest then, being what manner of man, I have been by nature well disposed to thee and thy children.

CLY. I know thee as being a faithful servant to my house.

OLD M. And that king Agamemnon received me among thy dowry.

CLY. Thou camest into Argos with us, and thou wast always mine.

OLD M. So it is, and I am well disposed to thee, but less so to thy husband.

CLY. Unfold now at least to me what words you are saying.

OLD M. The father who begat her is about to slay thy daughter with his own hand.

CLY. How? I deprecate thy words, old man, for thou thinkest not well.

OLD M. Cutting the fair neck of the hapless girl with the sword.

CLY. O wretched me! Is my husband mad?

OLD M. He is in his right mind, save with respect to thee and thy daughter, but in this he is not wise.

CLY. Upon what grounds? What maddening fiend impels him?

OLD M. The oracles, as at least Calchas says, in order that the army may be able to proceed.

CLY. Whither? Wretched me, and wretched she whom her father is about to slay?

OLD M. To the house of Dardanus, that Menelaus may recover Helen.

CLY. To the destruction, then, of Iphigenia, was the return of Helen foredoomed?

OLD M. Thou hast the whole story. Her father is going to offer thy daughter to Diana.

CLY. What! what pretext had the marriage, that brought me from home?

OLD M. That thou rejoicing mightest bring thy child, as if about to wed her to Achilles.

CLY. O daughter, both thou and thy mother are come to meet with destruction.

OLD M. Ye twain are suffering sad things, and dreadful things hath Agamemnon dared.

CLY. I wretched am undone, and my eyes no longer restrain the tear.

OLD M. For bitter 'tis to mourn, deprived of one's children.

CLY. But whence, old man, sayest thou that thou hast learned and knowest these things?

OLD M. I went to bear a letter to thee, in reference to what was before written.

CLY. Not allowing, or bidding me to bring my child, that she might die?

OLD M. [It was] that you should not bring her, for your husband then thought well.

CLY. And how was it then, that, bearing the letter, thou gavest it not to me?

OLD M. Menelaus, who is the cause of these evils, took it from me.

CLY. O child of Nereus' daughter, O son of Peleus, dost hear these things?

ACH. I hear that thou art wretched, and I do not bear my part indifferently.

CLY. They will slay my child, having deceived her with thy nuptials.

ACH. I also blame thy husband, nor do I bear it lightly.

CLY. I will not be ashamed to fall down at thy knee, mortal, to one born of a Goddess. For wherefore should I make a show of pride? Or what should I study more than my children? But, O son of the Goddess, aid me in my unhappiness, and her who is called thy wife, vainly indeed, but nevertheless, having decked her out, I led her as if to be married, but now I lead her to sacrifice, and reproach will come upon thee, who gavest no aid. For though thou wast not yoked in nuptials, at least thou wast called the beloved husband of the hapless virgin. By thy beard, by thy right hand, by thy mother [I beseech] thee, for thy name hath undone me, to whom thou shouldst needs give assistance. I have no other altar to fly to, but thy knee, nor is any friend near me,[70] but thou hearest the cruel and all-daring conduct of Agamemnon. But I a woman, as thou seest, have come to a naval host, uncontrolled, and bold for mischief, but useful, when they are willing. But if thou wilt venture to stretch thine hand in my behalf, we are saved, but if not, we are not saved.

CHOR. A terrible thing it is to be a mother, and it bears a great endearment, and one common to all, so as to toil on behalf of their children.

ACH. My mind is high-lifted in its thoughts,[71] and knows both how to grieve [moderately] in troubles, and to rejoice moderately in high prosperity. For the discreet among mortals are such as pass through life correctly with wisdom. Now there are certain cases where it is pleasant not to be too wise, and also where it is useful to possess wisdom. But I, being nurtured [in the dwelling] of a most pious man, Chiron, have learned to possess a candid disposition. And I will obey the Atrides, if indeed they order well, but when not well, I obey not. But here in Troy showing a free nature I will glorify Mars with the spear, as far as I can. But, O thou who hast suffered wretchedly at the hands of those dearest, in whatever can be done by a youth, I, showing so much pity, will set thee right, and thy daughter, having been called my bride, shall never be sacrificed by her father, for I will not furnish thy husband with my person to weave stratagems upon. For my name, even if he lift not up the sword, will slay thy daughter, but thy husband is the cause. But my body is no longer pure, if on my account, and because of my marriage, there perish a virgin who has gone through sad and unbearable troubles, and has been marvelously and undeservedly ill treated. I were the worst man among the Greeks, I were of naught (but Menelaus would be among men), not as born from Peleus, but from some fiend, if my name acts the murderer for thy husband.[72] By Nereus, nurtured in the damp waves, the father of Thetis, who begat me, king Agamemnon shall not lay hands on thy daughter, not so much as with a little finger, so as to touch her garments. I' faith, Sipylus, a fortress of barbarians, whence the [royal] generals trace their descent, shall be deemed a city, but the name of Phthia shall nowhere be named. And the seer Calchas will to his cost consecrate the sacrificial cakes and lustral waters. (But what man is a prophet?) who tells[73] a few things true, (but many falsely,) when he has made a hit, but when he fails, is undone. These words are not spoken for the sake of my wedding, (ten thousand girls are hunting after alliance with me,) but [because] king Agamemnon has been guilty of insult toward me. But it behooved him to ask [the use of] my name from me, as an enticement for his daughter, and Clytæmnestra would have been most readily persuaded to give her daughter to me as a husband. And I would have given her up to the Greeks, if on this account their passage to Troy had been impeded: I would not have refused to augment the common interest of those with whom I set out on the expedition. But now I am held as of no account by the generals, and it is a matter of indifference whether I benefit them or not. Soon shall my sword witness, which, before death came against the Phrygians,[74] I stained with spots of blood, whether any one shall take thy daughter from me. But keep quiet, I have appeared to thee as a most mighty God, though not [a God,] but nevertheless I will be such.

CHOR. O son of Peleus, thou hast spoken both worthily of thyself, and of the marine deity, hallowed Goddess.

CLY. Alas! how can I praise thee neither too much in words, nor, being deficient in this respect, [not] lose thy favor? For in a certain wise the praised dislike their praisers, if they praise too much. But I am ashamed at alleging pitiable words, being troubled in myself, while thou art not diseased with my ills. But in fact the good man has some reason, even though he be unconnected with them, for assisting the unfortunate. But pity us, for we have suffered pitiably; I, who, in the first place, thinking to have thee for a kinsman, cherished a vain hope.—Moreover, my child, by dying, might perchance become an omen to thy future bridals,[75] which thou must needs avoid. But well didst thou speak both first and last, for, if thou art willing, my child will be saved. Dost wish that she embrace thy knee as a suppliant? Such conduct is not virgin-like, but if thou wilt, she shall come, with her noble face suffused with modesty. Or shall I obtain these things from thee, without her presence?

ACH. Let her remain within doors, for with dignity she preserves her dignity.

CLY. Yet one must needs have modesty [only] as far as circumstances allow.

ACH. Do thou neither bring forth thy daughter into my sight, lady, not let us fall into reproach for inconsiderate conduct, for our assembled army, being idle from home occupations, loves evil and slanderous talk. But at all events you will accomplish the same, whether you come to me as a suppliant, or do not supplicate, for a mighty contest awaits me, to release you from these evils. Wherefore, having heard one thing, be persuaded that I will not speak falsely. But if I speak falsely, and vainly amuse you, may I perish; but may I not perish, if I preserve the virgin.

CLY. Mayest thou be blest, ever assisting the unhappy.

ACH. Hear me then, that the matter may be well.

CLY. What is this thou sayest? for one must listen to thee.

ACH. Let us again persuade her father to be wiser.

CLY. He is a coward, and fears the army too much.

ACH. But words can conquer words.

CLY. Chilly is the hope, but tell me what I must do.

ACH. Beseech him first not to slay his child, but if he oppose this, you must come to me. For if he will be persuaded what you wish, there is no occasion for my efforts, for this very [consent] contains her safety. And I also shall appear in a better light with my friend, and the army will not blame me, if I transact matters by discretion rather than force. And if this turn out well, these things, even without my help, may turn out satisfactorily to thy friends and thyself.[76]

CLY. How wisely hast thou spoken! But what thou sayest must be done. But if I do not obtain what I seek, where shall I again see thee? Where must I wretched woman, coming, find thee an assistant in my troubles?

ACH. We guards will watch thee when there is occasion, lest any one behold thee going in agitation through the host of the Greeks. But do not shame thy ancestral home, for Tyndarus is not worthy of an evil reputation, seeing he is great among the Greeks.

CLY. These things shall be. Command; it is meet that I obey thee. But if there are Gods, you, being a just man, will receive a good reward; but if not, why should one toil?

CHOR. What was that nuptial song that raised[77] its strains on the Libyan reed, and with the dance-loving lyre, and the reedy syrinx, when o'er Pelion at the feast of the Gods the fair-haired muses, striking their feet with golden sandals against the ground, came to the wedding of Peleus, celebrating with melodious sounds Thetis, and the son of Æacus, on the mountains of the Centaurs, through the Palian wood.

But the Dardan,[78] [Phrygian Ganymede,] dear delight of Jove's bed, poured out the nectar in the golden depths of the goblets, and along the white sands the fifty daughters of Nereus, entwining in circles, adorned the nuptials of Nereus with the dance. But with darts of fir, and crowns of grass, the horse-mounted troop of the Centaurs came to the banquet of the Gods and the cup of Bacchus. And the Thessalian girls shouted loud,[79] "O daughter of Nereus," and the prophet Phœbus, and Chiron, skilled in letters, declared, "Thou shalt bring forth a mighty light, who shall come to the [Trojan] land with Myrmidons armed with spear and shield, to burn the renowned city of Priam, around his body armed with a covering of golden arms wrought by Vulcan, having them as a gift from his Goddess Thetis, who begat him blessed." Then the deities celebrated the nuptials of the noble daughter of Nereus first,[80] and of Peleus. But thee, [O Iphigenia,] they will crown on the head with flowery garlands, like as a pure spotted heifer from a rocky cave, making bloody the mortal throat [of one] not trained up with the pipe, nor amidst the songs of herdsmen, but as a bride[81] prepared by thy mother for some one of the Argives. Where has the face of shame, or virtue any power to prevail? Since impiety indeed has influence, but virtue is left behind and disregarded by mortals, and lawlessness governs law, and it is a common struggle for mortals, lest any envy of the Gods befall.

CLY. I have come out of the house to seek for my husband, who has been absent, and has quitted the house a long time. But my hapless daughter is in tears, casting forth many a change of complaint, having heard the death her father devises for her. But I was mindful of Agamemnon who is now coming hither,[82] who will quickly be detected doing evil deeds against his own children.

AG. Daughter of Leda, opportunely have I found you without the house, that I may tell thee, apart from the virgin, words which it is not meet for those to hear who are about to marry.

CLY. And what is it, on which your convenience lays hold?

AG. Send forth thy daughter from the house with her father, since the lustral waters are ready prepared, and the salt-cakes to scatter with the hands upon the purifying flame, and heifers, which needs must be slain in honor of the Goddess Diana before the marriage solemnities, a shedding of black gore.

CLY. In words, indeed, thou speakest well, but for thy deeds, I know not how I may say thou speakest well. But come without, O daughter, for thou knowest all that thy father meditates, and beneath thy robes bring the child Orestes, thy brother. See, she is here present to obey thee. But the rest I will speak on her behalf and mine.

AG. Child, why weepest thou, and no longer beholdest me cheerfully, but fixing thy face upon the ground, keepest thy vest before it?

CLY. Alas! What commencement of my sorrows shall I take? For I may use them all as first, [both last, and middle throughout.[83]]

AG. But what is it? How all of you are come to one point with me, bearing disturbed and alarmed countenances.

CLY. Wilt thou answer candidly, husband, if I ask thee?

AG. There needs no admonition: I would fain be questioned.

CLY. Art thou going to slay thy child and mine?

AG. Ah! wretched things dost thou say, and thinkest what thou shouldst not.

CLY. Keep quiet, and first in turn answer me that.

AG. But if thou askest likely things, thou wilt hear likely.

CLY. I ask no other things, nor do thou answer me others.

AG. O revered destiny, and fate, and fortune mine!

CLY. Ay, and mine too, and this child's, one of three unfortunates!

AG. But in what art thou wronged?

CLY. Dost thou ask me this? This thy wit hath no wit.[84]

AG. I am undone. My secret plans are betrayed.

CLY. I know and have learned all that you are about to do to me, and the very fact of thy silence, and of thy groaning much, is a proof that you confess it. Do not take the trouble to say any thing.

AG. Behold, I am silent: for what need is there that, falsely speaking, I add shamelessness to misfortune?

CLY. Listen, then, for I will unfold my story, and will no longer make use of riddles away from the purpose. In the first place, that I may first reproach thee with this—thou didst wed me unwilling, and obtain me by force, having slain Tantalus, my former husband, and having dashed[85] my infant living to the ground, having torn him by force from my breast. And the twin sons of Jove, my brothers, glorying in their steeds, made war [against thee] but my old father Tyndarus saved you, when you had become a suppliant, and thou again didst possess me as a wife. When I, being reconciled to thee in respect to thy person and home, thou wilt bear witness how blameless a wife I was, both modest in respect to affection, and enriching thy house, so that thou both going within and without thy doors wast blessed. And 'tis a rare prize for a man to obtain such a wife, but there is no lack of getting a bad spouse. And I bear thee this son, besides three virgins, of one of whom thou art cruelly going to deprive me. And if any one ask thee on what account thou wilt slay her, say, what will you answer? or must I needs make your plea, "that Menelaus may obtain Helen?" A pretty custom, forsooth, that children must pay the price of a bad woman. We gain the most hateful things at the hand of those dearest. Come, if thou wilt set out, leaving me at home, and then wilt be a long time absent, what sort of feelings dost think I shall experience, when I behold every seat empty of this child's presence, and every virgin chamber empty, but myself sit in tears alone, ever mourning her [in such strains as these:] "My child, thy father, who begat thee, hath destroyed thee, himself, no other, the slayer, by no other hand, leaving such a reward for [my care of] the house."[86] Since there wants but a little reason for me and my remaining daughters to give thee such a reception as you deserve to receive. Do not, by the Gods, either compel me to act evilly toward thee, nor do thou thyself be so. Ah well! thou wilt sacrifice thy daughter—what prayers wilt thou then utter? What good thing wilt thou crave for thyself, slaying thy child? An evil return, seeing, forsooth, thou hast disgracefully set out from home. But is it right that I should pray for thee any good thing? Verily we must believe the Gods are senseless, if we feel well disposed to murderers. But wilt thou, returning to Argos, embrace thy children? But 'tis not lawful for thee. Will any of your children look upon you, if thou offerest one of them for slaughter? Thus far have I proceeded in my argument. What! does it only behoove thee to carry about thy sceptre and marshal the army?— whose duty it were to speak a just speech among the Greeks: "Do ye desire, O Greeks, to sail against the land of the Phrygians? Cast lots, whose daughter needs must die"— for this would be on equal terms, but not that you should give thy daughter to the Greeks as a chosen victim. Or Menelaus, whose affair it was, ought to slay Hermione for her mother's sake. But now I, having cherished thy married life, shall be bereaved of my child, but she who has sinned, bearing her daughter under her care to Sparta, will be blest. As to these things, answer me if I say aught not rightly, but if I have spoken well, do not then slay thy child and mine, and thou wilt be wise.

CHOR. Be persuaded, Agamemnon, for 'tis right to join in saving one's children. No one of mortals will gainsay this.

IPH. If, O father, I possessed the eloquence of Orpheus, that I might charm by persuasion, so that rocks should follow me, and that I might soften whom I would by my words, to this would I have resorted. But now I will offer tears as all my skill, for these I can. And, as a suppliant bough, I press against thy knees my body, which this [my mother] bore thee, [beseeching] that thou slay me not before my time, for sweet it is to behold the light, nor do thou compel me to visit the places beneath the earth. And I first[87] hailed thee sire, and thou [didst first call] me daughter, and first drawing nigh to thy knees, I gave and in turn received sweet tokens of affection. And such, were thy words: "My daughter, shall I some time behold thee prospering in a husband's home, living and flourishing worthily of me?" And mine in turn ran thus, as I hung about thy beard, which now with my hand I embrace: "But how shall I [treat] thee? Shall I receive thee when an old man, O father, with the hearty reception of my house, repaying thee the careful nurture of my youth?" Of such words have remembrance, but thou hast forgotten them, and fain wouldst slay me. Do not, [I beseech you] by Pelops and by thy father Atreus, and this my mother, who having before brought me forth with throes, now suffers this second throe. What have I to do with the marriage of Paris and Helen? Whence came he, father, for my destruction? Look upon me; give me one look, one kiss, that this memorial of thee at least I, dying, may possess, if thou wilt not be persuaded by my words. Brother, thou art but a little helpmate to those dear, yet weep with me, beseech thy sire that thy sister die not. Even in babes there is wont to be some sense of evil. Behold, O father, he silently implores thee. But respect my prayer, and have pity on my years. Yea, by thy beard we, two dear ones, implore thee; the one is yet a nursling, but the other grown up. In one brief saying I will overcome all arguments. This light of heaven is sweetest of things for men to behold, but that below is naught; and mad is he who seeks to die. To live dishonorably is better than to die gloriously.

CHOR. O wretched Helen, through thee and thy nuptials there is come a contest for the Atrides and their children.

AG. I can understand what merits pity, and what not; and I love my children, for [otherwise] I were mad. And dreadful 'tis for me[88] to dare these things, O woman, and dreadful not to do so—for so I must needs act. Thou seest how great is this naval host, and how many are the chieftains of brazen arms among the Greeks, to whom there is not a power of arriving at the towers of Troy, unless I sacrifice you, as the seer Calchas says, nor can we take the renowned plain of Troy. But a certain passion has maddened the army of the Greeks, to sail as quickly as possible upon the land of the barbarians, and to put a stop to the rapes of Grecian wives. And they will slay my daughters at Argos, and you, and me, if I break through the commands of the Goddess. It is not Menelaus who has enslaved me, O daughter, nor have I followed his device, but Greece, for whom I, will or nill, must needs offer thee. And I am inferior on this head. For it behooves her, [Helen,] as far as thou, O daughter, art concerned, to be free, nor for us, being Greeks, to be plundered perforce of our wives by barbarians.

CLY. O child! O ye stranger women! O wretched me for thy death! Thy father flees from thee, giving thee up to Hades.

IPH. Alas for me! mother, mother. The same song suits both of us on account of our fortunes, and no more to me is the light, nor this bright beam of the sun. Alas! alas! thou snow-smitten wood of Troy, and mountains of Ida, where once on a time Priam exposed a tender infant, having separated him from his mother, that he might meet with deadly fate, Paris, who was styled Idæan, Idæan [Paris] in the city of the Phrygians. Would that the herdsman Paris, who was nurtured in care of steers, had ne'er dwelt near the white stream, where are the fountains of the Nymphs, and the meadow flourishing with blooming flowers, and roseate flowers and hyacinths for Goddesses to cull. Where once on a time came Pallas, and artful Venus, and Juno, and Hermes, the messenger of Jove; Venus indeed, vaunting herself in charms, and Pallas in the spear, and Juno in the royal nuptials of king Jove, [these came] to a hateful judgment and strife concerning beauty; but my death, my death, O virgins, bearing glory indeed to the Greeks, Diana hath received as first-fruits [of the expedition] against Troy.[89] But he that begot me wretched, O mother, O mother, has departed, leaving me deserted. O hapless me! having †beheld† bitter, bitter, ill-omened Helen, I am slain, I perish, by the impious slaughter of an impious sire. Would[90] for me that Aulis had never received the poops of the brazen-beaked ships into these ports, the fleet destined for Troy, nor that Jove had breathed an adverse wind over Euripus, softening one breeze so that some mortals might rejoice in their [expanded] sails, but to others a pain, to others difficulty, to some to set sail, to others to furl their sails, but to others to tarry. In truth the race of mortals is full of troubles, is full of troubles, and it necessarily befalls men to find some misfortune. Alas! alas! thou daughter of Tyndarus, who hast brought many sufferings, and many griefs upon the Greeks.

CHOR. I indeed pity you having met with an evil calamity, such as thou never shouldst have met with.

IPH. O mother, to whom I owe my birth, I behold a crowd of men near.

CLY. Ay, the son of the Goddess, my child, for whom thou camest hither.

IPH. Open the house, ye servants, that I may hide myself.

CLY. But why dost thou fly hence, my child?

IPH. I am ashamed to behold this Achilles.

CLY. On what account?

IPH. The unfortunate turn-out of my nuptials shames me.

CLY. Thou art not in a state to give way to delicacy in the present circumstances. But do thou remain, there is no use for punctilio, if we can [but save your life.]

ACH. O hapless lady, daughter of Leda.

CLY. Thou sayest not falsely.

ACH. Terrible things are cried out among the Greeks.

CLY. What cry? tell me.

ACH. Concerning thy child.

CLY. Thou speakest a word of ill omen.

ACH. That it is necessary to slay her.

CLY. Does no one speak the contrary to this?

ACH. Ay, I myself have got into trouble.

CLY. Into what [trouble,] O friend?

ACH. Of having my body stoned with stones.

CLY. What, in trying to save my daughter!

ACH. This very thing.

CLY. And who would have dared to touch thy person?

ACH. All the Greeks.

CLY. And was not the host of the Myrmidons at hand for thee?

CI

ACH. That was the first that showed enmity.

CLY. Then are we utterly undone, my daughter.

ACH. For they railed at me as overcome by a betrothed—

CLY. And what didst thou reply?

ACH. That they should not slay my intended bride.

CLY. For so 'twas right.

ACH. [She] whom her father had promised me.

CLY. Ay, and had sent for from Argos.

ACH. But I was worsted by the outcry.

CLY. For the multitude is a terrible evil.

ACH. But nevertheless I will aid thee.

CLY. And wilt thou, being one, fight with many?

ACH. Dost see these men bearing [my] arms?

CLY. Mayest thou gain by thy good intentions.

ACH. But I will gain.

CLY. Then my child will not be slain?

ACH. Not, at least, with my consent.

CLY. And will any one come to lay hands on the girl?

ACH. Ay, a host of them, but Ulysses will conduct her.

CLY. Will it be the descendant of Sisyphus?

ACH. The very man.

CLY. Doing it of his own accord, or appointed by the army?

ACH. Chosen willingly.

CLY. A wicked choice forsooth, to commit slaughter!

ACH. But I will restrain him.

CLY. But will he lead her unwillingly, having seized her?

ACH. Ay, by her auburn locks.

CLY. But what must I then do?

ACH. Keep hold of your daughter.

CLY. As far as this goes she shall not be slain.

ACH. But it will come to this at all events.[91]

IPH. Mother, do thou hear my words, for I perceive that thou art vainly wrathful with thy husband, but it is not easy for us to struggle with things [almost] impossible. It is meet therefore to praise our friend for his willingness, but it behooves thee also to see that you be not an object of reproach to the army, and we profit nothing more, and he meet with calamity. But hear me, mother, thinking upon what has entered my mind. I have determined to die, and this I would fain do gloriously, I mean, by dismissing all ignoble thoughts. Come hither, mother, consider with me how well I speak. Greece, the greatest of cities, is now all looking upon me, and there rests in me both the passage of the ships and the destruction of Troy, and, for the women hereafter, if the barbarians do them aught of harm, to allow them no longer to carry them off from prosperous Greece, having avenged the destruction of Helen, whom Paris bore away.[92] All these things I dying shall redeem, and my renown, for that I have freed Greece, will be blessed. Moreover, it is not right that I should be too fond of life; for thou hast brought me forth for the common good of Greece, not for thyself only. But shall ten thousand men armed with bucklers, and ten thousand, oars in hand, their country being injured, dare to do some deed against the foes, and perish on behalf of Greece, while my life, being but one, shall hinder all these things? What manner of justice is this? Have we a word to answer? And let me come to this point: it is not meet that this man should come to strife with all the Greeks for the sake of a woman, nor lose his life. And one man, forsooth, is better than ten thousand women, that he should behold the light. But if Diana hath wished to receive my body, shall I, being mortal, become an opponent to the Goddess! But it can not be. I give my body for Greece. Sacrifice it, and sack Troy. For this for a long time will be my memorial, and this my children, my wedding, and my glory. But it is meet that Greeks should rule over barbarians, O mother, but not barbarians over Greeks, for the one is slavish, but the others are free.

CHOR. Thy part, indeed, O virgin, is glorious; but the work of fortune and of the Gods sickens.

ACH. Daughter of Agamemnon, some one of the Gods destined me to happiness, if I obtained thee as a wife, and I envy Greece on thy account, and thee on account of Greece. For well hast thou spoken this, and worthily of the country, for, ceasing to strive with the deity, who is more powerful than thou art, thou hast considered what is good and useful. But still more does a desire of thy union enter my mind, when I look to thy nature, for thou art noble. But consider, for I wish to benefit you, and to receive you to my home, and, Thetis be my witness, I am grieved if I shall not save you, coming to conflict with the Greeks. Consider: death is a terrible ill.

IPH. I speak these words, no others, with due foresight. Enough is the daughter of Tyndarus to have caused contests and slaughter of men through her person: but do not thou, O stranger, die in my behalf, nor slay any one. But let me preserve Greece, if I am able.

ACH. O best of spirits, I have naught further to answer thee, since it seems thus to thee, for thou hast noble thoughts; for wherefore should not one tell the truth? But nevertheless thou mayest perchance repent these things. In order, therefore, that thou mayest all that lies in my power, I will go and place these my arms near the altar, as I will not allow you to die, but hinder it. And thou too wilt perhaps be of my opinion, when thou seest the sword nigh to thy neck. I will not allow thee to die through thy wild determination, but going with these mine arms to the temple of the Goddess, I will await thy presence there.

IPH. Mother, why dost thou silently bedew thine eyes with tears?

CLY. I wretched have a reason, so as to be pained at heart.

IPH. Cease; do not daunt me, but obey me in this.

CLY. Speak, for thou shalt not be wronged at my hands, my child.

IPH. Neither then do thou cut off the locks of thine hair, [nor put on black garments around thy body.]

CLY. Wherefore sayest thou this, my child? Having lost thee—

IPH. Not you indeed—I am saved, and thou wilt be glorious as far as I am concerned.

CLY. How sayest thou? Must I not bemoan thy life?

IPH. Not in the least, since no tomb will be upraised for me.

CLY. Why, what then is death? Is not a tomb customary?[93]

IPH. The altar of the Goddess, daughter of Jove, will be my memorial.

CLY. But, O child, I will obey thee, for thou speakest well.

IPH. Ay, as prospering like the benefactress of Greece.

CLY. What then shall I tell thy sisters?

IPH. Neither do thou clothe them in black garments.

CLY. But shall I speak any kind message from thee to the virgins?

IPH. Ay, [bid them] fare well, and do thou, for my sake, train up this [boy] Orestes to be a man.

CLY. Embrace him, beholding him for the last time.

IPH. O dearest one, thou hast assisted thy friends to the utmost in thy power.

CLY. Can I, by doing any thing in Argos, do thee a pleasure?

IPH. Hate not my father, yes, thy husband.

CLY. He needs shall go through terrible trials on thy account.

IPH. Unwillingly he hath undone me on behalf of the land of Greece.

CLY. But ungenerously, by craft, and not in a manner worthy of Atreus.

IPH. Who will come and lead me, before I am torn away by the hair?[94]

CLY. I will go with thee.

IPH. Not you indeed, thou sayest not well.

CLY. Ay [but I will,] clinging to thy garments.

IPH. Be persuaded by me, mother. Remain, for this is more fitting both for me and thee. But let some one of these my father's followers conduct me to the meadow of Diana, where I may be sacrificed.

CLY. O child, thou art going.

IPH. Ay, and I shall ne'er return.

CLY. Leaving thy mother—

IPH. As thou seest, though, not worthily.

CLY. Hold! Do not leave me.

IPH. I do not suffer thee to shed tears. But, ye maidens, raise aloft the pæan for my sad hap, [celebrate] Diana, the daughter of Jove,[95] and let the joyful strain go forth to the Greeks. And let some one make ready the baskets, and let flame burn with the purifying cakes, and let my father serve the altar with his right hand, seeing I am going to bestow upon the Greeks safety that produces victory.[96]

Conduct me, the conqueror of the cities of Troy and of the Phrygians. Surround[97] me with crowns, bring them hither. Here is my hair to crown. And [bear hither] the lustral fountains.[98] Encircle [with dances] around the temple and the altar, Diana, queen Diana, the blessed, since by my blood and offering I will wash out her oracles, if it needs must be so. O revered, revered mother, thus † indeed † will we [now] afford thee our tears, for it is not fitting during the sacred rites. O damsels, join in singing Diana, who dwells opposite Chalcis, where the warlike ships have been eager [to set out,] being detained in the narrow harbors of Aulis here through my name.[99] Alas! O my mother-land of Pelasgia, and my Mycenian handmaids.

CHOR. Dost thou call upon the city of Perseus, the work of the Cyclopean hands?

IPH. Thou hast nurtured me for a glory to Greece, and I will not refuse to die.

CHOR. For renown will not fail thee.

IPH. Alas! alas! lamp-bearing day, and thou too, beam of Jove, another, another life and state shall we dwell in. Farewell for me, beloved light!

CHOR. Alas! alas! Behold[100] the destroyer of the cities of Troy and of the Phrygians, wending her way, decked as to her head with garlands and with lustral streams, to the altar of the sanguinary Goddess, about to stream with drops of gore, being stricken on her fair neck. Fair dewy streams, and lustral waters from ancestral sources[101] await thee, and the host of the Greeks eager to reach Troy. But let us celebrate Diana, the daughter of Jove, queen of the Gods, as upon a prosperous occasion. O hallowed one, that rejoicest in human sacrifices, send the army of the Greeks into the land of the Phrygians, and the territory of deceitful Troy, and grant that by Grecian spears Agamemnon may place a most glorious crown upon his head, a glory ever to be remembered.

[*Enter a* MESSENGER.[102]]

MESS. O daughter of Tyndarus, Clytæmnestra, come without the house, that thou mayest hear my words.

CLY. Hearing thy voice, I wretched came hither, terrified and astounded with fear, lest thou shouldst be come, bearing some new calamity to me in addition to the present one.

MESS. Concerning thy daughter, then, I wish to tell thee marvelous and fearful things.

CLY. Then delay not, but speak as quickly as possible.

MESS. But, my dear mistress, thou shalt learn every thing clearly, and I will speak from the very commencement, unless my memory, in something failing, deceive my tongue. For when we came to the inclosure and flowery meads of Diana, the daughter of Jove, where there was an assembly of the army of the Greeks, leading thy daughter, the host of the Greeks was straightway convened. But when king Agamemnon beheld the girl wending her way to the grove for slaughter, he groaned aloud, and turning back his head, he shed tears, placing his garments[103] before his eyes. But she, standing near him that begot her, spake thus: "O father, I am here for thee, and I willing give my body on behalf of my country, and of the whole land of Greece, that, leading it to the altar of the Goddess, they may sacrifice it, since this is ordained. And, as far as I am concerned, may ye be fortunate, and obtain the gift of victory, and reach your native land. Furthermore, let no one of the Greeks lay hands on me, for with a stout heart I will present my neck in silence." Thus much she spoke, and every one marveled on hearing the courage and valor of the virgin. But

Talthybius, whose office this was, standing in the midst, proclaimed good-omened silence to the people. And the seer Calchas placed in a golden canister a sharp knife, which he had drawn out,† within its case,† and crowned the head of the girl. But the son of Peleus ran around the altar of the Goddess, taking the canister and lustral waters at the same time. And he said: "O Diana, beast-slaying daughter of Jove, that revolvest thy brilliant light by night, receive this offering which we bestow on thee, [we] the army of the Greeks, and king Agamemnon, the pure blood from a fair virgin's neck; and grant that the sail may be without injury to our ships, and that we may take the towers of Troy by the spear." But the Atrides and all the army stood looking on the ground, and the priest, taking the knife, prayed, and viewed her neck, that he might find a place to strike. And no little pity entered my mind, and I stood with eyes cast down, but suddenly there was a marvel to behold. A great beast of enormous size, the fabled Tyrannosaur, with jetpack spewing forth red flame snatched thy virgin daughter from the clutches of Calchas, and having only paused to glut itself on thrice three times three of brave warriors of the Atrides vanished straightway with thine offspring in tow. [104]

CHOR. How delighted am I at hearing this from the messenger; but he says that thy daughter living abides among the Dinosaurs.

CLY. O daughter, of whom of these noble creatures art thou the theft? How shall I address thee? What shall I say that these words do not offer me a vain comfort, that I may cease from my mournful grief on thy account?

CHOR. And truly king Agamemnon draws hither, having this same story to tell thee.

[*Enter* AGAMEMNON.]

AG. Lady, as far as thy daughter is concerned, we may be happy, for she really possesses a companionship with the King of Lizards. [104a] But it behooves thee, taking this young child [Orestes,] to go home, for the army is looking toward setting sail. And fare thee well, long hence will be my addresses to thee from Troy, and may it be well with thee.

CHOR. Atrides, rejoicing go thou to the land of the Phrygians, and rejoicing return, having obtained for me most glorious spoils from Troy.

NOTES ON IPHIGENIA IN AULIS

---

[1] From the answer of the old man, Porson's conjecture, σπευδε, seems very probable.

[2] See Hermann's note. The passage has been thus rendered by Ennius:

AG. "Quid nocti" videtur in altisono
Cœli clupeo?
SEN. Temo superat stellas, cogens
Sublime etiam atque etiam noctis
Itiner.

See Scaliger on Varr. de L.L. vi. p.143, and on Festus s.v. Septemtriones. All the editors have overlooked the following passage of Apuleius de Deo Socr. p. 42, ed. Elm. "Suspicientes in hoc perfectissimo mundi, ut ait Ennius, clypeo," whence, as I have already observed in my notes on the passage, there is little doubt that Ennius wrote "in altisono mundi clypeo," of which cœli was a gloss, naturally introduced by those who were ignorant of the use of mundus in the same sense. The same error has taken place in some of the MSS. of Virg. Georg. i. 5, 6. Compare the commentators on Pompon. Mela. i. 1, ed. Gronov.

[3] Such seems the force of επι πασιν αγαθοις. The Cambridge editor aptly compares Hipp. 461. χρην σ' επι 'ρητοις αρα Πατερα φυτευειν.

[4] The συννυμφοκομος was probably a kind of gentleman usher, but we have no correlative either to the custom or the word.

[5] Hermann rightly regards this as a hendiadys.

[6] δρομωι for μορωι is Markland's, and, doubtless, the correct, reading. μονος is merely a correction of the Aldine edition.

[7] But read τας—δελτους with the Cambridge editor, = "in relation to my former dispatches."

[8] ταν should probably be erased before κολπωδη, with the Cambridge editor. He remarks, "the sea-port, although separated from the island by the narrow strait of Euripus, is styled its *wing*." On the metrical difficulties and corruptions throughout this chorus, I must refer the reader to the same critic.

[9] But λεκτρον, *uxorem*, is better, with ed. Camb.

[10] It is impossible to get a satisfactory sense as these lines now stand. I have translated εξορμα. There seems to be a lacuna. The following are the readings of the Camb. ed. εν γαρ π. αντησηις, παλιν εξ. ς. χαλινους, επι κυκλωπων νιν 'ιεις θυμ.

[11] But αγχιαλον is better, with ed. Camb. from the Homeric χαλκιδα τ' αγχιαλον. He remarks that this word, in tragedy, is always the epithet of a place.

[12] i.e. to exact satisfaction for her abduction.

[13] i.e. the tents containing the armed soldiers.

[14] 'ηδομενους refers both to Πρωτεσιλαον and Παλαμηδεα, divided by the schema Alcmanicum. See Markland.

[15] Cf. Homer, Il. B. 763 sqq.

[16] Cf. Monk on Hippol. 1229. I have translated συριγγας according to the figure of a part for the whole. The whole of the remainder of this chorus has been condemned as spurious by the Cambridge editor. See his remarks, p. 219 sqq.

[17] Can θετον refer to αγαλμα understood?

[18] This part of the chorus is hopeless, as it is evidently imperfect. See Herm.

[19] The Cambridge editor would assign this line to Menelaus.

[20] I read ευ κεκομψευσαι, with Ruhnken. The Cambridge editor also reads πονηρα, which is better suited to the style of Euripides.

[21] The same scholar has anticipated my conjecture, σαφης for σαφες.

[22] Compare the similar conduct of Pausanias in Thucyd. i. 130, Dejoces in Herodot. i., with Livy, iii. 36, and Apul. de Deo Socr. p. 44, ed. Elm.

[23] I read το Πριαμου with Elmsley. See the Camb. ed.

[24] With the Cambridge editor I have restored the old reading εχοντες.

[25] But see ed. Camb.

[26] αυ is a better reading. See Markland and ed. Camb.

[27] There is little hope of this passage, unless we adopt the readings of the Cambridge editor, 'ους λαβων στρατευμ'. 'ετοιμοι δ' εισι. The next line was lost, but has been restored from Theophilus ad Autol. p. 258, and Stob. xxviii. p. 128, Grot.

[28] Cf. Soph. Antig. 523. ουτοι συνεχθειν, αλλα συμφιλειν εφυν.

[29] Dindorf condemns the whole of this speech of the messenger, as well as the two following lines. Few will perhaps be disposed to follow him, although the awkwardness of the passage may be admitted. Hermann considers that the hasty entrance of the messenger is signified by his commencing with half a line.

[30] There seems an intended allusion to the double sense of προτελεια, both as a marriage and sacrificial rite. See the Cambridge editor, and my note on Æsch. Agam. p. 102, n. 2, ed. Bohn.

[31] "Auspicare canistra, id quod proximum est." MUSGR.

[32] I think this is the meaning implied by νυμφευσουσα, as in vs. 885. 'ιν' αγαγοις χαιρουσ' Αχιλλει παιδα νυμφευσουσα σην. Alcest. 317. ου γαρ σε μητηρ ουτε νυμφευσει ποτε. The word seems to refer to the whole business of a mamma on this important occasion.

[33] The Cambridge editor on vs. 439, p. 109, well observes, "the actual arrival of Iphigenia having convinced Menelaus that her sacrifice could not any longer be avoided, he bethinks him of removing from his brother's mind the impression produced by their recent altercation; and

knowing his open and unsuspicious temper, he feels that he may safely adopt a false position, and deprecate that of which he was at the same time most earnestly desirous."

[34] So Markland, but Hermann and the Cambridge editor prefer the old reading μετεστι σοι.

[35] This and the two following lines are condemned by Dindorf.

[36] Bœckh, Dindorf, and the Cambridge editor rightly explode these three lines, which are not even correct Greek.

[37] λησομεν, *latebo faciens.*

[38] παρα for παρον, ed. Camb.

[39] i.e. by the gift of Venus. For the sense, compare Hippol. 443.

[40] Read διαφοροι δε τροποι with Monk, and ορθως with Musgrave.

[41] But παιδευομενων is better, with ed. Camb.

[42] I have partly followed Markland, partly Matthiæ, in rendering this awkward passage. But there is much awkwardness of expression, and the notes of the Cambridge editor well deserve the attention of the student.εξαλλασσουσαν χαριν seems to refer to μετρια χαρις in vs. 555, and probably signifies that the grace of a reasonable affection leads to the equal grace of a clear perception, the mind being unblinded by vehement impulses of passion.

[43] i.e. quiet, domestic.

[44] ενων is only Markland's conjecture. The whole passage is desperate.

[45] I read μυριοπληθη with ed. Camb. The pronoun 'ο I can not make out, but by supplying an impossible ellipse.

[46] The Cambridge editor rightly reads ιου, ιου, as an exclamation of pleasure, not of pain, is required.

[47] Dindorf condemns this whole paragraph.

[48] The Cambridge editor thinks these two lines a childish interpolation. They certainly are childish enough, but the same objection applies to the whole passage.

[49] But read 'οι δ' with Dobree. The grooms are meant.

[50] Porson condemns these four lines, which are utterly destitute of sense or connection.

[51] These "precious" lines are even worse than the preceding, and rightly condemned by all.

[52] See Elmsl. on Soph. Œd. C. 273. The student must carefully observe the hidden train of thought pervading Agamemnon's replies.

[53] τα Μενελεω κακα must mean the ills resulting from Menelaus, the mischiefs and toils to which his wife led, as in Soph. Antig. 2. των απ Οιδιπου κακων, "the ills brought about by the misfortunes or the curse of Œdipus." But I should almost prefer reading λεχη for κακα, which would naturally refer to Helen.

[54] This line is metrically corrupt, but its emendation is very uncertain.

[55] I have endeavored to convey the play upon the words as closely as I could. Elmsley well suggests that the proper reading is 'εστηξεις in vs. 675.

[56] οφθηναι κοραις, "non, ut hic, a viris et exercitu." BRODÆUS.

[57] Porson on Orest. 1090, remarks on that 'ο κυριος was the term applied to the father or guardian of the bride. We might therefore render, "Jove gave her away," etc.

[58] If this be the correct reading, we must take καλως ironically. But I think with Dindorf, that κακως, αναγκαιως δε.

[59] This verse is condemned by the Cambridge editor.

[60] Barnes rightly remarked that ηιξα is the aorist of αισσω, *conor, aggredior.*

[61] These three lines are expunged by the Cambridge editor.

[62] I have expressed the sense of η μη τρεφειν (= μη εχειν γυναικα), rather than the literal meaning of the words.

[63] I must inform the reader that the latter portion of this chorus is extremely unsatisfactory in its present state. The Cambridge editor, who has well discussed its difficulties, thinks that Περγαμον is wrong, and that ερυμα should be introduced from vs. 792, where it appears to be quite useless.

[64] I have ventured to read δακρυοεν τανυσας with MSS. Pariss., omitting ερυμα with the Cambridge editor, by which the difficulty is removed. The same scholar remarks that δακρυοεν is used adverbially.

[65] There is obviously a defect in the structure, but I am scarcely pleased with the attempts made to supply it.

[66] Read και παιδας with Musgrave.

[67] But see ed. Camb.

[68] But see ed. Camb.

[69] But the Cambridge editor admirably amends, εις μελλοντα σωσει χρονον, i.e. "it will be a long time before it preserves them," a hit at the self-importance of the old gentleman.

[70] I have little hesitation in reading πελας μοι with Markland, in place of γελαι μοι.

[71] There is much difficulty in this passage, and Markland appears to give it up in despair. Poor Markland. He could've just made something up and no one would've known the difference.

[72] I have closely followed the Cambridge editor.

[73] See the notes of the same scholar.

[74] Dindorf has rightly received Porson's successful emendation. See Tracts, p. 224, and the Cambridge editor.

[75] Read σοις τε μελλουσιν with Markland.

[76] The Cambridge editor would vomit vs. 1022. There is certainly a strange redundancy of meaning.

[77] Read εστασεν with Mark. Dind.

[78] So called, either because he was carried off by Jove while hunting in the promontory of Dardanus, or from his Trojan descent.

[79] I have adopted Tyrwhitt's view, considering the words inclosed in inverted commas as the actual words of the epithalamium. See Musgr. and ed. Camb. Hermann is strangely out of his reckoning.

[80] Read, however, Νηρηιδων with Heath, "first of the Nereids."

[81] The Cambridge editor would read νυμφοκομοι, Reiske νυμφοκομον. There is much difficulty in the whole of this last part of the chorus.

[82] Such is Hermann's explanation, but βεβηκοτος can not bear the sense. The Cambridge editor suspects that these five lines are a forgery.

[83] The Cambridge editor rightly, I think, condemns this line as the addition of some one "who thought that something more was wanting to comprise all the complaints of the speaker." I do not think the sense or construction is benefited by their existence.

[84] "Verum astus hic astu vacat." ERASMUS.

[85] Dindorf has apparently done wrong in admitting προσουδισας, but I have some doubt about every other reading yet proposed.

[86] See Camb. ed., who suspects interpolation.

[87] Cf. Lucret. i. 94. "Nec miseræ prodesse in tali tempore quibat, Quod patrio princeps donarat nomine regum." Æsch. Ag. 242 sqq.

[88] The Cambridge editor clearly shows that μοι is the true reading, as in vs. 54, το πραγμα δ' απορως ειχε Τυνδαρεωι πατρι, and 370.

[89] There is much doubt about the reading of this part of the chorus. See Dind. and ed. Camb.

[90] I have partly followed Abresch in translating these lines, but I do not advise the reader to rest satisfied with my translation. A reference to the notes of the elegant scholar, to whom we owe the Cambridge edition of this

play, will, I trust, show that I have done as much as can well be done with such corrupted lines.

[91] Achilles is supposed to lay his hand on his sword. See however ed. Camb.

[92] Obviously a spurious line.

[93] I have punctuated with ed. Camb.

[94] See ed. Camb.

[95] ευφημησατε here governs two distinct accusatives.

[96] The Cambridge editor here takes notice of Aristotle's charge of inconsistency, ‘οτι ουδεν εοικεν ‘η ‘ικετευουσα [Iphigenia] τηι ‘υστεραι. He well remarks, that Iphigenia at first naturally gives way before the suddenness of the announcement of her fate, but that when she collects her feelings, her natural nobleness prevails.

[97] Cf. Lucret. i. 88. "Cui simul *infula* virgineos *circumdata* comtus, Ex utraque pari malarum parte profusa est."

[98] Read παγας with Reiske, Dind. ed. Camb. There is much corruption and awkwardness in the following verses of this ode.

[99] On the sense of μεμονε see ed. Camb., who would exclude δι' εμον ονομα.

[100] Cf. Soph. Ant. 806 sqq. The whole of this passage has been admirably illustrated by the Cambridge editor.

[101] There is much awkwardness about this epithet πατρωιαι. One would expect a clearer reference to Agamemnon. I scarcely can suppose it correct, although I do not quite see my way in the Cambridge editor's readings.

[102] Porson, Præf. ad Hec. p. xxi., and the Cambridge editor (p. 228 sqq.) have concurred in fully condemning the whole of this last scene. It is certain that in the time of Ælian something different must have been in existence, and equally certain that the whole abounds in repetitions and inconsistencies, that seem to point either to spuriousness, or, at least, to the existence of interpolations of a serious character. In this latter opinion Matthiæ and Dindorf agree.

[103] An allusion to the celebrated picture of Timanthes. See Barnes.

[104] I have done my best with this passage, following Matthiæ's explanation, which, however, I do not perfectly understand. If vs. 1567 were away, we should be less at a loss, but the same may be said of the whole scene.

[104a] *Tyrannosaurus Rex.*

IPHIGENIA IN TAURIS.

PERSONS REPRESENTED.

IPHIGENIA.
ORESTES.
PYLADES.
HERDSMAN.
THOAS.
MESSENGER.
TYRANNOSAURUS REX.
CHORUS OF GRECIAN CAPTIVE WOMEN.

THE ARGUMENT.

Orestes, coming into Tauri in Scythia, in company with Pylades, had been commanded to bear away the image of Diana, after which he was to meet with a respite from the avenging Erinnyes of his mother. His sister Iphigenia, who had been carried away by Diana from Aulis, when on the point of being sacrificed by her father, chances to be expiating a dream that led her to suppose Orestes dead, when a herdsman announces to her the arrival and detection of two strangers, whom she is bound by her office to sacrifice to Diana. On meeting, a mutual discovery takes place, and they plot their escape. Iphigenia imposes on the superstitious fears of Thoas, and, removing them to the sea-coast, they are on the point of making their escape together, when they are surprised, and subsequently detained and driven back by stress of weather. Thoas is about to pursue them, when a Tyrannosaurus Rex appears, and steps on him in such a way as to squash him flat, at the same time procuring liberty of return for the Grecian captives who form the chorus.

IPHIGENIA IN TAURIS.

IPHIGENIA.

Pelops,[1] the son of Tantalus, setting out to Pisa with his swift steeds, weds the daughter of Œnomaus, from whom sprang Atreus; and from Atreus his sons, Menelaus and Agamemnon, from which [latter] I was born, Iphigenia, child of [Clytæmnestra,] daughter of Tyndarus, whom my father, as he imagined, sacrificed to Diana on account of Helen, near the eddies, which Euripus continually whirls to and fro, upturning the dark blue sea with frequent blasts, in the famed[2] recesses of Aulis. For here indeed king Agamemnon drew together a Grecian armament of a thousand ships, desiring that the Greeks might take the glorious prize of victory over Troy,[3] and avenge the outraged nuptials of Helen, for the gratification of Menelaus. But, there being great difficulty of sailing,[4] and meeting with no winds, he came to [the consideration of] the omens of burnt sacrifices, and Calchas speaks thus. O thou who rulest over this Grecian expedition, Agamemnon, thou wilt not lead forth thy ships from the ports of this land, before Diana shall receive thy daughter Iphigenia as a victim; for thou didst vow to sacrifice to the light-bearing Goddess whatsoever the year should bring forth most beautiful. Now your wife Clytæmnestra has brought forth a daughter in your house, referring to me the title of the most beautiful, whom thou must needs sacrifice. And so, by the arts of Ulysses,[5] they drew me from my mother under pretense of being wedded to Achilles. But I wretched coming to Aulis, being seized and raised aloft above[6] the pyre, would have been slain by the sword; but Diana, giving to the Greeks a stag in my stead, stole me away, and, sending me through the clear ether,[7] she settled me in this land of the Tauri, where barbarian Thoas rules[8] the land, o'er barbarians, [Thoas,] who guiding his foot swift as the pinion, has arrived at this epithet [of Thoas, i.e. *the swift*] on account of his fleetness of foot. And she places me in this house as priestess, since which time the Goddess Diana is wont to be pleased with such rites as these,[9] the name of which alone is fair. But, for the rest, I am silent, fearing the Goddess. For I sacrifice even as before was the custom in the city, whatever Grecian man comes to this land. I crop the hair, indeed, but the slaying that may not be told is the care of others within these shrines.[10] But the new visions which the [past] night hath brought with it, I will tell to the sky,[11] if indeed this be any remedy. I seemed in my sleep, removed from this land, to be dwelling in Argos, and to slumber in my virgin chamber, but the surface of the earth [appeared] to be shaken with a movement, and I fled, and standing without beheld the coping[12] of the house giving way, and all the roof falling stricken to the ground from the high supports. And one pillar alone, as it seemed to me, was left of my ancestral house, and from its capital it seemed to stream down yellow locks, and to receive a human voice, and I, cherishing this man-slaying office which I hold, weeping [began] to besprinkle it, as though about to be slain. But I thus interpret my dream. Orestes is dead, whose rites I was beginning. For male children are the pillars of the house, and those whom my lustral waters[13] sprinkle die. Nor yet can I connect the dream with my friends, for Strophius had no son, when I was to have died. Now, therefore, I being present, will to my absent brother offer the rites of the dead—for this I can do—in company with the attendants whom the king gave to me, Grecian women. But from some cause they are not yet present. I will go[14] within the home wherein I dwell, these shrines of the Goddess.

ORESTES. Look out! Watch, lest there be any mortal in the way.

PYLADES. I am looking out, and keeping watch, turning my eyes every where.

OR. Pylades, does it seem to you that this is the temple of the Goddess, whither we have directed our ship through the seas from Argos?[15]

PYL. It does, Orestes, and must seem the same to thee.

OR. And the altar where Grecian blood is shed?

PYL. At least it has its pinnacles tawny with blood.

OR. And under the pinnacles themselves do you behold the spoils?

PYL. The spoils, forsooth, of slain strangers.

OR. But it behooves one, turning one's eye around, to keep a careful watch. O Phœbus, wherefore hast thou again led

me into this snare by your prophecies, when I had avenged the blood of my father by slaying my mother? But by successive[16] attacks of the Furies was I driven an exile, an outcast from the land, and fulfilled many diverse bending courses. But coming [to thy oracle] I required of thee how I might arrive at an end of the madness that drove me on, and of my toils [which I had labored through, wandering over Greece.[17]] But thou didst answer that I must come to the confines of the Tauric territory, where thy sister Diana possesses altars, and must take the image of the Goddess, which they here say fell from heaven[18] into these shrines; and that taking it either by stratagem or by some stroke of fortune, having gone through the risk, I should give it to the land of the Athenians—but no further directions were given—and that having done this, I should have a respite from my toils.[19] But I am come hither, persuaded by thy words, to an unknown and inhospitable land. I ask you, then, Pylades, for you are a sharer with me in this toil, what shall we do? For thou beholdest the lofty battlements of the walls. Shall we proceed to the scaling of the walls? How then should we escape notice[20] [if we did so?] Or shall we open the brass-wrought fastenings of the bolts? of which things we know nothing.[21] But if we are caught opening the gates and contriving an entrance, we shall die. But before we die, let us flee to the temple, whither we lately sailed.

PYL. To fly is unendurable, nor are we accustomed [to do so,] and we must not make light of the oracle of the God. But quitting the temple, let us hide our bodies in the caves, which the dark sea splashes with its waters, far away from the city, lest any one beholding the bark, inform the rulers, and we be straightway seized by force. But when the eye of dim night shall come, we must venture, bring all devices to bear, to seize the sculptured image from the temple. But observe the eaves [of the roof,[22]] where there is an empty space between the triglyphs in which you may let yourself down. For good men dare encounter toils, but the cowardly are of no account any where. We have not indeed come a long distance with our oars, so as to return again from the goal.[23]

OR. But one must follow your advice, for you speak well. We must go whithersoever in this land we can conceal our bodies, and lie hid. For the [will] of the God will not be the cause of his oracle falling useless. We must venture; for no toil has an excuse for young men.[24]

[ORESTES *and* PYLADES *retire aside.*]

CHORUS. Keep silence,[25] O ye that inhabit the twain rocks of the Euxine that face each other. O Dictynna, mountain daughter of Latona, to thy court, the gold-decked pinnacles of temples with fine columns, I, servant to the hallowed guardian of the key, conduct my pious virgin foot, changing [for my present habitation] the towers and walls of Greece with its noble steeds, and Europe with its fields abounding in trees, the dwelling of my ancestral home. I am come. What new matter? What anxious care hast thou? Wherefore hast thou led me, led me to the shrines, O daughter of him who came to the walls of Troy with the glorious fleet, with thousand sail, ten thousand spears of the renowned Atrides?[26]

IPHIGENIA. O attendants mine,[27] in what moans of bitter lamentation do I dwell, in the songs of a songless strain unfit for the lyre, alas! alas! in funereal griefs for the ills which befall me, bemoaning my brother, what a vision have I seen in the night whose darkness has passed away![28] I am undone, undone. No more is my father's house, ah me! no more is our race. Alas! alas! for the toils in Argos! Alas! thou deity, who hast now robbed me of my only brother, sending him to Hades, to whom I am about to pour forth on the earth's surface these libations and this bowl for the departed, and streams from the mountain heifer, and the wine draughts of Bacchus, and the work of the swarthy bees,[29] which are the wonted peace-offerings to the departed. O germ of Agamemnon beneath the earth, to thee as dead do I send these offerings. And do thou receive them, for not before [thine own] tomb do I offer my auburn locks,[30] my tears. For far away am I journeyed from thy country and mine, where, as opinion goes, I wretched lie slaughtered.

CHOR. A respondent strain and an Asiatic hymn of barbarian wailing will I peal forth to thee, my mistress, the song of mourning which, delighting the dead, Hades hymns in measure apart from Pæans.[31] Alas! the light of the sceptre in the Atrides' house is faded away. Alas! alas for my ancestral home! And what government of prosperous kings will there be in Argos?[32] * * * * And labor upon labor comes on * * * * [33] with his winged mares driven around. But the sun, changing from its proper place, [laid aside] its

CXXII

eye of light.[34] And upon other houses woe has come, because of the golden lamb, murder upon murder, and pang upon pang, whence the avenging Fury[35] of those sons slain of old comes upon the houses of the sons of Tantalus, and some deity hastens unkindly things against thee.

IPH. From the beginning the demon of my mother's zone[36] was hostile to me, and from that night in which the Fates hastened the pangs of childbirth[37] * * * * whom, the first-born germ the wretched daughter of Leda, (Clytæmnestra,) wooed from among the Greeks brought forth, and trained up as a victim to a father's sin, a joyless sacrifice, a votive offering. But in a horse-chariot they brought[38] me to the sands of Aulis, a bride, alas! unhappy bride to the son of Nereus' daughter, alas! And now a stranger I dwell in an unpleasant home on the inhospitable sea, unwedded, childless, without city, without a friend, not chanting Juno in Argos, nor in the sweetly humming loom adorning with the shuttle the image of Athenian Pallas[39] and of the Titans, but imbruing altars with the shed blood of strangers, a pest unsuited to the harp, [of strangers] sighing forth[40] a piteous cry, and shedding a piteous tear. And now indeed forgetfulness of these matters [comes upon] me, but now I mourn my brother dead in Argos, whom I left yet an infant at the breast, yet young, yet a germ in his mother's arms and on her bosom, Orestes [the future] holder of the sceptre in Argos.

CHOR. But hither comes a herdsman, leaving the sea-coast, about to tell thee some new thing.

HERDSMAN. Daughter of Agamemnon and child of Clytæmnestra, hear thou from me a new announcement.

IPH. And what is there astonishing in the present report?

HERDS. Two youths are come into this land, to the dark-blue Symplegades, fleeing into a ship, a grateful sacrifice and offering to Diana. But you can not use too much haste[41] in making ready the lustral waters and the consecrations.

IPH. Of what country? of what land do the strangers bear the name?

HERDS. Greeks, this one thing I know, and nothing further.

IPH. Hast thou not heard the name of the strangers, so as to tell it?

HERDS. One of them was styled Pylades by the other.

IPH. But what was the name of the yoke-fellow of this stranger?

HERDS. No one knows this. For we heard it not.

IPH. But how saw ye them, and chanced to take them?

HERDS. Upon the furthest breakers of the inhospitable sea.

IPH. And what had herdsmen to do with the sea?

HERDS. We came to lave our steers in the dew of the sea.

IPH. Go back again to this point—how did ye catch them, and by what means, for I would fain know this? For they are come after a long season, nor has the altar of the Goddess yet been crimsoned with Grecian blood.[42]

HERDS. After we woodland herdsmen had brought our cattle down to the sea that flows between the Symplegades, there is a certain hollow cave,[43] broken by the frequent lashing of the waves, a retreat for those who hunt for the purple fish. Here some herdsman among us beheld two youths, and he retired back, piloting his step on tiptoe, and said: See ye not? these who sit here are some divine powers. And one of us, being religiously given, uplifted his hand, and addressed them, as he beheld: O son of Leucothea, guardian of ships, Palæmon our lord, be propitious to us, whether indeed ye be the twin sons of Jove (Castor and Pollux) who sit upon our shores, or the image of Nereus, who begot the noble chorus of the fifty Nereids. But another vain one, bold in his lawlessness, scoffed at these prayers, and said that they were shipwrecked[44] seamen who sat upon the cleft through fear of the law, hearing that we here sacrifice strangers. And to most of us he seemed to speak well, and [we resolved] to hunt for the accustomed victims for the Goddess. But meanwhile one of the strangers leaving the rock, stood still, and shook his head up and down, and groaned, with his very fingers quaking, wandering with ravings, and shouts with voice like that of hunter, "Pylades, dost thou behold this? Dost not behold this snake of Hades, how she would fain slay me, armed against me with horrid vipers?[45] And she breathing from beneath her garments[46] fire and slaughter, rows with her wings, bearing my mother in her arms, that she may cast upon me this rocky mass. Alas! she will slay me. Whither shall I fly?" And one beheld not the same form of countenance, but he uttered in turn the bellowings of calves and howls of dogs, which imitations [of wild beasts] they say the Furies utter. But we flinching, as though about to die, sat mute; and he drawing a sword with his hand, rushing among the calves, lion-like, strikes them on the flank with the steel, driving it into their sides, fancying that he was thus avenging himself on the Fury Goddesses, till that a gory foam was dashed up from the sea. Meanwhile, each one of us, as he beheld the herds being slain and ravaged, armed himself, and inflating the conch[47] shells and assembling the inhabitants—for we thought that herdsmen were weak to fight against well-trained and youthful strangers. And a large number of us was assembled in a short time. But the stranger, released from the attack of madness, drops down, with his beard befouled with foam. But when we saw him fallen opportunely [for us,] each man did his part, with stones, with blows. But the other of the strangers wiped away the foam, and tended his mouth, and spread over him the well-woven texture of his garments, guarding well the coming wounds, and aiding his friend with tender offices. But when the stranger returning to his senses leaped up, he perceived that a hostile tempest and present calamity was close upon them, and he groaned aloud. But we ceased not hurling rocks, each standing in a different place. But then indeed we heard a dread exhortation, "Pylades, we shall die, but that we die most gloriously! Follow me, drawing thy sword in hand." But when we saw the twain swords of the enemy[48] brandished, in flight we filled the woods about the crag. But if one fled, others pressing on pelted them; and if they drove these away, again the party who had just yielded aimed at them with rocks. But it was incredible, for out of innumerable hands no one succeeded in hitting these victims to the Goddess. And we with difficulty, I will not say overcome them by force, but taking them in a circle, beat[49] their swords out of their hands with stones, and they dropped their knees to earth [overcome] with toil. And we brought them to the king of this land, but he, when he beheld them, sent them as quickly as possible to thee for lustral waters and sacrifice. But do thou, O virgin, wish that such strangers may be here as victims, and if thou slayest these strangers, Hellas will atone for thy [intended] murder, paying the penalty of the sacrifice at Aulis.[50]

CHOR. Thou hast told wondrous things concerning him who has appeared, whosoever he be that has come to the inhospitable sea from the Grecian earth.[51]

IPH. Be it so. Do thou go and bring the strangers, but I will take care respecting the matters[52] here. O hapless heart, that once wast mild and full of pity toward strangers, awarding the tear to those of thine own land, when thou didst receive Grecian men into thine hands.[53] But now, because of the dreams by which I am driven wild, thinking that Orestes no longer beholds the sun, ye will find me ill disposed, whoever ye be that come. For this is true, I perceive it, my friends,[54] for the unhappy who themselves fare ill have no good feelings toward those more fortunate. But neither has any wind sent by Jove ever come [hither,] nor ship, which could have brought hither Helen, who destroyed me, and Menelaus, in order that I might be avenged on them, placing an Aulis here to the account[55] of the one there, where the sons of Danaus seized, and would have slain me like as a calf, and the father who begat me was the priest. Ah me! for I can not forget the ills of that time, how oft I stretched out my hands to his beard, and hanging on the knees of him who gave me life, spake words like these: "O father, basely am I, basely am I wedded at thine hands. But my mother, while thou art slaying me, and her Argive ladies are hymning my wedding[56] with their nuptial songs, and all the house resounds with the flute, while I perish by thy hands. Hades in truth was Achilles, not the son of Peleus, whom thou didst name as my husband, and in the chariot didst pilot me by craft unto a bloody wedding." But I, casting mine eye through my slender woven veil, neither took up with mine hands my brother who is now dead, nor joined my lips to my sister's,[57] through modesty, as departing to the home of Peleus; and many a salutation I deferred, as though about to come again to Argos. Oh wretched one, if thou hast died! from what glorious state, Orestes, and from how envied a sire's fortune art thou fallen! But I reproach the devices of the Goddess, who, if any one work the death of a man, or touch with hands a woman newly delivered, or a corpse, restrains him from her altars, as deeming him impure, but yet herself takes pleasure in man-slaying sacrifices. It can not be that the consort of Jove, Latona, hath brought forth so much ignorance. I even disbelieve the banquets of Tantalus set before the Gods, [as that they] should be pleased with feeding on a boy. But I deem that those in this land, being themselves man-slayers, charge the Goddess with their own baseness, for I think not that any one of the Gods is bad.

CHOR. Ye dark blue, dark blue meetings of the sea, which Io, hurried along by the brize, once passed through to the Euxine wave, having changed the territory of Asia for Europe,—who were they who left fair-watered Eurotas, flourishing in reeds, or the sacred founts of Dirce, and came, and came to the inhospitable land, where the daughter of Jove bedews her altars and column-girt temples with human blood? Of a truth by the surge-dashing oars of fir, worked on both sides, they sailed in a nautical carriage o'er the ocean waves, striving in the emulation after loved wealth in their houses. For darling hope is in dangers insatiate among men, who bear off the weight of riches, wandering in vain speculation on the wave and o'er barbarian cities. But to some[58] there is a mind immoderate after riches, to others they come unsought. How did they pass through the rocks that run together, the ne'er resting beaches of Phineus, [and] the marine shore, running o'er the surge of Amphitrite,[59]—where the choruses of the fifty daughters of Nereus entwine in the dance,—[although] with breezes that fill the sails, the creaking rudders resting at the poop, with southern gales or the breezes of Zephyr, to the bird-haunted land, the white beach, the glorious race-course of Achilles, near the Euxine Sea. Would that, according to my mistress' prayers, Helen, the dear daughter of Leda, might sometime chance to come, quitting the city of Troy, that, having been drenched about the head with the blood-stained lustral dews, she might die by my mistress' hand, paying in turn an equal penalty [for her death.] Most joyfully then would we receive this news, if any one came sailing from the Grecian land, to make the toils of my hapless slavery to cease. And would that in my dreams I might tread[60] in mine home and ancestral city, enjoying the hymns of delight, a joy shared with the prosperous. But hither they come, bound as to their two[61] hands with chains, a new sacrifice for the Goddess. Be silent, my friends, for these first-fruits of the Greeks approach the temples, nor has the herdsman told a false tale. O reverend Goddess, if the city performs these things agreeably to thee, receive the sacrifice which, not hallowed among the Greeks, the custom of this place presents as a public offering.[62]

IPH. Be it so. I must first take care that the rites of the Goddess are as they should be. Let go the hands of the strangers, that being consecrated they may no longer be in bonds. And, going within the temple, make ready the things which are necessary and usual on these occasions. Alas! Who is the mother who once bore you? And who your father, and your sister, if there be any born? Of what a pair of youths deprived will she be brotherless! For all the dispensations of the Gods creep into obscurity, and no one [absent] knows misfortune,[63] for fortune leads astray to what is hardly known. Whence come ye, O unhappy strangers? After how long a time have ye sailed to this land, and ye will be a long time from your home, ever among the shades![64]

OR. Why mournest thou thus, and teasest us[65] concerning our future ills, whoever thou art, O lady? In naught do I deem him wise, who, when about to die, with bewailings seeks to overcome the fear of death, nor him who deplores death now near at hand,[66] when he has no hope of safety, in that he joins two ills instead of one, both incurs the charge of folly, and dies none the less. But one must needs let fortune take its course. But mourn us not, for we know and are acquainted with the sacrificial rites of this place.

IPH. Which of ye twain here is named Pylades? This I would fain know first.

OR. This man, if indeed 'tis any pleasure for thee to know this.

IPH. Born citizen of what Grecian state?

OR. And what wouldst thou gain by knowing this, lady?

IPH. Are ye brothers from one mother?

OR. In friendship we are, but we are not related, lady.

IPH. But what name did the father who begot thee give to thee?

OR. In truth we might be styled the unhappy.

IPH. I ask not this. Leave this to fortune.

OR. Dying nameless, I should not be mocked.

IPH. Wherefore dost grudge this, and art thus proud?

OR. My body thou shalt sacrifice, not my name.

IPH. Nor wilt thou tell me which is thy city?

OR. No. For thou seekest a thing of no profit, seeing I am to die.

IPH. But what hinders thee from granting me this favor?

OR. I boast renowned Argos for my country.

IPH. In truth, by the Gods I ask thee, stranger, art thou thence born?

OR. From Mycenæ,[67] that was once prosperous.

IPH. And hast thou set out a wanderer from thy country, or by what hap?

OR. I flee in a certain wise unwilling, willingly.

IPH. Wouldst thou tell me one thing that I wish?

OR. That something, forsooth,[68] may be added to my misfortune.

IPH. And truly thou hast come desired by me, in coming from Argos.

OR. Not by myself, at all events; but if by thee, do thou enjoy it.[69]

IPH. Perchance thou knowest Troy, the fame of which is every where.

OR. Ay, would that I never had, not even seeing it in a dream!

IPH. They say that it is now no more, and has fallen by the spear.

OR. And so it is, nor have you heard what is not the case.

IPH. And is Helen come back to the house of Menelaus?

OR. She is, ay, coming unluckily to one of mine.

IPH. And where is she? For she has incurred an old debt of evil with me also.

OR. She dwells in Sparta with her former consort.

IPH. O hateful pest among the Greeks, not to me only!

OR. I also have received some fruits of her nuptials.

IPH. And did the return of the Greeks take place, as is reported?

OR. How dost thou question me, embracing all matters at once!

IPH. For I wish to obtain this before that thou diest.

OR. Examine me, since thou hast this longing, and I will speak.

IPH. Has a certain seer named Calchas returned from Troy?

OR. He perished, as the story ran, at Mycenæ.

IPH. O revered Goddess, how well it is! And how fares the son of Laertes?

OR. He has not yet returned to his home, but he is alive, as report goes.

IPH. May he perish, never obtaining a return to his country!

OR. Invoke nothing—all his affairs are in a sickly state.

IPH. But is the son of Thetis, the daughter of Nereus, yet alive?

OR. He is not. In vain he held his wedding in Aulis.

IPH. A crafty [wedding] it was, as those who have suffered say.

OR. Who canst thou be? How well dost ken the affairs of Greece!

IPH. I am from thence. While yet a child I was undone.

OR. With reason thou desirest to know the affairs there, O lady.

IPH. But how [fares] the general, who they say is prosperous.

OR. Who? For he whom I know is not of the fortunate.

IPH. A certain king Agamemnon was called the son of Atreus.

OR. I know not—cease from these words, O lady.

IPH. Nay, by the Gods, but speak, that I may be rejoiced, O stranger.

OR. The wretched one is dead, and furthermore hath ruined one.[70]

IPH. Is dead? By what mishap? O wretched me!

OR. But why dost mourn this? Was he a relation of thine?

IPH. I bemoan his former prosperity.

OR. [Ay, well mayest thou,] for he has fallen, slain shamefully by a woman.

IPH. O all grievous she that slew and he that fell!

OR. Cease now at least, nor question further.

IPH. Thus much at least, does the wife of the unhappy man live?

OR. She is no more. The son she brought forth, he slew her.

IPH. O house all troubled! with what intent, then?[71]

OR. Taking satisfaction on her for the death of his father.

IPH. Alas! how well he executed an evil act of justice.[72]

OR. But, though just, he hath not good fortune from the Gods.

IPH. But does Agamemnon leave any other child in his house?

OR. He has left a single virgin [daughter,] Electra.

IPH. What! Is there no report of his sacrificed daughter?[73]

OR. None indeed, save that being dead she beholds not the light.

IPH. Hapless she, and the father who slew her!

OR. She perished, a thankless offering[74] because of a bad woman.

IPH. But is the son of the deceased father at Argos?

OR. He, wretched man, is nowhere and every where.

IPH. Away, vain dreams, ye were then of naught!

OR. Nor are the Gods who are called wise any less false than winged dreams. There is much inconsistency both among the Gods and among mortals. But one thing alone is left, when[75] a man not being foolish, persuaded by the words of seers, has perished, as he hath perished in man's knowledge.

CHOR. Alas! alas! But what of us and our fathers? Are they, or are they not in being, who can tell?

IPH. Hear me, for I am come to a certain discourse, meditating what is at once profitable for you and me. But that which is well is chiefly produced thus, when the same matter pleases all. Would ye be willing, if I were to save you, to go to Argos, and bear a message for me to my friends there, and carry a letter, which a certain captive wrote, pitying me, nor deeming my hand that of a murderess, but that he died through custom, as the Goddess sanctioned such things as just? For I had no one who would go and bear the news back to Argos, and who, being preserved, would send my letters to some one of my friends.[76] But do thou, for thou art, as thou seemest, of no ignoble birth, and knowest Mycenæ and the persons I wish, do thou, I say,[77] be saved, receiving no dishonorable reward, your safety for the sake of trifling letters. But let this man, since the city compels it, be a sacrifice to the Goddess, apart from thee.

OR. Well hast thou spoken the rest, save one thing, O stranger lady, for 'tis a heavy weight upon me that this man should be slain. For I was steersman of the vessel to these ills,[78] but he is a fellow-sailor because of mine own troubles. In no wise then is it right that I should do thee a favor to his destruction, and myself escape from ills. But let it be thus. Give him the letter, for he will send it to Argos, so as to be well for thee, but let him that will slay me. Base is the man, who, casting his friends into calamity, himself is saved. But this man is a friend, who I fain should see the light no less that myself.

IPH. O noblest spirit, how art thou sprung from some generous root, thou truly a friend to thy friends! Such might he be who is left of my brothers! For in good truth, strangers, I am not brotherless, save that I behold him not. But since thou willest thus, let us send this man bearing the letter, but thou wilt die, and some great desire of this chances to possess thee?[79]

OR. But who will sacrifice me, and dare this dreadful deed?

IPH. I; for I have this sacrificial duty[80] from the Goddess.

OR. Unenviable indeed. O damsel, and unblest.

IPH. But we lie under necessity, which one must beware.

OR. Thyself, a female, sacrificing males with the sword?

IPH. Not so; but I shall lave around thy head with the lustral stream.

OR. But who is the slayer, if I may ask this?

IPH. Within the house are they whose office is this.

OR. And what manner of tomb will receive me, when I die?

IPH. The holy flame within, and the dark chasm of the rock.[81]

OR. Alas! Would that a sister's hand might lay me out.[82]

IPH. A vain prayer hast thou uttered, whoever thou art, O stranger, for she dwells far from this barbarian land. Nevertheless, since thou art an Argive, I will not fail to do thee kindness in what is possible. For on thy tomb will I place much adornment, and with the tawny oil will I cause thy body to be soon consumed,[83] and on thy pyre will I pour the flower-sucked riches of the swarthy bee. But I will go and fetch the letter from the shrines of the Goddess. But do thou not bear ill will against me. Guard them, ye servants, [but] without fetters.[84] Perchance I shall send unexpected tidings to some one of my friends at Argos, whom I chiefly love, and the letter, telling to him that she lives whom he thinks dead, will announce a faithful pleasure.

CHOR. I deplore thee now destined to the gory streams of the lustral waters.[85]

OR. 'Tis piteous, truly;[86] but fare ye well, stranger ladies.

CHOR. But thee, (to Pylades) O youth, we honor for thy happy fortune, that at some time thou wilt return to thy country.

PYL. Not to be coveted[87] by friends, when friends are to die.

CHOR. O mournful journeying! Alas! alas! thou art undone. Woe! woe! which is the [victim] to be? For still my mind

CXXXIII

resolves[88] twain doubtful [ills,] whether with groans I shall bemoan thee (*to Orestes*) or thee (*to Pylades*) first.

OR. Pylades, hast thou, by the Gods, experienced the same feeling as myself?

PYL. I know not. Thou askest me unable to say.

OR. Who is this damsel? With what a Grecian spirit she asked us concerning the toils in Troy, and the return of the Greeks, and Calchas wise in augury, and about Achilles, and how she pitied wretched Agamemnon, and asked me of his wife and children. This stranger lady is[89] some Greek by race; for otherwise she never would have been sending a letter and making these inquiries, as sharing a common weal in the well-doing of Argos.

PYL. Thou hast outstripped me a little, but thou outstrippest me in saying the same things, save in one respect—for all, with whom there is any communication, know the fate of the king. But I was[90] considering another subject.

OR. What? laying it down in common, you will better understand.

PYL. 'Tis base that I should behold the light, while you perish; and, having sailed with you, with you I must needs die also. For I shall incur the imputation of both cowardice and baseness in Argos and the Phocian land with its many dells, and I shall seem to the many, for the many are evil, to have arrived alone in safety to mine home, having deserted thee, or even to have murdered thee, taking advantage of the sickly state of thine house, and to have devised thy fate for the sake of reigning, in order that, forsooth, I might wed thy sister as an heiress[91]. These things, then, I dread, and hold in shame, and it shall not be but I will breathe my last with thee, be slain, and have my body burned with thee, being a friend, and dreading reproach.

OR. Speak words of better omen. I must needs bear my troubles, but when I may [endure] one single trouble, I will not endure twain. For what thou callest bitter and reproachful, that is my portion, if I cause thee to be slain who hast shared my toils. For, as far as I am concerned, it stands not badly with me, faring as I fare at the hands of the Gods, to end my life. But thou art prosperous, and hast a home pure, not sickening, but I [have] one impious and unhappy. And living thou mayest raise children from my sister, whom I gave thee to have[92] as a wife, and my name might exist, nor would my ancestral house be ever blotted out. But go, live, and dwell in my father's house; and when thou comest to Greece and chivalrous Argos, by thy right hand, I commit to thee this charge. Heap up a tomb, and place upon it remembrances of me, and let my sister offer tears and her shorn locks upon my sepulchre. And tell how I died by an Argive woman's hand, sacrificed as an offering by the altar's side. And do thou never desert my sister, seeing my father's connections and home bereaved. And fare thee well! for I have found thee best among my friends. Oh thou who hast been my fellow-huntsman, my mate! Oh thou who hast borne the weight of many of my sorrows! But Phœbus, prophet though he be, has deceived me. For, artfully devising, he has driven me as far as possible from Greece, in shame of his former prophecies. To whom I, yielding up mine all, and obeying his words, having slain my mother, myself perish in turn.

PYL. Thou shalt have a tomb, and never will I, hapless one, betray thy sister's bed, since I shall hold thee more a friend dead than living. But the oracle of the God has never yet wronged thee, although thou art indeed on the very verge of death. But excessive mischance is very wont, is very wont to present changes, when the matter so falls.

OR. Be silent—the words of Phœbus avail me naught, for the lady is coming hither without the temple.

IPH. Depart ye, and go and make ready the things within for those who superintend the sacrifice. These, O stranger, are the many-folded inclosures of the letter, but hear thou what I further wish. No man is the same in trouble, and when he changes from fear into confidence. But I fear, lest he having got away from this land, will deem my letter of no account, who is about to bear this letter to Argos.[93]

OR. What wouldst thou? Concerning what art thou disturbed?

IPH. Let him make me oath that he will ferry these writings to Argos, to those friends to whom I wish to send them.

OR. Wilt thou in turn make the same assertion to him?

IPH. That I will do, or will not do what thing? say.

OR. That you will release him from this barbarian land, not dying.

IPH. Thou sayest justly; for how could he bear the message?

OR. But will the ruler also grant this?

IPH. Yea. I will persuade him, and will myself embark him on the ship's hull.

OR. Swear, but do thou commence such oath as is holy.

IPH. Thou must say "I will give this [letter] to my friends."

PYL. I will give this letter to thy friends.

IPH. And I will send thee safe beyond the Cyanean rocks.

PYL. Whom of the Gods dost thou call to witness of thine oath in these words?

IPH. Diana, in whose temple I hold office.

PYL. But I [call upon] the king of heaven, hallowed Jove.

IPH. But if, deserting thine oath, thou shouldst wrong me—

PYL. May I not return? But thou, if thou savest me not—

IPH. May I never living set footprint in Argos.

PYL. Hear now then a matter which we have passed by.

IPH. There will be opportunity hereafter, if matters stand aright.

PYL. Grant me this one exception. If the vessel suffer any harm, and the letter be lost[94] in the storm, together with the goods, and I save my person only, that this mine oath be no longer valid.[95]

IPH. Knowest thou what I will do?[96] for the many things contained in the folds of the letter bear opportunity for many things.[97] I will tell you in words all that you are to convey to my friends, for this plan is safe. If indeed thou preservest the letter, it will itself silently tell the things written, but if these letters be lost at sea, saving thy body, thou wilt preserve my message.

PYL. Thou hast spoken well on behalf of the Gods[98] and of myself. But tell me to whom at Argos I must needs bear these epistles, and what hearing from thee, I must tell.

IPH. Bear word to Orestes, the son of Agamemnon, (*reading*) "she[99] that was sacrificed at Aulis gives this commission, Iphigenia alive, but no longer alive as far as those in Argos are concerned."

OR. But where is she? Does she come back again having died?

IPH. She, whom you see. Do not confuse me with speaking. (*Continues reading*) "Bear me to Argos, my brother, before I die, remove me from this barbarian land and the sacrifices of the Goddess, in which I have the office of slaying strangers."

OR. Pylades, what shall I say? where shall we be found to be?[100]

IPH. (*still reading*) "Or I will be a cause of curses upon thine house, Orestes," (*with great stress upon the name and turning to Pylades,*) "that thou, twice hearing the name, mayest know it."

PYL. O Gods!

IPH. Why callest thou upon the Gods in matters that are mine?

PYL. 'Tis nothing. Go on. I was wandering to another subject. Perchance, inquiring of thee, I shall arrive at things incredible.[101]

IPH. (*continues reading*) "Say that the Goddess Diana saved me, giving in exchange for me a hind, which my father sacrificed, thinking that it was upon me that he laid the sharp sword, and she placed me to dwell in this land." This is the burden of my message, these are the words written in my letter.

PYL. O thou who hast secured me in easy oaths, and hast sworn things fairest, I will not delay much time, but I will firmly accomplish the oath I have sworn. Behold, I bear and deliver to thee a letter, O Orestes, from this thy sister.

OR. I receive it. And letting go the opening of the letter, I will first seize a delight not in words (*attempts to embrace her*). O dearest sister mine, in amazement, yet nevertheless embracing thee with a doubting arm, I go to a source of delight, hearing things marvelous to me.[102]

CHOR. Stranger,[103] thou dost not rightly pollute the servant of the Goddess, casting thine arm around her garments that should ne'er be touched.

OR. O fellow-sister born of one sire, Agamemnon, turn not from me, possessing a brother whom you never thought to possess.

IPH. I [possess] thee my brother? Wilt not cease speaking? Both Argos and Nauplia are frequented by him.[104]

OR. Unhappy one! thy brother is not there.

IPH. But did the Lacedæmonian daughter of Tyndarus beget thee?

OR. Ay, to the grandson of Pelops, whence I am sprung.[105]

IPH. What sayest thou? Hast thou any proof of this for me?

OR. I have. Ask something relative to my ancestral home.

IPH. Thou must needs then speak, and I learn.

OR. I will first speak from hearsay from Electra, this.[106] Thou knowest the strife that took place between Atreus and Thyestes?

IPH. I have heard of it, when it was waged concerning the golden lamb.

OR. Dost thou then remember weaving [a representation of] this on the deftly-wrought web?

IPH. O dearest one. Thou art turning thy course near to my own thoughts.[107]

OR. And [dost thou remember] a picture on the loom, the turning away of the sun?

IPH. I wove this image also in the fine-threaded web.

OR. And didst thou receive[108] a bath from thy mother, sent to Aulis?

IPH. I know it: for the wedding, though good, did not take away my recollection.[109]

OR. But what? [Dost thou remember] to have given thine hair to be carried to thy mother?

IPH. Ay, as a memorial for the tomb[110] in place of my body.

OR. But the proofs which I have myself beheld, these will I tell, viz. the ancient spear of Pelops in my father's house, which brandishing in his hand, he [Pelops] won Hippodameia, having slain Ænomaus, which is hidden in thy virgin chamber.

IPH. O dearest one, no more, for thou art dearest. I hold thee, Orestes, one darling son[111] far away from his fatherland, from Argos, O thou dear one!

OR. And I [hold] thee that wast dead, as was supposed. But tears, yet tearless,[112] and groans together mingled with joy, bedew thine eyelids, and mine in like manner.

IPH. This one, this, yet a babe I left, young in the arms of the nurse, ay, young in our house. O thou more fortunate than my words[113] can tell, what shall I say? This matter has turned out beyond marvel or calculation.

OR. [Say this.] May we for the future be happy with each other!

IPH. I have experienced an unaccountable delight, dear companions, but I fear lest it flit[114] from my hands, and escape toward the sky. O ye Cyclopean hearths, O Mycenæ, dear country mine. I am grateful to thee for my life, and grateful for my nurture, in that thou hast trained for me this brother light in my home.

OR. In our race we are fortunate, but as to calamities, O sister, our life is by nature unhappy.

IPH. But I wretched remember when my father with foolish spirit laid the sword upon my neck.

OR. Ah me! For I seem, not being present, to behold you there.[115]

IPH. Without Hymen, O my brother, when I was being led to the fictitious nuptial bed of Achilles. But near the altar were tears and lamentations. Alas! alas, for the lustral waters there!

OR. I mourn aloud for the deed my father dared.

IPH. I obtained a fatherless, a fatherless lot. But one calamity follows upon another.[116]

OR. [Ay,] if thou hadst lost thy brother, O hapless one, by the intervention of some demon.

IPH. O miserable for my dreadful daring! I have dared horrid, I have dared horrid things. Alas! my brother. But by a little hast thou escaped an unholy destruction, stricken by my hands. But what will be the end after this? What fortune will befall me? What retreat can I find for thee away from this city? can I send you out of the reach of slaughter to your country Argos, before that my sword enter on the contest concerning thy blood?[117] This is thy business, O hapless soul, to discover, whether over the land, not in a ship, but by the gust[118] of your feet thou wilt approach death, passing through[119] barbarian hordes, and through ways not to be traversed? Or[120] [wilt thou pass] through the Cyanean creek, a long journey in the flight of ships. Wretched, wretched one! Who then or God, or mortal, or [unexpected event,[121]] having accomplished a way out of inextricable difficulties, will show forth to the sole twain Atrides a release from ills?

CHOR. Among marvels and things passing even fable are these things which I shall tell as having myself beheld, and not from hearsay.

PYL. It is meet indeed that friends coming into the presence of friends, Orestes, should embrace one another with their hands, but, having ceased from mournful matters, it behooves you also to betake you to those measures by which we, obtaining the glorious name of safety, may depart from this barbarian earth. For it is the part of wise men, not wandering from their present chance, when they have obtained an opportunity, to acquire further delights.[122]

OR. Thou sayest well. But I think that fortune will take care of this with us. For if a man be zealous, it is likely that the divine power will have still greater power.

IPH. Do not restrain or hinder me from your words, not first to know what fortune of life Electra has obtained, for this were pleasant to me [to hear.][123]

OR. She is partner with this man, possessing a happy life.

IPH. And of what country is he, and son of what man born?

OR. Strophius the Phocian is styled his father.

IPH. And he is of the daughter of Atreus, a relative of mine?

CXL

OR. Ay, a cousin, my only certain friend.

IPH. Was he not in being, when my father sought to slay me?

OR. He was not, for Strophius was childless some time.

IPH. Hail! O thou spouse of my sister.

OR. Ay, and my preserver, not relation only.

IPH. But how didst thou dare the terrible deeds in respect to your mother?

OR. Let us be silent respecting my mother—'twas in avenging my father.

IPH. And what was the reason for her slaying her husband?

OR. Let go the subject of my mother. Nor is it pleasant for you to hear.

IPH. I am silent. But Argos now looks up to thee.

OR. Menelaus rules: I am an exile from my country.

IPH. What, did our uncle abuse our house unprospering?

OR. Not so, but the fear of the Erinnyes drives me from my land.

IPH. For this then wert thou spoken of as being frantic even here on the shore.

OR. We were beheld not now for the first time in a hapless state.

IPH. I perceive. The Goddesses goaded thee on because of thy mother.

OR. Ay, so as to cast a bloody bit[124] upon me.

IPH. For wherefore didst thou pilot thy foot to this land?

OR. I came, commanded by the oracles of Phœbus—

IPH. To do what thing? Is it one to be spoken of or kept in silence?

OR. I will tell you, but these are the beginning for me of many[125] woes. After these evil things concerning my mother, on which I keep silence, had been wrought, I was driven an exile by the pursuits of the Erinnyes, when Loxias sent my foot[126] to Athens, that I might render satisfaction to the deities that must not be named. For there is a holy council, that Jove once on a time instituted for Mars on account of some pollution of his hands.[127] And coming thither, at first indeed no one of the strangers received me willingly, as being abhorred by the Gods, but they who had respect to me, afforded me[128] a stranger's meal at a separate table, being under the same house roof, and silently devised in respect to me, unaddressed by them, how I might be separated from their banquet[129] and cup, and, having filled up a share of wine in a separate vessel, equal for all, they enjoyed themselves. And I did not think fit to rebuke my guests, but I grieved in silence, and did not seem to perceive [their conduct,] deeply groaning, because I was my mother's slayer.[130] But I hear that my misfortunes have been made a festival at Athens, and that this custom still remains, that the people of Pallas honor the Libation Vessel.[131] But when I came to the hill of Mars, and stood in judgment, I indeed occupying one seat, but the eldest of the Erinnyes the other, having spoken and heard respecting my mother's death, Phœbus saved me by bearing witness, but Pallas counted out for me[132] the equal votes with her hand, and I came off victor in the bloody trial.[133] As many then as sat [in judgment,] persuaded by the sentence, determined to hold their dwelling near the court itself.[134] But as many of the Erinnyes as did not yield obedience to the sentence passed, continually kept driving me with unsettled wanderings, until I again returned to the holy ground of Phœbus, and lying stretched before the adyts, hungering for food, I swore that I would break from life by dying on the spot, unless Phœbus, who had undone, should preserve me. Upon this Phœbus, uttering a voice from the golden tripod, sent me hither to seize the heaven-sent image, and place it in the land of Athens. But that safety which he marked out for me do thou aid in. For if we can lay hold on the image of the Goddess, I both shall cease from my madness, and embarking thee in the bark of many oars, I shall settle thee again in Mycenæ. But, O beloved one, O sister mine, preserve my ancestral home, and preserve me, since all my state and that of the Pelopids is undone, unless we seize on the heavenly image of the Goddess.

CHOR. Some dreadful wrath of the Gods hath burst forth, and leads the seed of Tantalus through troubles.[135]

IPH. I entertained the desire to reach Argos, and behold thee, my brother, even before thou camest. But I wish, as you do, both to save thee, and to restore again our sickening ancestral home from troubles, in no wise wrath with him who would have slain me. For I should both release my hand from thy slaughter, and preserve mine house. But I fear how I shall be able to escape the notice of the Goddess and the king, when he shall find the stone pedestal bared of the image. And how shall I escape death? What account can I give? But if indeed these matters can be effected at once, and thou wilt bear away the image, and lead me in the fair-pooped ship, the risk will be a glorious one. But separated from this I perish, but you, arranging your own affairs, would obtain a prosperous return. Yet in no wise will I fly, not even if I needs must perish, having preserved thee. In no wise, I say;[136] for a man who dies from among his household is regretted, but a woman is of little account.

OR. I would not be the murderer both of thee and of my mother. Her blood is enough, and being of the same mind with you, [with you] I should wish, living or dying, to obtain an equal lot. †But I will lead thee, even though I myself fall here, to my house, or, remaining with thee, will die.[137]† But hear my opinion. If this had been disagreeable to Diana, how would Loxias have answered, that I should remove the image of the Goddess to the city of Pallas, and behold thy face? For, putting all these matters together, I hope to obtain a return.

IPH. How then can it happen that neither you die, and that we obtain what we wish? For it is in this respect that our journey homeward is at fault, but the will is not wanting.

OR. Could we possibly destroy the tyrant?

IPH, Thou tellest a fearful thing, for strangers to slay their receivers.

OR. But if it will preserve thee and me, one must run the risk.

IPH. I could not—yet I approve your zeal.

OR. But what if you were secretly to hide me in this temple?

IPH. In order, forsooth, that, taking advantage of darkness, we might be saved?

OR. For night is the time for thieves, the light for truth.

IPH. But within are the sacred keepers,[138] whom we can not escape.

OR. Alas! we are undone. How can we then be saved?

IPH. I seem to have a certain new device.

OR. Of what kind? Make me a sharer in your opinion, that I also may learn.

IPH. I will make use of thy ravings as a contrivance.

OR. Ay, cunning are women to find out tricks.

IPH. I will say that thou, being slayer of thy mother, art come from Argos.

OR. Make use of my troubles, if you can turn them to account.

IPH. I will say that it is not lawful to sacrifice thee to the Goddess.

OR. Having what pretext? For I partly suspect.

IPH. As not being pure, but I will [say that I will][139] give what is holy to sacrifice.

OR. How then the more will the image of the Goddess be obtained?

IPH. I [will say that I] will purify thee in the fountains of the sea.

OR. The statue, in quest of which, we have sailed, is still in the temple.

IPH. And I will say that I must wash that too, as if you had laid hands on it.

OR. Where then is the damp breaker of the sea of which you speak?

IPH. Where thy ship rides at anchor with rope-bound chains.

OR. But wilt thou, or some one else, bear the image in their hands?

IPH. I, for it is lawful for me alone to touch it.

OR. But in what part of this contrivance will our friend Pylades[140] be placed?

IPH. He will be said to bear the same pollution of hands as thyself.

OR. And wilt thou do this unknown to, or with the knowledge of the king?

IPH. Having persuaded him by words, for I could not escape notice.

OR. And truly the well-rowed ship is ready for sailing.[141]

IPH. You must take care of the rest, that it be well.

OR. There lacks but one thing, namely, that these women who are present preserve our secret. But do thou beseech them, and find words that will persuade. A woman in truth has power to move pity. But all the rest will perchance fall out well.

IPH. O dearest women, I look to you, and my affairs rest in you, as to whether they turn out well, or be of naught, and I be deprived of my country, my dear brother, and dearest sister. And let this first be the commencement of my words. We are women, a race well inclined to one another, and most safe in keeping secret matters of common interest. Do ye keep silence for us, and labor out our escape. Honorable is it for the man who possesses a faithful tongue. But behold how one fortune holds the three most dear, either a return to our father-land, or to die. But, being preserved, that thou also mayest share my fortune, I will restore thee safe to Greece. But, by thy right hand, thee, and thee [addressing the women of the chorus in succession] I beseech, and thee by thy beloved cheek, and thy knees, and those most dear at home, mother, and father, and children, to whom there are such.[142] What say ye? Who of you will, or will not [speak!] these things.[143] For if ye assent not to my words, I am undone, and my wretched sister.

CHOR. Be of good cheer, dear mistress, and think only of being saved, since on my part all shall be kept secret, the mighty Jove be witness! in the things thou enjoinest.

IPH. May your words profit ye, and may ye be blest. 'Tis thy part now, and thine [to the different women] to enter the house, as the ruler of this land will straightway come, inquiring concerning the sacrifice of the strangers, whether it is over. O revered Goddess, who in the recesses of Aulis didst save me from the dire hand of a slaying father, now also save me and these, or the voice of Loxias will through thee be no longer truthful among mortals. But do thou with good will quit the barbarian land for Athens, for it becomes thee not to dwell here, when you can possess a blest city.

CHORUS. Thou bird, that by the rocky cliffs of the sea, halcyon,[144] dost chant thy mournful elegy, a sound well understood by the skilled, namely, that thou art ever bemoaning thine husband in song, I, a wingless bird, compare my dirge with thine, longing for the assemblies[145] of the Greeks, longing for Lucina, who dwells along the Cynthian height, and near the palm[146] with its luxuriant foliage, and the rich-springing laurel, and the holy shoot of the deep blue olive, the dear place of Latona's throes,[147] and the lake that rolls its waters in a circle,[148] where the melodious swan honors the muses. O ye many tricklings of tears which fell upon my cheeks, when, our towers being destroyed, I traveled in ships beneath the oars and the spears of the foes.[149] And through a bartering of great price I came a journey to a barbarian land,[150] where I serve the daughter of Agamemnon, the priestess of the Goddess, and the sheep-slaughtering[151] altars, envying her who has all her life been unfortunate;[152] for she bends not under necessity, who is familiar with it. Unhappiness is wont to change,[153] but to fare ill after prosperity is a heavy life for mortals. And thee indeed, O mistress, an Argive ship of fifty oars will conduct home, and the wax-bound reed of mountain Pan with Syrinx tune cheer on the oarsmen, and prophet Phœbus, plying the tones of his seven-stringed lyre, with song will lead thee prosperously to the rich land of Athens. But leaving me here thou wilt travel by the dashing oars. And the halyards by the prow,[154] will stretch forth the sails to the air, above the beak, the sheet lines of the swift-journeying ship. Would that I might pass through the glittering course, where the fair light of the sun wends its way, and over my own chamber might rest from rapidly moving the pinions on my shoulders.[155] And would that I might stand in the dance, where also [I was wont to stand,] a virgin sprung from honorable nuptials,[156] wreathing the dances of my companions at the foot of my dear mother,[157] bounding to the rivalry of the graces, to the wealthy strife respecting [beauteous] hair, pouring my variously-painted garb and tresses around, I shadowed my cheeks.[158]

[*Enter* THOAS.]

THOAS. Where is the Grecian woman who keeps the gate of this temple? Has she yet begun the sacrifice of the strangers, and are the bodies burning in the flame within the pure recesses?

CHOR. Here she is, O king, who will tell thee clearly all.

TH. Ah! Why art thou removing in your arms this image of the Goddess from its seat that may not be disturbed, O daughter of Agamemnon?

IPH. O king, rest there thy foot in the portico.

TH. But what new matter is in the house, Iphigenia?

IPH. I avert the ill—for holy[159] do I utter this word.

TH. What new thing art thou prefacing? speak clearly.

IPH. O king, no pure offerings hast thou hunted out for me.

TH. What hath taught you this? or dost thou speak it as matter of opinion?

IPH. The image of the Goddess hath again turned away from her seat.[160]

TH. Of its own accord, or did an earthquake turn it?

IPH. Of its own accord, and it closed its eyes.

TH. But what is the cause? is it pollution from the strangers?

IPH. That very thing, naught else, for they have done dreadful things.

TH. What, did they slay any of the barbarians upon the shore?

IPH. They came possessing the stain of domestic murder.

TH. What? for I am fallen into a longing to learn this.

IPH. They put an end to a mother's life by conspiring sword.

TH. Apollo! not even among barbarians would any one have dared this.

IPH. By persecutions they were driven out of all Greece.

TH. Is it then on their account that thou bearest the image without?

IPH. Ay, under the holy sky, that I may remove it from blood stains.

TH. But how didst thou discover the pollution of the strangers?

IPH. I examined them, when the image of the Goddess turned away.

TH. Greece hath trained thee up wise, in that thou well didst perceive this.

IPH. And now they have cast out a delightful bait for my mind.

TH. By telling thee any charming news of those at Argos?

IPH. That my only brother Orestes fares well.

TH. So that, forsooth, thou mightest preserve them because of their pleasant news!

IPH. And that my father lives and fares well.

TH. But thou hast with reason attended to the interest of the Goddess.

IPH. Ay, because hating all Greece that destroyed me.

TH. What then shall we do, say, concerning the two strangers?

IPH. We needs must respect the established law.

TH. Are not the lustral waters and thy sword already engaged?[161]

IPH. First I would fain lave them in pure cleansings.

TH. In the fountains of waters, or in the dew of the sea?

IPH. The sea washes out all the ills of men.

TH. They would certainly fall in a more holy manner before the Goddess.

IPH. And my matters would be in a more fitting state.[162]

TH. Does not the wave dash against the very temple?

IPH. There is need of solitude, for we have other things to do.

TH. Lead them whither thou wilt, I crave not to see things that may not be told.

IPH. The image of the Goddess also must be purified by me.

TH. If indeed the stain of the matricide hath fallen on it.

IPH. For otherwise I should not have removed it from its pedestal.

TH. Just piety and foresight! How reasonably doth all the city marvel at thee!

IPH. Knowest thou then what must be done for me?

TH. 'Tis thine to explain this.

IPH. Cast fetters upon the strangers.

TH. Whither could they escape from thee?

IPH. Greece knows nothing faithful.

TH. Go for the fetters, attendants.

IPH. Ay, and let them bring the strangers hither.

TH. This shall be.

IPH. Having enveloped their heads in robes.

TH. Against the scorching of the sun?

IPH. And send thou with me of thy followers—

TH. These shall accompany thee.

IPH. And send some one to signify to the city—

TH. What hap?

IPH. That all remain in their homes.

TH. Lest they encounter homicide?

IPH. For such things are unclean.

TH. Go thou, and order this.

IPH. That no one come into sight.

TH. Thou carest well for the city.

IPH. Ay, and more particularly friends must not be present.[163]

TH. This you say in reference to me.

IPH. But do thou, abiding here before the temple of the Goddess—

TH. Do what?

IPH. Purify the house with a torch.

TH. That it may be pure when thou comest back to it?

IPH. But when the strangers come out,

TH. What must I do?

IPH. Place your garment before your eyes.

TH. Lest I contract contagion?

IPH. But if I seem to tarry very long,

TH. What limit of this shall I have?

IPH. Wonder at nothing.

TH. Do thou rightly the business of the Goddess at thy leisure.

IPH. And may this purification turn out as I wish!

TH. I join in your prayer.

IPH. I now see these strangers coming out of the house, and the adornments of the Goddess, and the young lambs, in order that I may wash out foul slaughter by slaughter, and the shining light of lamps, and the other things, as many as I ordered as purifications for the strangers and the Goddess. But I proclaim to the strangers to get out of the way of this pollution, if any gate-keeper of the temples keeps pure hands for the Gods, or is about to join in nuptial alliance, or is pregnant, flee, get out of the way, lest this pollution fall on any. O thou queen, virgin daughter of Jove and Latona, if I wash away the blood-pollution from these men, and sacrifice where 'tis fitting, thou wilt occupy a pure house, and we shall be prosperous. But although I do not speak of the rest, I nevertheless signify my meaning to the Gods who know most things,[164] and to thee, O Goddess.

CHORUS.[165] Of noble birth is the offspring of Latona, whom once on a time in the fruitful valleys of Delos, Phœbus with his golden locks, skilled on the lyre, (and she who rejoices in skill of the bow,) his mother bore while yet an infant[166] from the sea-side rock, leaving the renowned place of her delivery, destitute of waters,[167] the Parnassian height haunted by Bacchus, where the ruddy-visaged serpent, with spotted back, † brazen † beneath the shady laurel with its rich foliage, an enormous prodigy of the earth, guarded the subterranean oracle. Him thou, O Phœbus, while yet an infant, while yet leaping in thy dear mother's arms, didst slay, and entered upon thy divine oracles, and thou sittest on the golden tripod, on the throne that is ever true, distributing to mortals prophecies from the divine adyts beneath the Castalian streams, dwelling hard by, occupying a dwelling in the middle of the earth.[168] But when, having gone against Themis, daughter of earth, he expelled her from the divine oracles, earth begot dark phantoms of dreams, which to many mortals explain what first, what afterward, what in future will happen, during their sleep in the couches of the dusky earth.[169] But † the earth † deprived Phœbus of the honor of prophecies, through anger on her daughter's account, and the swift-footed king, hastening to Olympus, stretched forth his little hand to the throne of Jove.[170] [beseeching him] to take away the earth-born[171] wrath of the Goddess, † and the nightly responses. † But he laughed, because his son had come quickly to him, wishing to obtain the wealthy office, and he shook his hair, and put an end to the nightly dreams,[172] and took away nightly divination from mortals, and again conferred the honor on Loxias, and confidence to mortals from the songs of oracles [proclaimed] on this throne, thronged to by many strangers.[173]

[*Enter* A MESSENGER.]

MESS. O ye guardians of the temple and presidents of the altars, where in this land has king Thoas gone? Do ye, opening the well-fastened gates, call the ruler of this land outside the house.

CHOR. But what is it, if I may speak when I am not bidden?

MESS. The two youths have escaped, and are gone by the contrivances of Agamemnon's daughter, endeavoring to fly from this land, and taking the sacred image in the bosom of a Grecian ship.

CHOR. Thou tellest an incredible story, but the king of this country, whom you wish to see, is gone, having quitted the temple.

MESS. Whither? For he needs must know what has been done.

CHOR. We know not. But go thou and pursue him to wheresoever, having met with him, thou mayest recount this news.

MESS. See, how faithless is the female race! and ye are partners in what has been done.

CHOR. Art thou mad? What have we to do with the flight of the strangers? Will you not go as quickly as possible to the gates of the rulers?

MESS. Not at least before some distinct informer[174] tell me this, whether the ruler of the land is within or not within. Ho there! Open the fastenings, I speak to those within, and tell the master that I am at the gates, bearing a weight of evil news.

THOAS. (*coming out*) Who makes this noise near the temple of the Goddess, hammering at the door, and sending fear within?

MESS. These women told me falsely, (and tried to drive me from the house,) that you were away, while you really were in the house.

TH. Expecting or hunting after what gain?

MESS. I will afterward tell of what concerns them, but hear the present, immediate matter. The virgin, she that presided over the altars here, Iphigenia, has gone out of the land with the strangers, having the sacred image of the Goddess; but the expiations were pretended.

TH. How sayest thou? possessed by what breath of calamity?[175]

MESS. In order to preserve Orestes, for at this thou wilt marvel.

TH. What [Orestes]? Him, whom the daughter of Tyndarus bore?

MESS. Him whom she consecrated to the Goddess at these altars.

TH. Oh marvel! How can I rightly[176] call thee by a greater name?

MESS. Do not turn thine attention to this, but listen to me; and having perceived and heard, clearly consider what pursuit will catch the strangers.

TH. Speak, for thou sayest well, for they do not flee by the way of the neighboring sea, so as to be able to escape my fleet.

MESS. When we came to the sea-shore, where the vessel of Orestes was anchored in secret, to us indeed, whom thou didst send with her, bearing fetters for the strangers, the daughter of Agamemnon made signs that we should get far out of the way, as she was about to offer the secret[177] flame and expiation, for which she had come. But she, holding the fetters of the strangers in her hands, followed behind them. And these matters were suspicious, but they satisfied your attendants, O king. But at length, in order forsooth that she might seem to us to be doing something, she screamed aloud, and chanted barbarian songs like a sorceress, as if washing out the stain of murder. But after we had remained sitting a long time, it occurred to us whether the strangers set at liberty might not slay her, and take to flight. And through fear lest we might behold what was not fitting, we sat in silence, but at length the same words were in every body's mouth, that we should go to where they were, although not permitted. And upon this we behold the hull of the Grecian ship, [the rowing winged with well-fitted oars,[178]] and fifty sailors holding their oars in the tholes, and the youths, freed from their fetters, standing [on the shore] astern of the ship.[179] But some held in the prow with their oars, and others from the epotides let down the anchor, and others hastily applying the ladders, drew the stern-cables through their hands, and giving them to the sea, let them down to the strangers.[180] But we unsparing [of the toil,] when we beheld the crafty stratagem, laid hold of the female stranger and of the cables, and tried to drag the rudders from the fair-prowed ship from the steerage-place. But words ensued: "On what plea do ye take to the sea, stealing from this land the images and priestess? Whose son art thou, who thyself, who art carrying this woman from the land?" But he replied, "Orestes, her brother, that you may know, the son of Agamemnon, I, having taken this my sister, whom I had lost from my house, am bearing her off." But naught the less we clung to the female stranger, and compelled them by force to follow us to thee, upon which arose sad smitings of the cheeks. For they had not arms in their hands, nor had we; but fists were sounding against fists, and the arms of both the youths at once were aimed against our sides and to the liver, so that we at once were exhausted[181] and worn out in our limbs. But stamped with horrid marks we fled to a precipice, some having bloody wounds on the head, others in the eyes, and standing on the heights, we waged a safer warfare, and pelted stones. But archers, standing on the poop, hindered us with their darts, so that we returned back. And meanwhile—for a tremendous wave drove the ship against the land, and there was alarm [on board] lest she might dip her sheet-line[182]— Orestes, taking his sister on his left shoulder, walked into the sea, and leaping upon the ladder, placed her within the well-banked ship, and also the image of the daughter of Jove, that fell from heaven. And from the middle of the ship a voice spake thus, "O mariners of the Grecian ship, seize[183] on your oars, and make white the surge, for we have obtained the things on account of which we sailed o'er the Euxine within the Symplegades." But they shouting forth a pleasant cry, smote the brine. The ship, as long indeed as it was within the port, went on; but, passing the outlet, meeting with a strong tide, it was driven back. For a terrible gale coming suddenly, drives [the bark winged with well-fitted oars] poop-wise,[184] but they persevered, kicking against the wave, but an ebbing tide brought them again aground. But the daughter of Agamemnon stood up and prayed, "O daughter of Latona, bring me, thy priestess, safe into Greece from a barbarian land, and pardon the stealing away of me. Thou also, O Goddess, lovest thy brother, and think thou that I also love my kindred." But the sailors shouted a pæan in assent to the prayers of the girl, applying on a given signal the point of the shoulders,[185] bared from their hands, to the oars. But more and more the vessel kept nearing the rocks, and one indeed leaped into the sea with his feet, and another fastened woven nooses.[186] And I was immediately sent hither to thee, to tell thee, O king, what had happened there. But go, taking fetters and halters in your hands, for, unless the wave shall become tranquil, there is no hope of safety for the strangers. For the ruler of the sea, the revered Neptune, both favorably regards Troy, and is at enmity with the Pelopidæ. And he will now, as it seems, deliver up to thee and the citizens the son of Agamemnon, to take him into your hands, and his sister, who is detected ungratefully forgetting the Goddess in respect to the sacrifice at Aulis.[187]

CHOR. O hapless Iphigenia, with thy brother wilt thou die, again coming into the hands of thy masters.

TH. O all ye citizens of this barbarian land, will ye not, casting bridles on your horses, run to the shore, and receive the casting on of the Grecian ship? But hastening, by the favor of the Goddess, will ye not hunt down the impious men, and some of you haul the swift barks down to the sea, that by sea, and by horse-coursings on the land seizing them, we may either hurl them down the broken rock, or impale their bodies upon stakes. But you women, the accomplices in these plots, I will punish hereafter, when I have leisure, but now, having such a present duty, we will not remain idle...

[TYRANNOSAURUS REX *appears and steps on Thoas, squashing him like a pancake.* [180] *Everybody else goes back to their houses while Iphigenia and Orestes escape.*]

NOTES ON IPHIGENIA IN TAURIS

---

[1] This verse and part of the following are set down among the "oil cruet" verses by Aristophanes, Ran. 1232. Aristotle, Poet. § xvii. gives a sketch of the plot of the whole play, by way of illustrating the general form of tragedy. Hyginus, who constantly has Euripides in view, also gives a brief analysis of the plot, fab. cxx. For a description of the quadrigæ of Pelops, see Philostratus Imagg. i. 19. It must be observed, that Antoninus Liberalis, § 27, makes

Iphigenia only the supposititious daughter of Agamemnon, but really the daughter of Theseus and Helen. See Meurs. on Lycophron, p. 145.

[2] I must confess that I can not find what should have so much displeased the critics in this word. Iphigenia, in using such an epithet, evidently refers to her own intended sacrifice, which had rendered the recesses of Aulis a place of no small fame.

[3] But Lenting prefers Αχαιους, with the approbation of the Cambridge editor.

[4] See Reiske apud Dindorf. Compare my note on Æsch. Ag. 188, p. 101, ed. Bohn. So also Callimachus, Hymn. iii. μειλιον απλοϊης, 'οτε 'οι κατεδησας αητας.

[5] Sinon made the same complaint. Cf. Virg. Æn. ii. 90.

[6] Cf. Æsch. Ag. 235.

[7] This whole passage has been imitated by Ovid, de Ponto, iii. 2, 60. "Sceptra tenente illo, liquidas fecisse per auras, Nescio quam dicunt Iphigenian iter. Quam levibus ventis sub nube per aera vectam Creditur his Phœbe deposuisse locis." Cf. Lycophron, p. 16, vs. 3 sqq. Nonnus xiii. p. 332, 14 sqq.

[8] Observe the double construction of ανασσει. Orest. 1690. ναυταις μεδεουσα θαλασσης.

[9] The Cambridge editor would expunge this line, which certainly seems languid and awkward. Boissonade on Aristænet. Ep. xiii. p. 421, would simply read τα δ' αλλα ς. τ. θ. φοβουμενη: θυω γαρ. He also retains 'ιερειαν, referring to Gaisford on Hephæst. p. 216.

[10] The Cambridge editor would throw out vs. 41.

[11] The Cambridge editor refers to Med. 56, Androm. 91, Soph. El. 425. Add Plaut. Merc. i. 1, 3. "Non ego idem facio, ut alios in comœdiis vidi facere amatores, qui aut nocti, aut die, Aut Soli, aut Lunæ miserias narrant suas." Theognetus apud Athen. xv. p. 671. Casaub. πεφιλοσοφηκας γηι και ουρανωι λαλων. Cf. Davis, on Cicero, Tusc. Q. iii. 26, and Lomeier de Lustrat. § xxxvii.

[12] Θριγκον is properly the uppermost part of the walls of any building (Pollux, vii. 27) surrounding the roof, στεγος is the roof itself.

[13] Cf. Meurs. ad Lycophron, p. 148.

[14] I read ειμ' εισω with Hermann and the Cambridge editor.

[15] This line is condemned by the Cambridge editor. Burges has transposed it.

[16] But διαδρομαις, the correction of the Cambridge editor, seems preferable.

[17] An interpolation universally condemned.

[18] See Barnes, and Wetstein on Acts xix. 35.

[19] On the wanderings of Orestes see my note on Æsch. Eum. 238 sqq. p. 187, ed. Bohn.

[20] See the note of the Cambridge editor, with whom we must read εισβησομεσθα.

[21] 'ων ουδεν ισμεν ad interiora templi spectat. HERM.

[22] We must read γεισα τριγλυφων 'οποι, with Blomfield and the Cambridge editor. See Philander on Vitruv. ii. p. 35, and Pollux, vii. 27.

[23] The sense is ουτοι, μακραν ελθοντες, εκ τερματων (sc. a meta) νοστησομεν. ED. CAMB.

[24] The Cambridge editor appositely compares a fragment of our author's Cresphontes, iii. 2, αισχρον τε μοχθειν μη θελειν νεανιαν.

[25] On the whole of this chorus, which is corrupt in several places, the notes of the Cambridge editor should be consulted.

[26] This last lumbering line must be corrupt.

[27] Compare the similar scene in Soph. El. 86 sqq.

[28] Cf. Elect. 90. νυκτος δε τησδε προς ταφον μολων πατρος. Hecub. 76. Æsch. Pers. 179. Aristoph. Ran. 1331.

[29] Compare my note on Æsch. Pers. 610 sqq.

[30] See on Æsch. Choeph. 6.

[31] Markland's emendation has been unanimously adopted by the later editors.

[32] Schema Colophonium. The Cambridge editor compares vs. 244. Αργει σκηπτουχον. Phœn. 17. Θηβαισιν αναξ. Heracl. 361. Αργει τυραννος.

[33] I have marked lacunæ, as some mythological particulars have evidently been lost.

[34] An imperfect allusion to the Thyestean banquet. Cf. Seneca Thyest. 774. "O Phœbe patiens, fugeris retro licet, medioque ruptum merseris cœlo diem, sero occidisti—" vs. 787 sqq.

[35] Cf. Æsch. Ag. 1501 sqq. Seneca, Ag. 57 sqq.

[36] i.e. the demon allotted to me at my birth (cf. notes on Æsch. 1341, p. 135, ed. Bohn). Statius, Theb. i. 60, makes Œdipus invoke Tisiphone under the same character.—"Si me de matre cadentem Fovisti gremio."

[37] See the note of the Cambridge editor.

[38] εβησαν is active.

[39] The Cambridge editor aptly refers to Hecub. 464.

[40] These participles refer to the preceding αιμορραντων ξεινων.

[41] See on Heracl. 721.

[42] The Cambridge editor would omit these two lines.

[43] Cf. vs. 107. κατ' αντρ', 'α ποντιος νοτιδι διακλυζει μελας. On αγμος (Brodæus' happy correction for 'αρμος) the Cambridge editor quotes Nicander Ther. 146. κοιλη τε φαραγξ, και τρηχεες αγμοι, and other passages. The manner of hunting the purple fish is thus described by Pollux, i. 4, p. 24. They plat a long rope, to which they fasten, like bells, a number of hempen baskets, with an open entrance to admit the animal, but which does not allow of its egress. This they let down into the sea, the baskets being filled with such food as the murex delights in, and, having fastened the end of the rope to the rock, they leave it, and returning to the place, draw up the baskets full of the fish. Having broken the shells, they pound the flesh to form the dye.

[44] εφθαρμενους. Cf. Cycl. 300. Hel. 783. Ed. Camb.

[45] Compare Orest. 255 sqq.

[46] χιτωνων is probably corrupt.

[47] Cf. Lobeck on Aj. 17. Hesych. κοχλος τοις θαλαττιοις (i.e. κοχλοις) εχρωντο, προ της των σαλπιγγων ευρεσεως. Virg. Æn. vi. 171. "Sed tum forte cava dum personat æquora concha."

[48] "Moriamur, et in media arma ruamus." Virg. Æn. ii.

[49] Such seems to be the sense, but εξεκλεψαμεν is ridiculous, and Hermann's emendation more so. Bothe reads εξεκοψαμεν, which is better. The Cambridge editor thinks that the difficulty lies in πετροισι.

[50] I would omit this line as an evident gloss.

[51] See the Cambridge editor.

[52] Reiske's emendation, ʽοσια for ʽοια, seems deserving of admission.

[53] The Cambridge editor would omit these lines.

[54] This line also the Cambridge editor trusts "will never hereafter be reckoned among the verses of Euripides."

[55] Such is the proper sense of αντιθεισα.

[56] νιν is νυμφευματα.

[57] Read κασιγνητηι.

[58] I read τοις μεν and τοις δ' with the Cambridge editor. Hermann's emendation is unheard of.

[59] This clause interrupts the construction. δραμοντες must be understood with all the following sentence, as no finite verb is expressed except επερασαν.

[60] I have partly followed Hermann, reading επεβαιην ... απολαυων, but, as to reading ʽυπνων for ʽυμνων, the Cambridge editor well calls it "one of the wonders of his edition." I should prefer reading ολβου with the same elegant scholar.

[61] I follow the Cambridge editor in reading διδυμας, from Ovid, Ep. Pont. iii. 2, 71. "Protinus immitem Triviæ ducuntur ad aram, Evincti geminas ad sua terga manus."

[62] "*displays while she offers*" i.e. "*presents as a public offering*" ED. CAMB.

[63] I am but half satisfied with this passage.

[64] Read εσεσθε δη κατω with the Cambridge editor.

[65] We must read νω with Porson.

[66] Probably a spurious line.

[67] Read Μυκηνων γ', *αy, from Mycenæ*, with the Cambridge editor.

[68] Hermann seems rightly to read 'ος γ' εν.

[69] Dindorf rightly adopts Reiske's emendation συ τουδ' ερα.

[70] The Cambridge editor rightly reads τινά with an accent, as Orestes obviously means himself. Compare Soph. Ant. 751. 'ηδ' ουν θανειται, και θανουσ' ολει τινά.

[71] Such is the force of δη.

[72] I would read εξεπραξατο with Emsley, but I do not agree with him in substituting κακην. The oxymoron seems intentional, and by no means unlike Euripides.

[73] The Cambridge editor would read εστ' ουτις λογος.

[74] But χαριν, as Matthiæ remarks, is taken in two senses; as a preposition with γυναικος, *ob improbam mulierem*, and as a substantive, with αχαριν added. Cf. Æsch. Choeph. 44. Lucretius uses a similar oxymoron respecting the same subject, i. 99. "Sed *casta inceste* nubendi tempore in ipso Hostia concideret mactatu mæsta parentis."

[75] This passage is very corrupt. The Cambridge editor supposes something lost respecting the fortunes of Orestes. Hermann reads 'εν δε λυπεισθαι μονον, 'ο τ' ουκ αφρων ων. But I am very doubtful.

[76] These three lines are justly condemned as an absurd interpolation by Dindorf and the Cambridge editor.

[77] This seems the easiest way of expressing και συ after συ δ'.

[78] I am partly indebted to Potter's happy version. The Cambridge editor is as ingenious as usual, but he candidly allows that conjecture is scarcely requisite.

[79] i.e. thou seemest reckless of life.

[80] προστροπη, this mode of offering supplication, i.e. this duty of sacrifice.

[81] Diodorus, xx. 14. quotes this and the preceding line reading χθονος for πετρας. He supposes that Euripides derived the present account from the sacrifices offered to Saturn by the Carthaginians, who caused their children to fall from the hands of the statue εις τι χασμα πληρες πυρος. Compare Porphyr. de Abst. ii. 27. Justin, xviii. 6. For similar human sacrifices among the Gauls, Cæsar de B.G. vi. 16, with the note of Vossius. Compare also Saxo Grammaticus, Hist. Dan. iii. p. 42, and the passages of early historians quoted in Stephens' entertaining notes, p. 92.

[82] Cf. Tibull. i. 3, 5. "Abstineas, mors atra, precor, non hic mihi mater, Quæ legat in mæstos ossa perusta sinus; non soror, Assyrios cineri quæ dedat odores, et fleat effusis ante sepulchra comis."

[83] This must be what the poet *intends* by κατασβεσω, however awkwardly expressed. See Hermann's note.

[84] Compare vs. 468 sq.

[85] This line is hopelessly corrupt.

[86] I read μεν ουν with the Cambridge editor.

[87] αζηλα is in opposition to the whole preceding clause.

[88] See the note of the Cambridge editor on Iph. Aul. 1372.

[89] I should prefer εστι δη, "she surely is."

[90] We must evidently read either διηλθον with Porson, or διελθε with Jan., Le Fevre, and Markland.

[91] I almost agree with Dindorf in considering this line spurious.

[92] For this construction compare Ritterhus. ad Oppian, Cyn. i. 11.

[93] I can not help thinking this line is spurious, and the preceding θηται corrupt. One would expect θησηι.

[94] Cf. Kuinoel on Cydon. de Mort. Contem. § 1, p. 6, n. 18.

[95] Literally, "no longer a hinderance," i.e. "that I be no longer responsible for its fulfillment."

[96] The Cambridge editor, however, seems to have settled the question in favor of οισθ' ουν 'ο δρασον.

[97] I must candidly confess that none of the explanations of these words satisfy me. Perhaps it is best to regard them, with Seidler, as merely signifying the mutability of fortune.

[98] i.e. as far as the fulfilling of my oath is concerned.

[99] The letter evidently commences with the words 'η 'ν Αυλιδι σφαγεισα. I can not imagine how Markland and others should have made it commence with the previous line.

[100] i.e. in what company.

[101] This line is either spurious or out of place. See the Cambridge editor.

[102] The Cambridge editor in a note exhibiting his usual chastened and elegant judgment, regards these three lines as an absurd and trifling interpolation. For the credit of Euripides, I would fain do the same.

[103] The same elegant scholar justly assigns these lines to Iphigenia.

[104] So Erfurdt.

[105] See the Cambridge editor.

[106] This line seems justly condemned by the Cambridge editor.

[107] With καμπτεις understand δρομον = thou art fast arriving at the goal of the truth.

[108] Read απεδεξω with ed. Camb.

[109] "I remember it: for the wedding did not, by its happy result, take away the recollection of that commencement of nuptial ceremonies." CAMB. ED.

[110] i.e. Iphigenia sent it with a view to a cenotaph at Mycenæ, as she was about to die at Aulis. See Seidler.

[111] "This Homeric epithet of an only son is used, I believe, nowhere else in Attic poetry. Its adoption here seems owing to Hom. Il. I. 142 and 284. τισω δε μιν 'ισον Ορεστηι 'Ος μοι τηλυγετος τρεφεται θαλιηι ενι πολληι." ED. CAMB.

[112] This is Musgrave's elegant emendation, which Hermann, unwilling to let well alone, has attempted to spoil. See, however, the Cambridge editor, who possesses taste and clear perception, unbiased by self-love.

[113] Read εμοις with the Cambridge editor.

[114] But φυγηις, and ω φιλος, the emendation of Burges, seems far better, and is followed by the Cambridge editor.

[115] i.e. I can imagine your sufferings at Aulis.

[116] The Cambridge editor compares Hec. 684. 'ετερα δ' αφ' 'ετερων κακα κακων κυρει.

[117] This is Reiske's interpretation, taking the construction πριν ξιφος παλ. επι 'αιματι. But Seidler would recall the old reading πελασαι, comparing Hel. 361. αυτοσιδαρον εσω πελασω δια σαρκος 'αμιλλαν. This is better, but we must also read ετι for επι with the Cambridge editor.

[118] 'ριπαι ποδων is a bold way of expressing rapid traveling.

[119] Read ανα with Markland, for αρα.

[120] I read η δια κυαν. with the Cambridge editor. The following words are rendered thus by Musgrave, "Per ... est longum iter."

[121] Unintelligible, and probably spurious.

[122] The Cambridge editor finds fault with the obvious clumsiness of the expression, and proposes εχειν for λαβειν. I have still greater doubts about εκβαντας τυχης. The sense ought to be, "'tis the part of wise men, *when fortune favors*, not to lose the opportunity, but to gain other advantages."

[123] See Dindorf's notes. But the Cambridge editor has shown so decided a superiority to the German critics, that I should unhesitatingly adopt his reading, as follows: ου μη μ' επισχηις, ουδ' αποστησεις λογου, το μη ου πυθεσθαι ... φιλα γαρ ταυτα, (with Markland,) although πρωτον may perhaps be defended.

[124] See the Cambridge editor. The same elegant scholar has also improved the arrangement of the lines.

[125] "Quanquam animus meminisse horret, luctuque refugit, Incipiam." Virg. Æn. i.

[126] I read ενθ' εμον ποδα with Herm. and Dind.

[127] Cf. Elect. 1258 sqq., and Meurs. Areop. § i. ψηφος seems here used to denote the place where the council was held. The pollution of Mars was the murder of Hallirothius. Cf. Pausan. i. 21.

[128] An instance of the nominativus pendens.

[129] So Valckenaer, Diatr. p. 246, who quotes some passages relative to the treatment of Orestes at Athens.

[130] See the Cambridge editor.

[131] See Barnes, who quotes the Schol. on Arist. Eq. 95. Χους was the name of the festival.

[132] εμοι is the dativus commodi.

[133] I am indebted to Maltby for this translation.

[134] Cf. Piers, on Mœr. p. 351, and the Cambridge editor.

[135] But see ed. Camb.

[136] Such is the force, of ου γαρ αλλ'.

[137] These lines are very corrupt, and perhaps, as Dindorf thinks, spurious.

[138] Markland rightly reads 'ιεροφυλακες.

[139] "dicam me daturam." MARKLAND.

[140] 'οδ' is the correction of Brodæus.

[141] νεως πιτυλος seems not merely a periphrase, but implies that the oars are in the row-locks, as if ready for starting.

[142] But the Cambridge editor very elegantly reads ει τοι.

[143] Put φθεγξασθε in an inclosure, and join ταυτα with θελει. See ed. Camb.

[144] Schol. Theocr. Id. vii. 57. θρηνητικον το ζωιον, και παρα τοις αιγιαλοις νεοττευον. Cf. Aristoph. Ran. 1309, who perhaps had the passage in view.

[145] αγορος is a somewhat rare word for αγυρις.

[146] Cf. Hecub. 457 sqq.

[147] So Matthiæ, "locum ubi Latona partum edidit."

[148] Read κυκλιον with Seidler. On the λιμνη τροχοειδης at Delos, see Barnes.

[149] "I was conveyed by sailors and soldiers." ED. CAMB.

[150] The same scholar quotes Soph. Ph. 43. αλλ' η' πι φορβης νοστον εξεληλυθεν, vhere νοστος is used in the same manner as here, simply meaning "a journey."

[151] But see Camb. ed.

[152] I read ζηλουσα ταν with the same.

[153] The Cambridge critic again proposes μεταβολαι δ' ευδαιμονια, which he felicitously supports. Musgrave has however partly anticipated this emendation.

[154] Dindorf has shown so little care in editing this passage, that I have merely recalled the old reading, αερι δ' 'ιστια προτονοι κ. πρ. 'υπερ στολον εκπ., following the construction proposed by Heath, and approved, as it appears, by the Cambridge editor. Seidler's note is learned and instructive, but I have some doubts about his criticism.

[155] i.e. I wish I might become a bird and fly homeward.

[156] See ed. Camb.

[157] But see ibid. Dindorf's text is a hopeless display of bad readings and worse punctuation.

[158] Reading γεννας, I have done my best with this passage, but I can only refer to the Cambridge editor for a text and notes worthy of the play.

[159] I have recalled the old reading, 'οσια.

[160] On these sort of prodigies, see Musgrave, and Dansq. on Quintus Calaber, xii. 497 sqq.

[161] "in eo, ut" is the force of εν εργωι.

[162] Perhaps a sly allusion to their escape.

[163] See ed. Camb.

[164] But we must read τοις τε with the Cambridge editor = "who know more than men."

[165] I can not too early impress upon the reader the necessity of a careful attention to the criticisms of the Cambridge editor throughout this difficult chorus, especially to his masterly sketch of the whole, p. 146, 147.

[166] φερεν ινιν is Burges' elegant emendation, the credit of which has been unduly claimed by Seidler.

[167] i.e. the place afterward called Inopus. See Herm., whose construction I have followed.

[168] On the ομφαλος see my note on Æsch. Eum. p. 180, ed. Bohn. On the Delphic priesthood, compare ibid. p. 179.

[169] See, however, the Cambridge editor.

[170] Read ες θρονον with Barnes and Dind., or rather επι Ζηνος θρονον with Herm.

[171] But see Dindorf.

[172] See Dindorf's note, but still better the Cambridge editor.

[173] I follow Seidler.

[174] So ed. Camb.

[175] i.e. what evil inspiration of the Gods impelled her to this act? Thoas, who is represented as superstitious to the most barbarian extent, naturally regards the infidelity of Iphigenia as proceeding from the intervention of heaven.

[176] Cf. Monk. on Hippol. 828.

[177] Cf. vs. 1197. ερημιας δει.

[178] Dindorf and the Cambridge editor follow Hermann, corner him in an alley, and beat the living daylights out of him.

[179] So Musgrave. Soooooo Musgrave.

[180] This ancient figure of speech does not literally mean that the squashing which took place was similar to that which would occur were one to make an attempt at squashing a pancake. Pancakes, being inherently flat in nature, are altered very little by way of squashing actions. The meaning intended by this phrase is that Thoas, after being squashed by Tyrannosaurus Rex, or perhaps more correctly in the *process* of being squashed by Tryannosaurus Rex, became flattened in a manner not dissimilar to the pancakes native horizontal characteristics.

PHILOCTETES

PERSONS REPRESENTED

THE PERSONS
ODYSSEUS.
NEOPTOLEMUS.
CHORUS _of Mariners_.
PHILOCTETES.
Messenger, _disguised as a Merchantman_.
TYRANNOSAURUS REX, _appearing from the sky in a Zeppelin_.

THE ARGUMENT

SCENE. A desert shore of the Island of Lemnos.   It was fated that Troy should be taken by Neoptolemus, the son of Achilles, assisted by the bow of Heracles in the hands of Philoctetes. Now Philoctetes had been rejected by the army because of a trouble in his foot, which made his presence with them insufferable; and had been cast away by Odysseus on the island of Lemnos. But when the decree of fate was revealed by prophecy, Odysseus undertook to bring Philoctetes back, and took with him Neoptolemus, whose ambition could only be gratified through the return of Philoctetes with the bow. Philoctetes was resolutely set against returning, and at the opening of the drama Neoptolemus is persuaded by Odysseus to take him with guile. But when Philoctetes appears, the youth's ingenuous nature is so wrought upon through pity and remorse, that his sympathy and native truthfulness at length overcome his ambition. When the inward sacrifice is complete, a Tyrannosaurus appears in a bombing raid, sending all the players directly to Hades, so that all ends well.

PHILOCTETES

ODYSSEUS. NEOPTOLEMUS.

ODYSSEUS.[1] This coast of sea-girt Lemnos, where we
stand, Is uninhabited, untrodden of men.
And here, O noble son of noblest sire,
Achilles-born Neoptolemus, I erewhile,--
Ordered by those who had command,--cast forth
Trachinian Philoctetes, Poeas' son,
His foot dark-dripping with a rankling wound;
When with wild cries, that frighted holy rest,
Filling the camp, he troubled every rite,
That none might handle sacrifice, or pour
Wine-offering, but his noise disturbed our peace.
But why these words? No moment this for talk,
Lest he discern my coming, and I lose
The scheme, wherewith I think to catch him soon.
Now most behoves thy service, to explore
This headland for a cave with double mouth,
Whose twofold aperture, on wintry days,
Gives choice of sunshine, and in summer noons
The breeze wafts slumber through the airy cell.
Then, something lower down, upon the left,
Unless 'tis dried, thine eye may note a spring.
Go near now silently, and make me know
If still he persevere, and hold this spot,
Or have roamed elsewhere, that informed of this
I may proceed with what remains to say,
And we may act in concert.

NEOPTOLEMUS.[2] Lord Odysseus, Thy foremost errand
will not task me far. Methinks I see the cave whereof thou
speakest.

OD. Where? let me see it. Above there, or below?

NEO.[3] Yonder, above. And yet I hear no tread.

  [NEOPTOLEMUS _climbs up to the cave]

OD. Look if he be not lodged in slumber there.

NEO. I find no inmate, but an empty room.

OD. What? no provision for a dwelling-place?

NEO. A bed of leaves for some one harbouring here.

OD. Nought else beneath the roof? Is all forlorn?

NEO. A cup of wood, some untaught craftsman's skill,
And, close at hand, these embers of a fire.

OD. That store is his. I read the token clear.

NEO. Oh! and these festering rags give evidence,
Steeped as with dressing some malignant sore.

OD. The man inhabits here: I know it now.
And sure he's not far off. How can he range,
Whose limb drags heavy with an ancient harm?
But he's gone, either to bring forage home,
Or where he hath found some plant of healing power.
Send therefore thine attendant to look forth,
Lest unawares he find me. All our host
Were not so fair a prize for him as I.

NEO. My man is going, and shall watch the path.
What more dost thou require of me?
Speak on.

OD. Son of Achilles, know that thou art come
To serve us nobly, not with strength alone,
But, faithful to thy mission, if so be,
To do things strange, unwonted to thine ear.

NEO. What dost thou bid me?

OD. 'Tis thy duty now
To entrap the mind of Poeas' son with words.
When he shall ask thee, who and whence thou art,
Declare thy name and father.
'Tis not that I charge thee to conceal.
But for thy voyage,
'Tis homeward, leaving the Achaean host,
With perfect hatred hating them, because

They who had drawn thee with strong prayers from home,
Their hope for taking Troy, allowed thee not
Thy just demand to have thy father's arms,
But, e'er thy coming, wrongly gave them o'er
Unto Odysseus: and thereon launch forth
With boundless execration against me.
That will not pain me, but if thou reject
This counsel, thou wilt trouble all our host,
Since, if his bow shall not be ta'en, thy life
Will ne'er be crowned through Troy's discomfiture.
Now let me show, why thine approach to him
Is safe and trustful as mine cannot be
Thou didst sail forth, not to redeem thine oath,
Nor by constraint, nor with the foremost band.
All which reproaches I must bear: and he,
But seeing me, while master of his bow,
Will slay me, and my ruin will be thine.
This point then craves our cunning, to acquire
By subtle means the irresistible bow—
Thy nature was not framed, I know it well,
For speaking falsehood, or contriving harm.
Yet, since the prize of victory is so dear,
Endure it--We'll be just another day
But now, for one brief hour, devote thyself
To serve me without shame, and then for aye
Hereafter be the pearl of righteousness.

NEO. The thing that, being named, revolts mine ear,
Son of Laërtes, I abhor to do
'Tis not my nature, no, nor, as they tell,
My father's, to work aught by craft and guile.
I'll undertake to bring him in by force,
Not by deceit. For, sure, with his one foot,
He cannot be a match for all our crew
Being sent, my lord, to serve thee, I am loth
To seem rebellious. But I rather choose
To offend with honour, than to win by wrong.

OD. Son of a valiant sire, I, too, in youth,
Had once a slow tongue and an active hand.
But since I have proved the world,
I clearly see Words and not deeds give mastery over men.

NEO. What then is thy command? To lie? No more?

OD. To entangle Philoctetes with deceit.

NEO. Why through deceit? May not persuasion fetch him?

OD. Never. And force as certainly will fail.

NEO. What lends him such assurance of defence?

OD. Arrows, the unerring harbingers of Death.

NEO. Then to go near him is a perilous thing.

OD. Unless with subtlety, as I have said.

NEO. And is not lying shameful to thy soul?

OD. Not if by lying I can save my soul.

NEO. How must one look in speaking such a word?

OD. Where gain invites, this shrinking is not good.

NEO. What gain I through his coming back to Troy?

OD. His arms alone have power to take Troy-town.

NEO. Then am not I the spoiler, as ye said?

OD. Thou without them, they without thee, are powerless.

NEO. If it be so, they must be sought and won.

OD. Yea, for in this two prizes will be thine.

NEO. What? When I learn them, I will not refuse.

OD. Wisdom and valour joined in one good name.

NEO. Shame, to the winds! Come, I will do this thing.

OD. Say, dost thou bear my bidding full in mind?

NEO. Doubt not, since once for all I have embraced it.

OD. Thou, then, await him here. I will retire,
For fear my hated presence should be known,

And take back our attendant to the ship.
And then once more, should ye appear to waste
The time unduly, I will send again
This same man hither in disguise, transformed
To the strange semblance of a merchantman;
From dark suggestion of whose crafty tongue,
Thou, O my son, shalt gather timely counsel.
Now to my ship. This charge I leave to thee.
May secret Hermes guide us to our end,
And civic Pallas, named of victory,
The sure protectress of my devious way.

CHORUS[4] (_entering_).
Strange in the stranger land,
What shall I speak?
What hide From a heart suspicious of ill?
Tell me, O master mine!
Wise above all is the man,
Peerless in searching thought,
Who with the Zeus-given wand
Wieldeth a Heaven-sent power.
This unto thee, dear son,
Fraught with ancestral might,
This to thy life hath come.
Wherefore I bid thee declare,
What must I do for thy need?

 NEO. Even now methinks thou longest to espy
Near ocean's marge the place where he doth lie.
Gaze without fear. But when the traveller stern,
Who from this roof is parted, shall return,
Advancing still as I the signal give, To serve each moment's
mission thou shalt strive.

CH.
That, O my son, from of old
Hath been my care, to take note
What by thy beck'ning is told;
Still thy success to promote.
But for our errand to-day
Behoves thee, master, to say
Where is the hearth of his home;
Or where even now doth he roam?
O tell me, lest all unaware
He spring like a wolf from his lair
And I by surprise should be ta'en,

Where doth he move or remain,
Here lodging, or wandering away?

NEO. Thou seëst yon double doorway of his cell, Poor
habitation of the rock.

CH. 2.
But tell Where is the pain-worn wight[5] himself abroad?

NEO. To me 'tis clear, that, in his quest for food,
Here, not far off, he trails yon furrowed path.
For, so 'tis told, this mode the sufferer hath
Of sustenance, oh hardness! bringing low
Wild creatures with wing'd arrows from his bow;
Nor findeth healer for his troublous woe.

CH.
I feel his misery.
With no companion eye,
Far from all human care,
He pines with fell disease;
Each want he hourly sees
Awakening new despair.
How can he bear it still?
O cruel Heavens! O pain
Of that afflicted mortal train
 Whose life sharp sorrows fill!
 Born in a princely hall,
Highest, perchance, of all,
Now lies he comfortless
Alone in deep distress,
'Mongst rough and dappled brutes,
With pangs and hunger worn;
While from far distance shoots,
On airy pinion borne,
The unbridled Echo, still replying
To his most bitter crying.

NEO. At nought of this I marvel--for if I
Judge rightly, there assailed him from on high
That former plague through Chrysa's cruel sting[1]:
And if to-day he suffer anything
With none to soothe, it must be from the will
Of some great God, so caring to fulfil
The word of prophecy, lest he should bend
On Troy the shaft no mortal may forfend,

Before the arrival of Troy's destined hour,
When she must fall, o'er-mastered by their power.

CH. I.
Hush, my son!

NEO. Why so?

CH. I.
A sound Gendered of some mortal woe,
Started from the neighbouring ground.
Here, or there? Ah! now I know.
Hark! 'tis the voice of one in pain,
Travelling hardly, the deep strain
Of human anguish, all too clear,
That smites my heart, that wounds mine ear.

CH. 2.
From far it peals. But thou, my son!

NEO. What?

CH. 2.
Think again. He moveth nigh:
He holds the region: not with tone
Of piping shepherd's rural minstrelsy,
But belloweth his far cry,
Stumbling perchance with mortal pain,
Or else in wild amaze,
As he our ship surveys
Unwonted on the inhospitable main.

[Enter_ PHILOCTETES.]

PHILOCTETES. Ho!
What men are ye that to this desert shore,
Harbourless, uninhabited, are come
On shipboard? Of what country or what race
Shall I pronounce ye? For your outward garb
Is Grecian, ever dearest to this heart
That hungers now to hear your voices' tune.
Ah! do not fear me, do not shrink away
From my wild looks: but, pitying one so poor,
Forlorn and desolate in nameless woe,
Speak, if with friendly purpose ye are come.
Oh answer! 'Tis not meet that I should lose

This kindness from your lips, or ye from mine.

NEO. Then know this first, O stranger, as thou wouldest,
That we are Greeks.

PHI. O dear, dear name! Ah me!
In all these years, once, only once, I hear it!
My son, what fairest gale hath wafted thee?
What need hath brought thee to the shore?
What mission?
Declare all this, that I may know thee well.

NEO. The sea-girt Scyros is my native home.
Thitherward I make voyage:--Achilles' son,
Named Neoptolemus.--I have told thee all.

PHI. Dear is that shore to me, dear is thy father
O ancient Lycomedes' foster-child,
Whence cam'st thou hither?
How didst thou set forth?

NEO. From Troy we made our course in sailing hither.

PHI. How? Sure thou wast not with us, when at first
We launched our vessels on the Troyward way?

NEO. Hadst thou a share in that adventurous toil?

PHI. And know'st thou not whom thou behold'st in me,
Young boy?

NEO. How should I know him whom I ne'er Set eye on?

PHI. Hast not even heard my name,
Nor echoing rumour of my ruinous woe?

NEO. Nay, I know nought of all thy questioning.

PHI. How full of griefs am I, how Heaven-abhorred,
When of my piteous state no faintest sound
Hath reached my home, or any Grecian land!
But they, who pitilessly cast me forth,
Keep silence and are glad, while this my plague
Blooms ever, and is strengthened more and more.
Boy, great Achilles' offspring, in this form
Thou seest the man, of whom, methinks, erewhile

Thou hast been told, to whom the Hercúlean bow
Descended, Philoctetes, Poeas' son;
Whom the two generals and the Ithacan king
Cast out thus shamefully forlorn, afflicted
With the fierce malady and desperate wound
Made by the cruel basilisk's murderous tooth.
With this for company they left me, child!
Exposed upon this shore, deserted, lone.
From seaward Chrysa came they with their fleet
And touched at Lemnos. I had fallen to rest
From the long tossing, in a shadowy cave
On yonder cliff by the shore. Gladly they saw,
And left me, having set forth for my need,
Poor man, some scanty rags, and a thin store
Of provender. Such food be theirs, I pray! Imagine,
O my son, when they were gone,
What wakening, what arising, then was mine;
What weeping, what lamenting of my woe!
When I beheld the ships, wherewith I sailed,
Gone, one and all! and no man in the place,
None to bestead me, none to comfort me
In my sore sickness. And where'er I looked,
Nought but distress was present with me still.
No lack of that, for one thing!--Ah! my son,
Time passed, and there I found myself alone
Within my narrow lodging, forced to serve
Each pressing need. For body's sustenance
This bow supplied me with sufficient store,
Wounding the feathered doves, and when the shaft,
From the tight string, had struck, myself, ay me!
Dragging this foot, would crawl to my swift prey.
Then water must be fetched, and in sharp frost
Wood must be found and broken,--all by me.
Nor would fire come unbidden, but with flint
From flints striking dim sparks, I hammered forth
The struggling flame that keeps the life in me.
For houseroom with the single help of fire
Gives all I need, save healing for my sore.
Now learn, my son, the nature of this isle.
No mariner puts in here willingly.
For it hath neither moorage, nor sea-port,
For traffic or kind shelter or good cheer.
Not hitherward do prudent men make voyage.
Perchance one may have touched against his will.
Many strange things may happen in long time.
These, when they come, in words have pitied me,

And given me food, or raiment, in compassion.
But none is willing, when I speak thereof,
To take me safely home. Wherefore I pine
Now this tenth year, in famine and distress,
Feeding the hunger of my ravenous plague.
Such deeds, my son, the Atridae, and the might
Of sage Odysseus, have performed on me.
Wherefore may all the Olympian gods, one day,
Plague them with stern requital for my wrong!

CH.
Methinks my feeling for thee, Poeas' child,
Is like that of thy former visitants.

NEO. I, too, a witness to confirm his words,
Know them for verities, since I have found
The Atridae and Odysseus evil men.

PHI. Art thou, too, wroth with the all-pestilent sons
Of Atreus? Have they given thee cause to grieve?

NEO. Would that my hand might ease the wrath I feel!
Then Sparta and Mycenae should be ware
That Scyros too breeds valiant sons for war.

PHI. Brave youth! I love thee. Tell me the great cause
Why thou inveighest against them with such heat?

NEO. O son of Poeas, hardly shall I tell
What outrage I endured when I had come;
Yet I will speak it. When the fate of death
O'ertook Achilles--

PHI. Out, alas! no more!
Hold, till thou first hast made me clearly know,
Is Peleus' offspring dead?

NEO. Alas! he is,
Slain by no mortal, felled by Phoebus' shaft:
So men reported--

PHI. Well, right princely was he!
And princely is he who slew him. Shall I mourn
Him first, or wait till I have heard thy tale?

NEO. Methinks thou hast thyself enough to mourn,
Without the burden of another's woe.

PHI. Well spoken. Then renew thine own complaint,
And tell once more wherein they insulted thee.

NEO. There came to fetch me, in a gallant ship,
Odysseus and the fosterer of my sire[2],
Saying, whether soothly, or in idle show,
That, since my father perished, it was known
None else but I should take Troy's citadel.
Such words from them, my friend, thou may'st believe,
Held me not long from making voyage with speed,
Chiefly through longing for my father's corse,
To see him yet unburied,--for I ne'er
Had seen him[3]. Then, besides, 'twas a fair cause,
If, by my going, I should vanquish Troy.
One day I had sailed, and on the second came
To sad Sigeum with wind-favoured speed,
When straightway all the host, surrounding me
As I set foot on shore, saluted me,
And swore the dead Achilles was in life,
Their eyes being witness, when they looked on me.
He lay there in his shroud: but I, unhappy,
Soon ending lamentation for the dead,
Went near to those Atridae, as to friends,
To obtain my father's armour and all else
That had been his. And then,--alas the while,
That men should be so hard!--they spake this word:
'Seed of Achilles, thou may'st freely take
All else thy father owned, but for those arms,
Another wields them now, Laërtes' son.'
Tears rushed into mine eyes, and in hot wrath
I straightway rose, and bitterly outspake:
'O miscreant! What? And have ye dared to give
Mine arms to some man else, unknown to me?'
Then said Odysseus, for he chanced to be near,
'Yea, child, and justly have they given me these.
I saved them and their master in the field.'
Then in fierce anger all at once I launched
All terms of execration at his head,
Bating no word, being maddened by the thought
That I should lose this heirloom,--and to him!
He, at this pass, though not of wrathful mood,
Stung by such utterance, made rejoinder thus:
'Thou wast not with us here, but wrongfully

Didst bide afar. And, since thou mak'st so bold,
I tell thee, never shalt thou, as thou sayest,
Sail with these arms to Scyros.'--Thus reviled,
With such an evil echo in mine ear,
I voyage homeward, robbed of mine own right
By that vile offset of an evil tree[4].
Yet less I blame him than the men in power.
For every multitude, be it army or state,
Takes tone from those who rule it, and all taint
Of disobedience from bad counsel springs.
I have spoken. May the Atridae's enemy
Be dear to Heaven, as he is loved by me!

CH.
Mother of mightiest Zeus,
Feeder of all that live,
Who from thy mountainous breast
Rivers of gold dost give!
To thee, O Earth, I cried that shameful day,
When insolence from Atreus' sons went forth
Full on our lord: when they bestowed away
His father's arms to crown Odysseus' worth;
Thou, whom bull-slaughtering lions yoked bear,
O mighty mother, hear!

PHI. Your coming is commended by a grief
That makes you kindly welcome. For I feel
A chord that vibrates to your voice, and tells,
Thus have Odysseus and the Atridae wrought.
Full well I know, Odysseus' poisoned tongue
Shrinks from no mischief nor no guileful word
That leads to bad achievement in the end.
This moves not my main marvel, but if one
Saw this and bore it,--Aias of the shield.

NEO. Ah, friend, he was no more. Had he but lived,
This robbery had ne'er been wrought on me.

PHI. What? Is he too departed?

NEO. He is dead. The light no more beholds him.

PHI. Oh! alas! But Tydeus' offspring, and the rascal birth
Laërtes bought of Sisyphus, they live: I know it.
For their death were to be wished.

NEO. Yea, be assured, they live and flourish high
Exalted in the host of Argive men.

PHI. And Nestor, my old friend, good aged man,
Is he yet living?
Oft he would prevent
Their evils, by the wisdom of his thought.

NEO. He too is now in trouble, having lost Antilochus, the
comfort of his age.

PHI. There, there! In one brief word thou hast revealed
The mournful case of twain, whom I would last
Have chosen to hear of as undone. Ah me!
Where must one look? when these are dead, and he,
Odysseus, lives,--and in a time like this,
That craves their presence, and his death for theirs.

NEO. He wrestles cleverly; but, O my friend,
Even ablest wits are ofttimes snared at last.

PHI. Tell me, I pray, what was become of him,
Patroclus, whom thy father loved so well?

NEO. He, too, was gone. I'll teach thee in a word
One truth for all. War doth not willingly
Snatch off the wicked, but still takes the good.

PHI. True! and to prove thy saying, I will inquire
The fate of a poor dastard, of mean worth,
But ever shrewd and nimble with his tongue.

NEO. Whom but Odysseus canst thou mean by this?

PHI. I meant not him. But there was one Thersites,
Who ne'er made conscience to stint speech, where all
Cried 'Silence!' Is he living, dost thou know?

NEO. I saw him not, but knew he was alive.

PHI. He must be: for no evil yet was crushed.
The Heavens will ever shield it. 'Tis their sport
To turn back all things rancorous and malign
From going down to the grave, and send instead
The good and true. Oh, how shall we commend
Such dealings, how defend them?

When I praise Things god-like, I find evil in the Gods.

NEO. I, O thou child of a Trachinian sire,
Henceforth will take good care, from far away
To look on Troy and Atreus' children twain.
Yea, where the trickster lords it o'er the just,
And goodness languishes and rascals rule, --
Such courses I will nevermore endure.
But rock-bound Scyros henceforth shall suffice
To yield me full contentment in my home.
Now, to my vessel! And thou, Poeas' child,
Farewell, right heartily farewell! May Heaven
Grant thy desire, and rid thee of thy plague!
Let us be going, that when God shall give
Fair voyage, that moment we may launch away.

PHI. My son, are ye now setting forth?

NEO. Our time
Bids us go near and look to sail erelong.

PHI. Now, by thy father, by thy mother,--nay,
By all thy love e'er cherished in thy home,
Suppliant I beg thee, leave me not thus lone,
Forlorn in all my misery which thou seest,
In all thou hast heard of here surrounding me!
Stow me with other freightage.
Full of care, I know, and burdensome the charge may prove.
Yet venture! Surely to the noble mind
All shame is hateful and all kindness blest.
And shame would be thy meed, didst thou fail here
But, doing this, thou shalt have glorious fame,
When I return alive to Oeta's vale.
Come, 'tis the labour not of one whole day.
So thou durst take me, fling me where thou wilt
O' the ship, in hold, prow, stern, or wheresoe'er
I least may trouble those on board with me.
Ah! by great Zeus, the suppliant's friend, comply,
My son, be softened! See, where I am fall'n
Thus on my knees before thee, though so weak,
Crippled and powerless. Ah! forsake me not
Thus far from human footstep. Take me, take me!
If only to thy home, or to the town
Of old Chalcodon[5] in Euboea.—
From thence I have not far to Oeta, and the ridge
Of Trachis, and Spercheius' lordly flood.

So thou shalt bless my father with my sight.
And yet long since I fear he may be gone.
For oft I sent him suppliant prayers by men
Who touched this isle, entreating him to fetch
And bear me safely home with his own crew.
But either he is dead, or else, methinks, It well may be, my messengers made light
Of my concerns, and hastened onward home.
But now in thee I find both messenger
And convoy, thou wilt pity me and save. For, well thou knowest, danger never sleeps,
And fear of dark reverse is always nigh.
Mortals, when free, should look where mischief lurks,
And in their happiest hour consider well
Their life, lest ruin unsuspected come.

CH.
Pity him, O my king! Many a crushing woe
He telleth, such as I pray
None of my friends may know.
And if, dear master, thou mislikest sore
Yon cruel-hearted lordly pair, I would,
Turning their plan of evil to his good,
On swift ship bear him to his native shore,
Meeting his heart's desire; and free thy path
From fear of heavenly wrath.

NEO. Thou mak'st small scruple here; but be advised:
Lest, when this plague on board shall weary thee,
Thy voice should alter from this liberal tone.

CH.
No, truly! Fear not thou shalt ever have
Just cause to utter such reproach on me.

NEO. Then sure 'twere shame, should I more backward prove
Than thou, to labour for the stranger's need.
Come, if thou wilt, let us make voyage, and he,
Let him set forth with speed. Our ship shall take him.
He shall not be refused. Only may Heaven
Lead safely hence and to our destined port!

PHI. O morning full of brightness! Kindest friend,
Sweet mariners, how can I make you feel,
In act, how dearly from my heart I love you!

Ye have won my soul. Let us be gone, my son,--
First having said farewell to this poor cave,
My homeless dwelling-place, that thou may'st know,
How barely I have lived, how firm my heart!
Methinks another could not have endured
The very sight of what I bore.
But I Through strong necessity have conquered pain.

CH.
Stay: let us understand.
There come two men
A stranger, with a shipmate of thy crew.
When ye have heard them, ye may then go in.

[Enter_ Messenger, _disguised as a merchantman]

MERCHANTMAN. Son of Achilles, my companion here,
Who with two more remained to guard thy ship,
Agreed to help me find thee where thou wert,
Since unexpectedly, through fortune's will,
I meet thee, mooring by the self-same shore.
For like a merchantman, with no great sail,
Making my course from Ilion to my home,
Grape-clustered Peparethos, when I heard
The mariners declare that one and all
Were of thy crew, I would not launch again,
Without a word, till we had told our news.--
Methinks thou knowest nought of thine own case,
What new devices of the Argive chiefs
Surround thee; nor devices only now,
But active deeds, no longer unperformed.

NEO. Well, stranger, for the kindness thou hast shown,--
Else were I base,--my heart must thank thee still.
But tell me what thou meanest, that I may learn
What new-laid plot thou bring'st me from the camp.

MER. Old Phoenix, Acamas and Demophon
Are gone in thy pursuit with ships and men.

NEO. To bring me back with reasons or perforce?

MER. I know not. What I heard, I am here to tell.

NEO. How? And is this in act? Are they set forth
To please the Atridae, Phoenix and the rest?

MER. The thing is not to do, but doing now.

NEO. What kept Odysseus back, if this be so,
From going himself? Had he some cause for fear?

MER. He and the son of Tydeus, when our ship
Hoist sail, were gone to fetch another man.

NEO. For whom could he himself be sailing forth?

MER. For some one,--but first tell me, whispering low
Whate'er thou speakest,--who is this I see?

NEO. (_speaking aloud_). This, sir, is Philoctetes the
renowned.

 MER. (_aside to_ NEOPTOLEMUS).
Without more question, snatch thyself away
And sail forth from this land.

PHI. What saith he, boy?
Through what dark traffic is the mariner
Betraying me with whispering in thine ear?

NEO. I have not caught it, but whate'er he speaks
He must speak openly to us and thee.

MER. Seed of Achilles, let me not offend
The army by my words! Full many a boon,
Being poor, I reap from them for service done.

NEO. The Atridae are my foes; the man you see
Is my fast friend, because he hates them sore.
Then, if you come in kindness, you must hide
Nothing from him or me of all thou hast heard.

 MER. Look what thou doest, my son!

 NEO. I mark it well.

MER. Thou shalt be answerable.

NEO. Content: but speak.

MER. Then hear me. These two men whom I have named,
Diomedes and Odysseus, are set forth
Engaged on oath to bring this man by force
If reasons fail. The Achaeans every one
Have heard this plainly from Odysseus' mouth.
He was the louder and more confident.

NEO. Say, for what cause, after so long a time,
Can Atreus' sons have turned their thoughts on him,
Whom long they had cast forth? What passing touch
Of conscience moved them, or what stroke from
Heaven, Whose wrath requites all wicked deeds of men?

MER. Methinks thou hast not heard what I will now
Unfold to thee. There was a princely seer,
A son of Priam, Helenus by name,
Whom he for whom no word is bad enough,
Crafty Odysseus, sallying forth alone
One night, had taken, and in bonds displayed
'Fore all the Achaeans, a right noble prey.
He, 'mid his other prophecies, foretold
No Grecian force should sack Troy's citadel,
Till with fair reasons they had brought this man
From Lemnos isle, his lonely dwelling-place.
When thus the prophet spake, Laërtes' son
Straight undertook to fetch this man, and show him
To all the camp:--he hoped, with fair consent:
But else, perforce.--And, if he failed in this,
Whoever would might smite him on the head.
My tale is told, dear youth. I counsel speed
To thee and to the friend for whom thou carest.

 PHI. Ah me, unhappy! has that rascal knave
Sworn to fetch me with reasons to their camp?
As likely might his reasons bring me back,
Like his begetter, from the house of death.

MER. You talk of what I know not. I will go Shipward.
May God be with you for all good.   [_Exit_]

PHI. Is not this terrible, Laërtes' son
Should ever think to bring me with soft words
And show me from his deck to all their host?
No! Sooner will I listen to the tongue
Of the curs'd basilisk that thus hath maim'd me.
Ay, but he'll venture anything in word

Or deed. And now I know he will be here.
Come, O my son, let us be gone, while seas
And winds divide us from Odysseus' ship.
Let us depart. Sure timely haste brings rest
And quiet slumber when the toil is done.

NEO. Shall we not sail when this south-western wind
Hath fallen, that now is adverse to our course?

PHI. All winds are fair to him who flies from woe.

NEO. Nay, but this head-wind hinders them no less.

PHI. No head-wind hinders pirates on their way,
When violence and rapine lead them on.

NEO. Well, then, let us be going, if you will;
When you have taken from within the cave
What most you need and value.

PHI. Though my all Be little, there is that I may not lose.

NEO. What can there be that we have not on board?

PHI. A leaf I have found, wherewith I still the rage
Of my sore plague, and lull it quite to rest.

NEO. Well, bring it forth.--
What? Is there something more?

PHI. If any of these arrows here are fallen,
I would not leave them for a casual prey.

NEO. How? Do I see thee with the marvellous bow?

PHI. Here in my hand. The world hath only one.

NEO. And may one touch and handle it, and gaze
 With reverence, as on a thing from Heaven?

PHI. Thou mayest, my son. This and whate'er of mine
May stead thee, 'tis thy privilege to enjoy.

NEO. In very truth I long for it, but so,
That longing waits on leave.
Am I permitted?

PHI. Thou art, my son,--and well thou speakest,--thou art.
Thou, that hast given me light and life, the joy
Of seeing Mount Oeta and my father's home,
With all I love there, and his aged head,--
Thou that hast raised me far above my foes
Who triumphed! Thou may'st take it in thine hand,
And,--when thou hast given it back to me,--may'st vaunt
Alone of mortals for thine excellence To have held this in
thy touch. I, too, at first,
Received it as a boon for kindness done.

NEO. Well, go within.

PHI. Nay, I must take thee too.
My sickness craves thee for its comforter.

[PHILOCTETES _and_ NEOPTOLEMUS _go into
the cave]

CHORUS.
 In fable I have heard,
Though sight hath ne'er confirmed the word,
How he who attempted once the couch supreme,
To a whirling wheel by Zeus the all-ruler bound,
Tied head and heel, careering ever round,
Atones his impious unsubstantial dream.
Of no man else, through eye or ear,
Have I discerned a fate more full of fear
Than yonder sufferer's of the cureless wound:
Who did no violence, defrauded none:--
A just man, had he dwelt among the just
Unworthily behold him thrust
Alone to hear the billows roar
That break around a rugged shore!
How could he live, whose life was thus consumed with
moan?

Where neighbour there was none:
No arm to stay him wandering lone,
Unevenly, with stumbling steps and sore;
No friend in need, no kind inhabitant,
To minister to his importunate want,
No heart whereto his pangs he might deplore.
None who, whene'er the gory flow
Was rushing hot, might healing herbs bestow,

Or cull from teeming Earth some genial plant
To allay the anguish of malignant pain
And soothe the sharpness of his poignant woe.
Like infant whom the nurse lets go,
With tottering movement here and there,
He crawled for comfort, whensoe'er
His soul-devouring plague relaxed its cruel strain.
 Not fed with foison of all-teeming Earth

Whence we sustain us, ever-toiling men,
But only now and then
With wingèd things, by his wing'd shafts brought low,
He stayed his hunger from his bow.
Poor soul, that never through ten years of dearth
Had pleasure from the fruitage of the vine,
But seeking to some standing pool,
Nor clear nor cool,
Foul water heaved to head for lack of heartening wine.
But now, consorted with the hero's child,

He winneth greatness and a joyful change;
Over the water wild
Borne by a friendly bark beneath the range
Of Oeta, where Spercheius fills
Wide channels winding among lovely hills
Haunted of Melian nymphs, till he espies
The roof-tree of his father's hall,
And high o'er all Shines the bronze shield of him, whose
home is in the skies[6].

[NEOPTOLEMUS _comes out of the cave, followed
by_ PHILOCTETES _in pain]

NEO. Prithee, come on! Why dost thou stand aghast,
Voiceless, and thus astonied in thine air?

PHI. Oh! oh!

NEO. What?

PHI. Nothing. Come my son, fear nought.

 NEO. Is pain upon thee? Hath thy trouble come?

PHI. No pain, no pain! 'Tis past; I am easy now. Ye heavenly
powers!

NEO. Why dost thou groan aloud, And cry to Heaven?

PHI. To come and save. Kind Heaven! Oh, oh!

NEO. What is 't? Why silent? Wilt not speak? I see thy
misery.

PHI. Oh! I am lost, my son! I cannot hide it from you.
Oh! it shoots, It pierces. Oh unhappy!
Oh! my woe! I am lost, my son, I am devoured.
Oh me! Oh! Oh! Oh! Oh! Pain! pain! Oh pain! oh pain!
Child, if a sword be to thine hand, smite hard,
Shear off my foot! heed not my life! Quick, come!

NEO. What hath so suddenly arisen, that thus
Thou mak'st ado and groanest o'er thyself?

PHI. Thou knowest.

NEO. What know I?

PHI. O! thou knowest, my son!

NEO. I know not.

PHI. How? Not know? Ah me! Pain, pain!

NEO. Thy plague is a sore burden, heavy and sore.

PHI. Sore? 'Tis unutterable. Have pity on me!

NEO. What shall I do?

PHI. Do not in fear forsake me.
This wandering evil comes in force again,
Hungry as ere it fed.

NEO. O hapless one!
Thrice hapless in thy manifold distress!
What wilt thou?
Shall I raise thee on mine arm?

PHI. Nay, but receiving from my hand the bow,
As late thou didst desire me, keep it safe
And guard it, till the fury of my pain

CXC

Pass over me and cease. For when 'tis spent,
Slumber will seize me, else it ne'er would end.
I must sleep undisturbed. But if meanwhile
They come,--by Heaven I charge thee, in no wise,
Willingly nor perforce, let them have this!
Else thou wilt be the slayer of us both;
Of me thy suppliant, and of thyself.

NEO. Fear not my care. No hand shall hold these arms
But thine and mine. Give, and Heaven bless the deed!

PHI. I give them; there, my son! But look to Heaven
And pray no envy smite thee, nor such bane
In having them, as fell on me and him
Who bore them formerly.

NEO. O grant it, Gods!
And grant us fair and happy voyage, where'er
Our course is shaped and righteous Heaven shall guide.

PHI. Ah! but I fear, my son, thy prayer is vain:
For welling yet again from depths within,
This gory ooze is dripping. It will come! I know it will.
O, foot, torn helpless thing,
What wilt thou do to me?
Ah! ah! It comes, It is at hand.
'Tis here! Woe's me, undone!
I have shown you all. Stay near me.
Go not far: Ah! ah!
O island king, I would this agony
Might cleave thy bosom through and through!
Woe, woe! Woe! Ah! ye two commanders of the host,
Agamemnon, Menelaüs, O that ye,
Another ten years' durance in my room
Might nurse this malady! O Death, Death, Death!
I call thee daily--wilt thou never come? Will it not be?--
My son, thou noble boy,
If thou art noble, take and burn me there
Aloft in yon all-worshipped Lemnian fire!
Yea, when the bow thou keep'st was my reward,
I did like service for the child of Heaven.
How now, my son? What say'st?
Art silent? Where--where art thou, boy?

NEO. My heart is full, and groaning o'er thy woes.

PHI. Nay, yet have comfort. This affliction oft
Goes no less swiftly than it came. I pray thee,
Stand fast and leave me not alone!

NEO. Fear nought. We will not stir.

PHI. Wilt thou remain?

NEO. Be sure of it.

PHI. I'll not degrade thee with an oath, my son.

NEO. Rest satisfied. I may not go without thee.

PHI. Thy hand, to pledge me that!

NEO. There, I will stay.

PHI. Now, now, aloft!

NEO. Where mean'st thou?

PHI. Yonder aloft!

NEO. Whither? Thou rav'st. Why starest thou at the sky?

PHI. Now, let me go.

NEO. Where?

PHI. Let me go, I say!

NEO. I will not.

PHI. You will kill me. Let me go!

NEO. Well, thou know'st best I hold thee not.

PHI. O Earth, I die. receive me to thy breast!
This pain Subdues me utterly, I cannot stand.

NEO. Methinks he will be fast in slumber soon
That head sinks backward, and a clammy sweat
Bathes all his limbs, while from his foot hath burst
A vein, dark bleeding. Let us leave him, friends,
In quietness, till he hath fallen to sleep.

CXCII

CHORUS
Lord of the happiest life,
Sleep, thou that know'st not strife,
That know'st not grief,
Still wafting sure relief,
Come, saviour now!
Thy healing balm is spread
Over this pain worn head,
Quench not the beam that gives calm to his brow.
Look, O my lord, to thy path,
Either to go or to stay
How is my thought to proceed?
What is our cause for delay?
Look! Opportunity's power,
Fitting the task to the hour,
Giveth the race to the swift.

NEO. He hears not. But I see that to have ta'en
His bow without him were a bootless gain
He must sail with us. So the god hath said
Heaven hath decreed this garland for his head:
And to have failed with falsehood were a meed
Of shameful soilure for a shameless deed.

CH.
God shall determine the end--
But for thine answer, friend,
Waft soft words low!
All sick men's sleep, we know,
Hath open eye;
Their quickly ruffling mind
Quivers in lightest wind,
Sleepless in slumber new danger to spy.
Think, O my lord, of thy path,
Secretly look forth afar,
What wilt thou do for thy need?
How with the wise wilt thou care?
If toward the nameless thy heart
Chooseth this merciful part,
Huge are the dangers that drift.
The wind is fair, my son, the wind is fair,
The man is dark and helpless, stretched in night.
(O kind, warm sleep that calmest human care!)
Powerless of hand and foot and ear and sight,
Blind, as one lying in the house of death.

(Think well if here thou utterest timely breath.)
This, O my son, is all my thought can find,
Best are the toils that without frightening bind.

NEO. Hush! One word more were madness.
He revives. His eye hath motion.
He uplifts his head.

PHI. Fair daylight following sleep, and ye, dear friends,
Faithful beyond all hope in tending me!
I never could have dreamed that thou, dear youth,
Couldst thus have borne my sufferings and stood near
So full of pity to relieve my pain.
Not so the worthy generals of the host;--
This princely patience was not theirs to show.
Only thy noble nature, nobly sprung,
Made light of all the trouble, though oppressed
With fetid odours and unceasing cries.
And now, since this my plague would seem to yield
Some pause and brief forgetfulness of pain,
With thine own hand, my son, upraise me here,
And set me on my feet, that, when my strength
After exhaustion shall return again,
We may move shoreward and launch forth with speed.

NEO. I feel unhoped-for gladness when I see
Thy painless gaze, and hear thy living breath,
For thine appearance and surroundings both
Were deathlike. But arise! Or, if thou wilt,
These men shall raise thee. For they will not shrink
From toil which thou and I at once enjoin.

PHI. Right, right, my son! But lift me thine own self,
As I am sure thou meanest. Let these be,
Lest they be burdened with the noisome smell
Before the time. Enough for them to bear
The trouble on board.

NEO. I will; stand up, endure!

PHI. Fear not. Old habit will enable me.

NEO. O me! What shall I do? Now 'tis my turn to exclaim!

PHI. What canst thou mean? What change is here, my son?

NEO. I know not how to shift the troublous word. 'Tis
hopeless.

PHI. What is hopeless? Speak not so, Dear child!

NEO. But so my wretched lot hath fallen.

PHI. Ah! Can it be, the offence of my disease
Hath moved thee not to take me now on board?

NEO. All is offence to one who hath forced himself
From the true bent to an unbecoming deed.

PHI. Nought misbecoming to thyself or sire
Doest thou or speak'st, befriending a good man.

NEO. My baseness will appear. That wrings my soul.

PHI. Not in thy deeds. But for thy words, I fear me!

NEO. O Heaven! Must double vileness then be mine
Both shameful silence and most shameful speech?

PHI. Or my discernment is at fault, or thou
Mean'st to betray me and make voyage without me.

NEO. Nay, not without thee, there is my distress!
Lest I convey thee to thy bitter grief.

PHI. How? How, dear youth? I do not understand.

NEO. Here I unveil it. Thou art to sail to Troy,
To join the chieftains and the Achaean host.

PHI. What do I hear? Ah!

NEO. Grieve not till you learn.

PHI. Learn what? What wilt thou make of me?
What mean'st thou?

NEO. First to release thee from this plague, and then
With thee to go and take the realm of Troy.

PHI. And is this thine intent?

NEO. 'Tis so ordained Unchangeably.
Be not dismayed! 'Tis so.

PHI. Me miserable! I am betrayed, undone!
What guile is here? My bow! give back my bow!

NEO. I may not. Interest, and duty too,
Force me to obey commandment.

PHI. O thou fire, Thou terror of the world!
Dark instrument
Of ever-hateful guile!--
What hast thou done?
How thou hast cheated me!
Art not ashamed
To look on him that sued to thee for shelter?
O heart of stone, thou hast stolen my life away
With yonder bow!--Ah, yet I beg of thee,
Give it me back, my son, I entreat thee, give!
By all thy father worshipped, rob me not
Of life!--Ah me! Now he will speak no more,
But turns away, obdúrate to retain it.
O ye, my comrades in this wilderness,
Rude creatures of the rocks, O promontories,
Creeks, precipices of the hills, to you
And your familiar presence I complain
Of this foul trespass of Achilles' son.
Sworn to convey me home, to
Troy he bears me.
And under pledge of his right hand hath ta'en
And holds from me perforce my wondrous bow,
The sacred gift of Zeus-born Heracles,
Thinking to wave it midst the Achaean host
Triumphantly for his. In conquering me
He vaunts as of some valorous feat, and knows not
He is spoiling a mere corse, an empty dream,
The shadow of a vapour. In my strength
He ne'er had vanquished me. Even as I am,
He could not, but by guile. Now, all forlorn,
I am abused, deceived. What must I do?
Nay, give it me. Nay, yet be thy true self!
Thou art silent. I am lost. O misery!
Rude face of rock, back I return to thee
And thy twin gateway, robbed of arms and food,
To wither in thy cave companionless:--
No more with these mine arrows to destroy

Or flying bird or mountain-roving beast.
But, all unhappy! I myself must be
The feast of those on whom I fed, the chase
Of that I hunted, and shall dearly pay
In bloody quittance for their death, through one
Who seemed all ignorant of sinful guile.
Perish,--not till I am certain if thy heart
Will change once more,--if not, my curse on thee!

CH.
What shall we do, my lord? We wait thy word
Or to sail now, or yield to his desire.

NEO. My heart is pressed with a strange pity for him,
Not now beginning, but long since begun.

PHI. Ay, pity me, my son! by all above,
Make not thy name a scorn by wronging me!

NEO. O! I am troubled sore. What must I do?
Would I had never left mine island home!

PHI. Thou art not base, but seemest to have learnt
Some baseness from base men. Now, as 'tis meet,
Be better guided--leave me mine arms, and go.

NEO. (_to Chorus_). What shall we do?

[Enter_ ODYSSEUS]

ODYSSEUS. What art thou doing, knave?
Give me that bow, and haste thee back again.

PHI. Alas! What do I hear? Odysseus' voice?

OD. Be sure of that, Odysseus, whom thou seest.

PHI. Oh, I am bought and sold, undone!
'Twas he That kidnapped me, and robbed me of my bow.

OD. Yea. I deny it not. Be sure, 'twas I.

PHI. Give back, my son, the bow; release it!

OD. That, Though he desire it, he shall never do.
Thou too shalt march along, or these shall force thee.

PHI. They force me! O thou boldest of bad men!
They force me?

 OD. If thou com'st not willingly.

PHI. O Lemnian earth and thou almighty flame,
Hephaestos' workmanship, shall this be borne,
That he by force must drag me from your care?

OD. 'Tis Zeus, I tell thee, monarch of this isle,
Who thus hath willed. I am his minister.

PHI. Wretch, what vile words thy wit hath power to say!
The gods are liars when invoked by thee.

OD. Nay, 'tis their truth compels thee to this voyage.

PHI. I will not have it so.

OD. I will. Thou shalt.

PHI. Woe for my wretchedness! My father, then,
Begat no freeman, but a slave in me.

OD. Nay, but the peer of noblest men, with whom
Thou art to take and ravage Troy with might.

PHI. Never,--though I must suffer direst woe,--
While this steep Lemnian ground is mine to tread!

OD. What now is thine intent?

 PHI. Down from the crag
This head shall plunge and stain the crag beneath.

OD. (_to the Attendants_.) Ay, seize and bind him. Baffle
him in this.

PHI. Poor hands, for lack of your beloved string,
Caught by this craven! O corrupted soul!
How thou hast undermined me, having taken
To screen thy quest this youth to me unknown,
Far worthier of my friendship than of thine,
Who knew no better than to obey command.
Even now 'tis manifest he burns within

With pain for his own error and my wrong.
But, though unwilling and mapt for ill,
Thy crafty, mean, and cranny spying soul
Too well hath lessoned him in sinful lore.
Now thou hast bound me, O thou wretch, and thinkest
To take me from this coast, where thou didst cast me
Outlawed and desolate, a corpse 'mongst men.
Oh! I curse thee now, as ofttimes in the past:
But since Heaven yields me nought but bitterness,
Thou livest and art blithe, while 'tis my pain
To live on in my misery, laughed to scorn
By thee and Atreus' sons, those generals twain
Whom thou art serving in this chase. But thou
With strong compulsion and deceit was driven
Troyward, whilst I, poor victim, of free will
Took my seven ships and sailed there, yet was thrown
Far from all honour,--as thou sayest, by them,
But, as they turn the tale, by thee.--And now
Why fetch me hence and take me? To what end?
I am nothing, dead to you this many a year.
How, O thou Heaven-abhorred! am I not now
Lame and of evil smell? how shall ye vaunt
Before the gods drink-offering or the fat
Of victims, if I sail among your crew?
For this, as ye professed, was the chief cause
Why ye disowned me. Perish!--So ye shall,
For the wrong done me, if the Heavens be just.
And that they are, I know. Else had ye ne'er
Sailed on this errand for an outcast wretch,
Had they not pricked your heart with thoughts of me.
Oh, if ye pity me, chastising powers, And thou, the
Genius of my land, revenge, Revenge this crime on all their
heads at once! My life is pitiable; but if I saw
Their ruin, I would think me well and strong.

CH. How full of bitterness is his resolve,
Wrathfully spoken with unbending will!

OD. I might speak long in answer, did the time
Give scope, but now one thing is mine to say.
I am known to vary with the varying need;
And when 'tis tried, who can be just and good,
My peer will not be found for piety.
But though on all occasions covetous
Of victory, this once I yield to thee,
And willingly. Unhand him there. Let go!

CXCIX

Leave him to stay. What further use of thee,
When we have ta'en these arms?
Have we not Teucer, Skilled in this mystery?
Yea, I may boast
Myself thine equal both in strength and aim
To wield them. Fare thee well, then!
Thou art free To roam thy barren isle.
We need thee not. Let us be going!
And perchance thy gift
May bring thy destined glory to my brow.

PHI. What shall I do? Alas, shalt thou be seen
Graced with mine arms amongst Achaean men?

OD. No more! I am going.

PHI. O Achilles' child! Wilt thou, too, vanish?
Must I lose thy voice?

OD. Come on, and look not, noble though thou be,
Lest thou undo our fortune.

PHI. Mariners, Must ye, too, leave me thus disconsolate?
Will ye not pity me?

CH.
Our captain's here.
Whate'er he saith to thee, that we too speak.

NEO. My chief will call me weakling, soft of heart;
But go not yet, since our friend bids you stay.
Till we have prayed, and all be ready on board.
Meanwhile, perchance, he may conceive some thought
That favours our design. We two will start;
And ye, be swift to speed forth at our call.

[_Exit_ MONODY].

PHI. O cavern of the hollow rock,
Frosty and stifling in the seasons' change!
How I seem fated never more to range
From thy sad covert, that hath felt the shock
Of pain on pain, steeped with my wretchedness.
Now thou wilt be my comforter in death!
Grief haunted harbour, choked with my distress!
Tell me, what hope is mine of daily food,

Who will be careful for my good? I fail.
Ye cowering creatures of the sky,
Oh, as ye fly,
Snatch me, borne upward on the blast's sharp breath!

CH. 1.
Thou child of misery!
No mightier power hath this decreed,
But thine own will and deed
Hath bound thee thus in grief,
Since, when kind Heaven had sent relief
And shown the path of wisdom firm and sure,
Thou still hast chosen this evil to endure.

PHI. O hapless life, sore bruised with pain!
No more with living mortal may I dwell,
But ever pining in this desert cell
With lonely grief, all famished must remain
And perish; for what food is mine to share,
When this strong arm no longer wields my bow,
Whose fleet shafts flew to smite the birds of air
I was o'erthrown by words, words dark and blind,
Low-creeping from a traitorous mind!
O might I see him, whose unrighteous thought
This ruin wrought,
Plagued for no less a period with like woe!

CH. 2.
Not by our craft thou art caught,
But Destiny divine hath wrought
The net that holds thee bound.
Aim not at us the sound
Of thy dread curse with dire disaster fraught.
On others let that light! 'Tis our true care
Thou should'st not scorn our love in thy despair.

PHI. Now, seated by the shore
Of heaving ocean hoar,
He mocks me, waving high
The sole support of my precarious being,
The bow which none e'er held but I.
O treasure of my heart, torn from this hand,
That loved thy touch,--if thou canst understand,
How sad must be thy look in seeing
Thy master destined now no more,
Like Heracles of yore,

To wield thee with an archer's might!
But in the grasp of an all-scheming wight,
O bitter change! thou art plied;
And swaying ever by his side,
Shalt view his life of dark malignity,
Teeming with guileful shames, like those he wrought on me.

CH. 3.
Nobly to speak for the right
Is manly and strong;
But not with an envious blight
To envenom the tongue;
He to serve all his friends of the fleet,
One obeying a many-voiced word,
Through the minist'ring craft of our lord
Hath but done what was meet.

PHI.
Come, legions of the wild,
Of aspect fierce or mild,
Fowl from the fields of air,
And beasts that roam with bright untroubled gaze,
No longer bounding from my lair
Fly mine approach! Now freely without fear
Ye may surround my covert and come near,
Treading the savage rock-strewn ways.
The might I had is no more mine,
Stolen with those arms divine.
This fort hath no man to defend.
Come satisfy your vengeful jaws, and rend
These quivering tainted limbs!
Already hovering death bedims
My fainting sense. Who thus can live on air,
Tasting no gift of earth that breathing mortals share?

CH. 4.
Ah! do not shrink from thy friend,
If love thou reverest,
But know 'tis for thee to forfend
The fate which thou fearest.
The lot thou hast here to deplore,
Is sad evermore to maintain,
And hardship in sickness is sore,
But sorest in pain.

PHI. Kindest of all that e'er before

Have trod this shore,
Again thou mind'st me of mine ancient woe!
Why wilt thou ruin me?
What wouldst thou do?

CH. 5. How mean'st thou?

PHI. If to Troy, of me abhorred Thou e'er hast hoped to lead me with thy lord.

CH. 6. So I judge best.

PHI. Begone at once, begone!

CH. 7. Sweet is that word, and swiftly shall be done! Let us be gone, each to his place on board.

[The Chorus _make as if they were going]

PHI. Nay, by dear Zeus, to whom all suppliants moan Leave me not yet!

CH. 8. Keep measure in thy word.

PHI. Stay, by Heaven, stay!

CH. 9. What wilt thou say?

PHI. O misery! O cruel power
That rul'st this hour! I am destroyed. Ah me!
O poor torn limb, what shall I do with thee
Through all my days to be?
Ah, strangers, come, return, return!

CH. 10.
What new command are we to learn
Crossing thy former mind?

PHI. Ah! yet be kind.
Reprove not him, whose tongue, with grief distraught,
Obeys not, in dark storms, the helm of thought!

CH. 11. Come, poor friend, the way we call.

PHI. Never, learn it once for all!
Not though he, whom Heaven obeys,

Blast me with fierce lightning's blaze!
Perish Troy, and all your host,
That have chosen, to their cost,
To despise and cast me forth,
Since my wound obscured my worth!
Ah, but, strangers, if your sense
Hath o'er-mastered this offence,
Yield but one thing to my prayer!

CH. 12. What wouldst thou have?

PHI. Some weapon bare,
Axe or sword or sharpened dart,
Bring it to content my heart.

CH. 13. What is thy new intent?

PHI. To sever point by point
This body, joint from joint.
On bloody death my mind is bent.

CH. 14. Wherefore?

PHI. To see my father's face.

CH. 15. Where upon earth?

PHI. He hath no place
Where sun doth shine, but in the halls of night.
O native country, land of my delight,
Would I were blest one moment with thy sight!
Why did I leave thy sacred dew
And loose my vessels from thy shore,
To join the hateful Danaän crew
And lend them succour?
Oh, I am no more!

LEADER OF CH.
Long since thou hadst seen me nearing yonder ship,
Had I not spied Odysseus and the son
Of great Achilles hastening to our side.

OD. Wilt thou not tell me why thou art hurrying
This backward journey with reverted speed?

NEO. To undo what I have wrongly done to-day.

OD. Thy words appal me. What is wrongly done?

NEO. When in obeying thee and all the host--

OD. Thou didst what deed that misbecame thy life?

NEO. I conquered with base stratagem and fraud--

OD. Whom? What new plan is rising in thy mind?

NEO. Not new. But to the child of Poeas here--

OD. What wilt thou do? I quake with strange alarm.

NEO. From whom I took these weapons, back again----

OD. O Heaven! thou wilt not give them! Mean'st thou this?

NEO. Yea, for I have them through base sinful means.

OD. I pray thee, speak'st thou thus to anger me?

NEO. If the truth anger thee, the truth is said.

OD. Achilles' son! What word is fallen from thee?

NEO. Must the same syllables be thrice thrown forth?

OD. Once was too much. Would they had ne'er been said!

NEO. Enough. Thou hast heard my purpose clearly told.

OD. I know what power shall thwart thee in the deed.

NEO. Whose will shall hinder me?

OD. The Achaean host
And I among them.

NEO. Thou'rt sharp-witted, sure!
But little wit or wisdom show'st thou here.

OD. Neither thy words nor thy design is wise.

NEO. But if 'tis righteous, that is better far.

OD. How righteous, to release what thou hast ta'en By my device?

NEO. I sinned a shameful sin, And I will do mine utmost to retrieve it.

OD. How? Fear'st thou not the Achaeans in this act?

NEO. In doing right I fear not them nor thee.

OD. I call thy power in question.

NEO. Then I'll fight, Not with Troy's legions, but with thee.

OD. Come on! Let fortune arbitrate.

NEO. Thou seest my hand
Feeling the hilt.

OD. And me thou soon shalt see
Doing the like and dallying not!—
And yet I will not touch thee, but will go and tell
The army, that shall wreak this on thy head.

[_Exit_ NEO]
Thou show'st discretion: which if thou preserve,
Thou may'st maintain a path exempt from pain.
Ho! son of Poeas, Philoctetes, come
And leave thy habitation in the rock.

PHI. What noise again is troubling my poor cave?[6]
Why do ye summon me?
What crave[7] ye, sirs?
Ha! 'tis some knavery.
Are ye come to add
Some monster evil to my mountainous woe?

NEO. Fear not, but hearken to what now I speak.

PHI. I needs must fear thee, whose fair words erewhile
Brought me to bitter fortune.

NEO. May not men
Repent and change?

PHI. Such wast thou in thy talk,
When thou didst rob me of my bow,--so bright
Without, so black within.[8]

NEO. Ah, but not now, Assure thee!
Only let me hear thy will,
Is 't constant to remain here and endure,
Or to make voyage with us?

PHI. Stop, speak no more!
Idle and vain will all thine utterance be.[9]

NEO. Thou art so resolved?

PHI. More firmly than I say.

NEO. I would I might have brought thee to my mind,
But since my words are out of tune, I have done.

PHI. Thou wert best.
No word of thine can touch my soul
Or win me to thy love, who by deceit
Hast reft my life away. And then thou com'st
To school me,--of noblest father, basest son!
Perish, the Atridae first of all, and then Laërtes' child, and
thou!

NEO. Curse me no more,
But take this hallowed weapon from my hand.

PHI. What words are these? Am I again deceived?

NEO. No, by the holiest name of Zeus on high!

PHI. O voice of gladness, if thy speech be true!

NEO. The deed shall prove it. Only reach thy hand, And be
again sole master of thy bow.

[ODYSSEUS _appears]

OD. But I make protest, in the sight of Heaven, For Atreus'
sons, and all the Achaean host.

PHI. Dear son, whose voice disturbs us? Do I hear
Odysseus?

OD. Ay, and thou behold'st him nigh,
And he shall force thee to the Trojan plain,
Howe'er Achilles' offspring make or mar.

PHI. This shaft shall bear thee sorrow for that boast.

NEO. Let it not fly, by Heaven!

PHI. Dear child, let go Mine arm!

NEO. I will not.

[_Exit_ ODYSSEUS]

PHI. Ah! Why hast thou robbed
My bow of bringing down mine enemy?

NEO. This were ignoble both for thee and me.

PHI. One thing is manifest, the first o' the host
Lying forerunners of the Achaean band,
Are brave with words, but cowards with the steel.

NEO. Well, now the bow is thine.
Thou hast no cause
For blame or anger any more 'gainst me.

PHI. None. Thou hast proved thy birthright, dearest boy.
Not from the loins of Sisyphus thou earnest,
But from Achilles, who in life was held
Noblest of men alive, and now o' the dead.

NEO. It gladdens me that thou shouldst speak in praise
Both of my sire and me.
But hear me tell The boon for which I sue thee.—
Mortal men Must bear such evils as high Heaven ordains;
But those afflicted by self-chosen ills,
Like thine to-day, receive not from just men
Or kind indulgence or compassionate thought.
And thou art restive grown, and wilt not hearken,
But though one counsel thee with kind'st intent,
Wilt take him for a dark malignant foe.
Yet, calling Zeus to witness for my soul,
Once more I will speak. Know this, and mark it well:
Thou bear'st this sickness by a heavenly doom,

Through coming near to Chrysa's sentinel,
The lurking snake, that guards the sky-roofed fold[7].
And from this plague thou ne'er shall find reprieve
While the same Sun god rears him from the east
And droops to west again, till thou be come
Of thine own willing mind to Troia's plain,
Where our physicians, sons of Phoebus' child[8],
Shall soothe thee from thy sore, and thou with me
And with this bow shalt take Troy's citadel.
How do I know this? I will tell thee straight
We have a Trojan captive, Helenus,
Both prince and prophet, who hath clearly told
This must be so, yea, and ere harvest time
This year, great Troy must fall, else if his words
Be falsified, who will may slay the seer.
Now, since thou know'st of this, yield thy consent;
For glorious is the gain, being singled forth
From all the Greeks as noblest, first to come
To healing hands, and then to win renown
Unrivalled, vanquishing all tearful Troy.

PHI. Oh how I hate my life! Why must it keep
This breathing form from sinking to the shades?
How can I prove a rebel to his mind
Who thus exhorts me with affectionate heart?
And yet, oh misery! must I give way?
Then how could I endure the light of heaven?
With whom could I exchange a word?
Ay me! Eyes that have seen each act of my sad life,
How could ye bear it, to behold the sons
Of Atreus, my destroyers, comrades now
And friends! Laërtes' wicked son, my friend!
And less I feel the grief of former wrong
Than shudder with expectance of fresh harm
They yet may work on me. For when the mind
Hath once been mother of an evil brood,
It nurses nought but evils. Yea, at thee I marvel.
Thou should'st ne'er return to Troy,
Nor suffer me to go, when thou remember'st
What insult they have done thee, ravishing
Thy father's rights from thee. And wilt thou then
Sail to befriend them, pressing me in aid?
Nay, do not, son; but, even as thou hast sworn,
Convey me home, and thou, in Scyros dwelling,
Leave to their evil doom those evil men.
So thou shalt win a twofold gratitude

From me and from my father, and not seem,
Helping vile men, to be as vile as they.

NEO. 'Tis fairly spoken. Yet I would that thou
Relying on my word and on Heaven's aid,
Would'st voyage forth from Lemnos with thy friend.

PHI. Mean'st thou to Troy, and to the hateful sons
Of Atreus, me, with this distressful limb?

NEO. Nay, but to those that will relieve the pain
Of thy torn foot and heal thee of thy plague.

PHI. Thy words are horrible. What mean'st thou, boy?

NEO. The act I deem the noblest for us both.

PHI. Wilt thou speak so? Where is thy fear of Heaven?

NEO. Why should I fear, when I see certain gain?

PHI. Gain for the sons of Atreus, or for me?

NEO. Methinks a friend should give thee friendly counsel.

PHI. Friendly, to hand me over to my foes?

NEO. Ah, be not hardened in thy misery!

PHI. I know thou wilt ruin me by what thou speakest.

NEO. Not I. The case is dark to thee, I see.

PHI. I know the Atreidae cast me on this rock.

NEO. But how, if they should save thee afterward?

PHI. They ne'er shall make me see Troy with my will.

NEO. Hard is my fortune, then, if by no sleight
Of reasoning I can draw thee to my mind.
For me, 'twere easiest to end speech, that thou
Might'st live on as thou livest in hopeless pain.

PHI. Then leave me to my fate!--But thou hast touched
My right hand with thine own, and given consent

To bear me to my home. Do this, dear son!
And do not linger to take thought of Troy.
Enough that name hath echoed in my groans.

NEO. If thou wilt, let us be going.

PHI. Nobly hast thou said the word.

NEO. Lean thy steps on mine.

PHI. As firmly as my foot will strength afford.

NEO. Ah! but how shall I escape Achaean anger?

PHI. Do not care!

NEO. Ah! but should they spoil my country!

PHI. I to shield thee will be there.

NEO. How to shield me, how to aid me?

PHI. With the shafts of Heracles I will scare them.

NEO. Give thy blessing to this isle, and come in peace.

[TYRANNOSAURUS REX _appears from above in a
Zeppelin and carpet bombs the entire island of Lemnos
until the island falls into the sea. Having settled yet another
human philosophical dilemma, TYRANNOSAURUS REX
changes course and flies off to Disneyland.]

NOTES ON PHILOCTETES

---

[1] Yes, that Odysseus.

[2] Literally *New Ptolemus.*

[3] Literally *New.*

[4] Singular version of *Kouroi*.

[5] Either means *Ghost* or else is a frightful misspelling of the word white.

[6] Latin for *Dog*.

[7] Latin for *Drog*.

[8] In this passage, Philoctetes is referring to Eminem, the famous hip-hop artist.

[9] Unfortunately Philoctetes is correct. Everything you read previous to this point has been nothing but idle and useless.

[10] The Cambridge editor would throw out vs. 41.

[11] The Cambridge editor refers to Med. 56, Androm. 91, Soph. El. 425. Add Plaut. Merc. i. 1, 3. "Non ego idem facio, ut alios in comœdiis vidi facere amatores, qui aut nocti, aut die, Aut Soli, aut Lunæ miserias narrant suas." Theognetus apud Athen. xv. p. 671. Casaub. πεφιλοσοφηκας γηι και ουρανωι λαλων. Cf. Davis, on Cicero, Tusc. Q. iii. 26, and Lomeier de Lustrat. § xxxvii.

[12] Θριγκον is properly the uppermost part of the walls of any building (Pollux, vii. 27) surrounding the roof, στεγος is the roof itself.

[13] Cf. Meurs. ad Lycophron, p. 148.

[14] I read ειμ' εισω with Hermann and the Cambridge editor.

[15] This line is condemned by the Cambridge editor. Burges has transposed it.

[16] But διαδρομαις, the correction of the Cambridge editor, seems preferable.

[17] An interpolation universally condemned.

[18] See Barnes, and Wetstein on Acts xix. 35.

[19] On the wanderings of Orestes see my note on Æsch. Eum. 238 sqq. p. 187, ed. Bohn.

[20] See the note of the Cambridge editor, with whom we must read εισβησομεσθα.

[21] 'ων ουδεν ισμεν ad interiora templi spectat. HERM.

[22] We must read γεισα τριγλυφων 'οποι, with Blomfield and the Cambridge editor. See Philander on Vitruv. ii. p. 35, and Pollux, vii. 27.

[23] The sense is ουτοι, μακραν ελθοντες, εκ τερματων (sc. a meta) νοστησομεν. ED. CAMB.

[24] The Cambridge editor appositely compares a fragment of our author's Cresphontes, iii. 2, αισχρον τε μοχθειν μη θελειν νεανιαν.

[25] On the whole of this chorus, which is corrupt in several places, the notes of the Cambridge editor should be consulted.

[26] This last lumbering line must be corrupt.

[27] Compare the similar scene in Soph. El. 86 sqq.

[28] Cf. Elect. 90. νυκτος δε τησδε προς ταφον μολων πατρος. Hecub. 76. Æsch. Pers. 179. Aristoph. Ran. 1331.

[29] Compare my note on Æsch. Pers. 610 sqq.

[30] See on Æsch. Choeph. 6.

[31] Markland's emendation has been unanimously adopted by the later editors.

[32] Schema Colophonium. The Cambridge editor compares vs. 244. Αργει σκηπτουχον. Phœn. 17. Θηβαισιν αναξ. Heracl. 361. Αργει τυραννος.

[33] I have marked lacunæ, as some mythological particulars have evidently been lost.

[34] An imperfect allusion to the Thyestean banquet. Cf. Seneca Thyest. 774. "O Phœbe patiens, fugeris retro licet, medioque ruptum merseris cœlo diem, sero occidisti—" vs. 787 sqq.

[35] Cf. Æsch. Ag. 1501 sqq. Seneca, Ag. 57 sqq.

[36] i.e. the demon allotted to me at my birth (cf. notes on Æsch. 1341, p. 135, ed. Bohn). Statius, Theb. i. 60, makes

Œdipus invoke Tisiphone under the same character.—"Si me de matre cadentem Fovisti gremio."

[37] See the note of the Cambridge editor.

[38] εβησαν is active.

[39] The Cambridge editor aptly refers to Hecub. 464.

[40] These participles refer to the preceding αιμορραντων ξεινων.

[41] See on Heracl. 721.

[42] The Cambridge editor would omit these two lines.

[43] Cf. vs. 107. κατ' αντρ', 'α ποντιος νοτιδι διακλυζει μελας. On αγμος (Brodæus' happy correction for 'αρμος) the Cambridge editor quotes Nicander Ther. 146. κοιλη τε φαραγξ, και τρηχεες αγμοι, and other passages. The manner of hunting the purple fish is thus described by Pollux, i. 4, p. 24. They plat a long rope, to which they fasten, like bells, a number of hempen baskets, with an open entrance to admit the animal, but which does not allow of its egress. This they let down into the sea, the baskets being filled with such food as the murex delights in, and, having fastened the end of the rope to the rock, they leave it, and returning to the place, draw up the baskets full of the fish. Having broken the shells, they pound the flesh to form the dye.

[44] εφθαρμενους. Cf. Cycl. 300. Hel. 783. Ed. Camb.

[45] Compare Orest. 255 sqq.

[46] χιτωνων is probably corrupt.

[47] Cf. Lobeck on Aj. 17. Hesych. κοχλος τοις θαλαττιοις (i.e. κοχλοις) εχρωντο, προ της των σαλπιγγων ευρεσεως. Virg. Æn. vi. 171. "Sed tum forte cava dum personat æquora concha."

[48] "Moriamur, et in media arma ruamus." Virg. Æn. ii.

[49] Such seems to be the sense, but εξεκλεψαμεν is ridiculous, and Hermann's emendation more so. Bothe reads εξεκοψαμεν, which is better. The Cambridge editor thinks that the difficulty lies in πετροισι.

[50] I would omit this line as an evident gloss.

[51] See the Cambridge editor.

[52] Reiske's emendation, ʽοσια for ʽοια, seems deserving of admission.

[53] The Cambridge editor would omit these lines.

[54] This line also the Cambridge editor trusts "will never hereafter be reckoned among the verses of Euripides."

[55] Such is the proper sense of αντιθεισα.

[56] νιν is νυμφευματα.

[57] Read κασιγνητηι.

[58] I read τοις μεν and τοις δ' with the Cambridge editor. Hermann's emendation is unheard of.

[59] This clause interrupts the construction. δραμοντες must be understood with all the following sentence, as no finite verb is expressed except επερασαν.

[60] I have partly followed Hermann, reading επεβαιην ... απολαυων, but, as to reading ʽυπνων for ʽυμνων, the Cambridge editor well calls it "one of the wonders of his edition." I should prefer reading ολβου with the same elegant scholar.

[61] I follow the Cambridge editor in reading διδυμας, from Ovid, Ep. Pont. iii. 2, 71. "Protinus immitem Triviæ ducuntur ad aram, Evincti geminas ad sua terga manus."

ION[1]

PERSONS REPRESENTED

MERCURY
ION
CREUSA, daughter of Erechtheus
XUTHUS, husband of CREUSA
TUTOR
ATTENDANT
PRIESTESS OF APOLLO
TYRANNOSAURUS REX
CHORUS OF HANDMAIDENS OF CREUSA

Before the Temple of Apollo at Delphi. The sun is about to
rise. MERCURY enters.

MERCURY
Atlas, that on his brazen shoulders rolls
Yon heaven, the ancient mansion of the gods,
Was by a goddess sire to Maia; she
To supreme Jove bore me, and call'd me Hermes;
Attendant on the king, his high behests
I execute. To Delphi am I come,
This land where Phoebus from his central throne
Utters to mortals his high strain, declaring
The present and the future; this is the cause;
Greece hath a city of distinguish'd glory,
Which from the goddess of the golden lance
Received its name; Erechtheus was its king;
His daughter, call'd Creusa, to the embrace
Of nuptial love Apollo strain'd perforce,
Where northward points the rock beneath the heights
Crown'd with the Athenian citadel of Pallas,
Call'd Macrai by the lords of Attica.
Her growing burden, to her sire unknown
(Such was the pleasure of the god,) she bore,
Till in her secret chamber to a son
The rolling months gave birth: to the same cave,

Where by the enamour'd god she was compress'd,
Creusa bore the infant: there for death
Exposed him in a well-compacted ark
Of circular form, observant of the customs
Drawn from her great progenitors, and chief
From Erichthonius, who from the Attic earth
Deriv'd his origin: to him as guards
Minerva gave two dragons, and in charge
Consign'd him to the daughters of Aglauros:
This rite to the Erechthidae hence remains,
Mid serpents wreathed in ductile gold to nurse
Their children. What of ornament she had
She hung around her son, and left him thus
To perish. But to me his earnest prayer
Phoebus applied, "To the high-lineaged sons
Of glorious Athens go, my brother; well
Thou know'st the city of Pallas; from the cave
Deep in the hollow rock a new-born babe,
Laid as he is, and all his vestments with him;
Bring to thy brother to my shrine, and place
At the entrance of my temple; of the rest
(For, know, the child is mine) I will take care."
To gratify my brother thence I bore
The osier-woven ark, and placed the boy
Here at the temple's base, the wreathed lid
Uncovering, that the infant might be seen.
It chanced, as the orient sun the steep of heav'n
Ascended, to the god's oracular seat
The priestess entering, on the infant cast
Her eye, and marvelled, deeming that some nymph
Of Delphi at the fane had dared to lay
The secret burden of her womb: this thought
Prompts her to move it from the shrine: but soon
To pity she resign'd the harsh intent;
The impulse of the god secretly acting
In favour of the child, that in his temple
It might abide; her gentle hand then took it,
And gave it nurture; yet conceived she not
That Phoebus was the sire, nor who the mother
Knew aught, nor of his parents could the child
Give information. All his youthful years
Sportive he wandered round the shrine, and there
Was fed: but when his firmer age advanced
To manhood, o'er the treasures of the god
The Delphians placed him, to his faithful care
Consigning all; and in this royal dome

His hallow'd life he to this hour hath pass'd.
Meantime Creusa, mother of the child,
To Xuthus was espoused, the occasion this:-
On Athens from Euboean Chalcis roll'd
The waves of war; be join'd their martial toil,
And with his spear repell'd the foe; for this
To the proud honour of Creusa's bed
Advanc'd; no native, in Achaea sprung
From Aeolus, the son of Jove. Long time
Unbless'd with children, to the oracular shrine
Of Phoebus are they come, through fond desire
Of progeny: to this the god hath brought
The fortune of his son, nor, as was deem'd,
Forgets him; but to Xuthus, when he stands
This sacred seat consulting, will he give
That son, declared his offspring; that the child,
When to Creusa's house brought back, by her
May be agnized; the bridal rites of Phoebus
Kept secret, that the youth may claim the state
Due to his birth, through all the states of Greece
Named Ion, founder of the colonies
On the Asiatic coast. The laurell'd cave
Now will I visit, there to learn what fortune
Is to the boy appointed, for I see
This son of Phoebus issuing forth to adorn
The gates before the shrine with laurel boughs.
First of the gods I hail him by the name
Of Ion, which his fortune soon will give him.
MERCURY vanishes. ION and the attendants of the temple
enter.

ION chanting
Now flames this radiant chariot of the sun
High o'er the earth, at whose ethereal fire
The stars into the sacred night retreat:
O'er the Parnassian cliffs the ascending wheels
To mortals roll the beams of day; the wreaths
Of incense-breathing myrrh mount to the roof
Of Phoebus' fane; the Delphic priestess now
Assumes her seat, and from the hallow'd tripod
Pronounces to the Greeks the oracular strains
Which the god dictates. Haste, ye Delphic train,
Haste to Castalia's silver-streaming fount;
Bathed in its chaste dews to the temple go;
There from your guarded mouths no sound be heard
But of good omen, that to those who crave

Admission to the oracle, your voice
May with auspicious words expound the answers.
My task, which from my early infancy
Hath been my charge, shall be with laurel boughs
And sacred wreaths to cleanse the vestibule
Of Phoebus, on the pavement moistening dews
To rain, and with my bow to chase the birds
Which would defile the hallow'd ornaments.
A mother's fondness, and a father's care
I never knew: the temple of the god
Claims then my service, for it nurtured me.
The attendants leave. ION busies himself before the temple
as he continues to sing.

Haste, thou verdant new-sprung bough,
Haste, thy early office know;
Branch of beauteous laurel come,
Sweep Apollo's sacred dome,
Cropp'd this temple's base beneath,
Where the immortal gardens breathe,
And eternal dews that round
Water the delicious ground,
Bathe the myrtle's tresses fair.
Lightly thus, with constant care,
The pavement of the god I sweep,
When over the Parnassian steep
Flames the bright sun's mounting ray;
This my task each rising day.
Son of Latona, Paean, Paean, hail!
Never, O never may thy honours fail!

Grateful is my task, who wait
Serving, Phoebus, at thy gate;
Honouring thus thy hallow'd shrine,
Honour for the task is mine.
Labouring with unwilling hands,
Me no mortal man commands:
But, immortal gods, to you
All my pleasing toil is due.
Phoebus is to me a sire;
Grateful thoughts my soul inspire;
Nurtured by thy bounty here,
Thee, Apollo, I revere;
As a father's I repeat.
Son of Latona, Paean, Paean, hail!
Never, O never may thy honours fail!

Now from this labour with the laurel bough
I cease; and sprinkling from the golden vase
The chaste drops which Castalia's fountain rolls,
Bedew the pavement. Never may I quit
This office to the god; or, if I quit it,
Be it, good Fortune, at thy favouring call!
But see, the early birds have left their nests,
And this way from Parnassus wing their flight.
Come not, I charge you, near the battlements,
Nor near the golden dome. Herald of Jove,
Strong though thy beak beyond the feather'd kind,
My bow shall reach thee. Towards the altar, see,
A swan comes sailing: elsewhere wilt thou move
Thy scarlet-tinctured foot? or from my bow
The lyre of Phoebus to thy notes attuned
Will not protect thee; farther stretch thy wings;
Go, wanton, skim along the Delian lake,
Or wilt thou steep thy melody in blood.
Look, what strange bird comes onwards; wouldst thou fix
Beneath the battlements thy straw-built nest?
My singing bow shall drive thee hence; begone,
Or to the banks of Alpheus, gulfy stream,
Or to the Isthmian grove; there hatch thy young;
Mar not these pendent ornaments, nor soil
The temple of the god: I would not kill you:
'Twere pity, for to mortal man you bear
The message of the gods; yet my due task
Must be perform'd, and never will I cease
My service to the god who nurtured me.
The CHORUS enters. The following lines between ION
and the CHORUS are chanted responsively as they gaze
admiringly at the decorations on the temple.

CHORUS
The stately column, and the gorgeous dome
Raised to the gods, are not the boast alone
Of our magnificent Athens; nor the statues
That grace her streets; this temple of the god,
Son of Latona, beauteous to behold,
Beams the resplendent light of both her children.

ION
Turn thine eyes this way; look, the son of Jove
Lops with his golden scimitar the heads
Of the Lernean Hydra: view it well.

CHORUS
I see him.

ION
And this other standing nigh,
Who snatches from the fire the blazing brand.

CHORUS
What is his name? the subject, on the web
Design'd, these hands have wrought in ductile gold.

ION
The shield-supporting Iolaus, who bears
The toils in common with the son of Jove.
View now this hero; on his winged steed
The triple-bodied monster's dreadful force
He conquers through the flames his jaws emit.

CHORUS
I view it all attentively.

ION
Observe
The battle of the giants, on the walls
Sculptured in stone.

CHORUS
Let us note this, my friends.

ION
See where against Enceladus she shakes
Her gorgon shield.

CHORUS
I see my goddess, Pallas.

ION
Mark the tempestuous thunder's flaming bolt
Launch'd by the hand of Jove.

CHORUS
The furious Mimas
Here blazes in the volley'd fires: and there
Another earth-born monster falls beneath
The wand of Bacchus wreathed with ivy round,

No martial spear. But, as 'tis thine to tend
This temple, let me ask thee, is it lawful,
Leaving our sandals, its interior parts
To visit?

ION
Strangers, this is not permitted.

CHORUS
Yet may we make inquiries of thee?

ION
Speak;
What wouldst thou know?

CHORUS
Whether this temple's site
Be the earth's centre?

ION
Ay, with garlands hung,
And gorgons all around.

CHORUS
So fame reports.

ION
If at the gate the honey'd cake be offer'd,
Would you consult the oracle, advance
To the altar: till the hallow'd lamb has bled
In sacrifice, approach not the recess.

CHORUS
I am instructed: what the god appoints
As laws, we wish not to transgress: without
Enough of ornament delights our eyes.

ION
Take a full view of all; that is allow'd.

CHORUS
To view the inmost shrine was our lord's order.

ION
Who are you call'd? Attendants on what house?

CHORUS
Our lords inhabit the magnific domes
Of Pallas.-But she comes, of whom thou askest.
CREUSA and attendants enter.

ION
Lady, whoe'er thou art, that liberal air
Speaks an exalted mind: there is a grace,
A dignity in those of noble birth,
That marks their high rank. Yet I marvel much
That from thy closed lids the trickling tear
Water'd thy beauteous cheeks, soon as thine eye
Beheld this chaste oracular seat of Phoebus.
What brings this sorrow, lady? All besides,
Viewing the temple of the god, are struck
With joy; thy melting eye o'erflows with tears.

CREUSA
Not without reason, stranger, art thou seized
With wonder at my tears: this sacred dome
Awakes the sad remembrance of things past.
I had my mind at home, though present here.
How wretched is our sex! And, O ye gods,
What deeds are yours! Where may we hope for right,
If by the injustice of your power undone?

ION
Why, lady, this inexplicable grief?

CREUSA
It matters not; my mind resumes its firmless:
I say no more; cease thy concern for me.

ION
But say, who art thou? whence? what country boasts
Thy birth? and by what name may we address thee?

CREUSA
Creusa is my name, drawn from Erechtheus
My high-born lineage; Athens gave me birth.
Illustrious is thy state; thy ancestry
So noble that I look with reverence on thee.

CREUSA
Happy indeed is this, in nothing farther.

ION
But tell me, is it true what fame has blazon'd?

CREUSA
What wouldst thou ask? Stranger, I wish to know.

ION
Sprung the first author of thy line from the earth?

CREUSA
Ay, Erichthonius; but my race avails not.

ION
And did Minerva raise him from the earth?

CREUSA
Held in her virgin hands: she bore him not.

ION
And gave him as the picture represents?

CREUSA
Daughters of Cecrops these, charged not to see him.

ION
The virgins ope'd the interdicted chest?

CREUSA
And died, distaining with their blood the rock.

ION
But tell me, is this truth, or a vain rumour?

CREUSA
What wouldst thou ask? I am not scant of time.

ION
Thy sisters did Erechtheus sacrifice?

CREUSA
He slew the virgins, victims for their country.

ION
And thou of all thy sisters saved alone?

CREUSA

I was an infant in my mother's arms.

ION
And did the yawning earth swallow thy father?

CREUSA
By Neptune's trident smote; and so he perish'd.

ION
And Macrai call you not the fatal place?

CREUSA
Why dost thou ask? What thoughts hast thou recall'd?,

ION
Does Phoebus, do his lightnings honour it?

CREUSA
Honour! Why this? Would I had never seen it!

ION
Why? Dost thou hate the place dear to the god?

CREUSA
No: but for some base deed done in the cave.

ION
But what Athenian, lady, wedded thee?

CREUSA
Of Athens none, but one of foreign birth.

ION
What is his name? Noble he needs must be.

CREUSA
Xuthus, by Aeolus derived from Jove.

ION
How weds a stranger an Athenian born?

CREUSA
Euboea is a state neighbouring on Athens.

ION
A narrow sea flows, I have heard, between.

CREUSA
Joining the Athenian arms, that state he wasted.

ION
Confederate in the war, thence wedded thee?

CREUSA
The dowral meed of war, earn'd by his spear.

ION
Comest thou with him to Delphi, or alone?

CREUSA
With him, gone now to the Trophonian shrine.

ION
To view it, or consult the oracle?

CREUSA
Both that and this, anxious for one response.

ION
For the earth's fruits consult you, or for children?

CREUSA
Though wedded long, yet childless is our bed.

ION
Hast thou ne'er borne a child, that thou hast none?

CREUSA
My state devoid of children Phoebus knows.

ION
Bless'd in all else, luckless in this alone.

CREUSA
But who art thou? Bless'd I pronounce thy mother.

ION
Call'd as I am the servant of the god.

CREUSA
Presented by some state, or sold to this?

ION

I know not aught save this, I am the god's.

CREUSA

And in my turn, stranger, I pity thee.

ION

As knowing not my mother, or my lineage.

CREUSA

Hast thou thy dwelling here, or in some house?

ION

The temple is my house, ev'n when I sleep.

CREUSA

A child brought hither, or in riper years?

ION

An infant, as they say, who seem to know.

CREUSA

What Delphian dame sustain'd thee at her breast?

ION

I never knew a breast. She nourish'd me.

CREUSA

Who, hapless youth? Diseased, I find disease.

ION

The priestess: as a mother I esteem her.

CREUSA

Who to these manly years gave thee support?

ION

The altars, and the still-succeeding strangers.

CREUSA

Wretched, whoe'er she be, is she that bore thee.

ION

I to some woman am perchance a shame.

CREUSA

Are riches thine? Thou art well habited.

ION
Graced with these vestments by the god I serve.

CREUSA
Hast thou made no attempt to trace thy birth?

ION
I have no token, lady, for a proof.

CREUSA
Ah, like thy mother doth another suffer.

ION
Who? tell me: shouldst thou help me, what a joy

CREUSA
One for whose sake I come before my husband.

ION
Say for what end, that I may serve thee, lady.

CREUSA
To ask a secret answer of the god.

ION
Speak it: my service shall procure the rest.

CREUSA
Hear then the tale: but Modesty restrains me.

ION
Ah, let her not; her power avails not here.

CREUSA
My friend then says that to the embrace of Phoebus-

ION
A woman and a god! Say not so, stranger.

CREUSA
She bore a son: her father knew it not.

ION
Not so: a mortal's baseness he disdains.

CREUSA
This she affirms; and this, poor wretch, she suffer'd.

ION
What follow'd, if she knew the god's embrace?

CREUSA
The child, which hence had birth, she straight exposed.

ION
This exposed child, where is he? doth he live?

CREUSA
This no one knows; this wish I to inquire.

ION
If not alive, how probably destroyed?

CREUSA
Torn, she conjectures, by some beast of prey.

ION
What ground hath she on which to build that thought?

CREUSA
Returning to the place she found him not.

ION
Observed she drops of blood distain the path?

CREUSA
None, though with anxious heed she search'd around.

ION
What time hath pass'd since thus the child was lost?

CREUSA
Were he alive, his youth were such as thine.

ION
The god hath done him wrong: the unhappy mother-

CREUSA
Hath not to any child been mother since.

ION
What if in secret Phoebus nurtures him!

CREUSA
Unjust to enjoy alone a common right.

ION
Ah me! this cruel fate accords with mine.

CREUSA
For thee too thy unhappy mother mourns.

ION
Ah, melt me not to griefs I would forget!

CREUSA
I will be silent: but impart thy aid.

ION
Seest thou what most the inquiry will suppress?

CREUSA
And to my wretched friend what is not ill?

ION
How shall the god what he would hide reveal?

CREUSA
As placed on the oracular seat of Greece.

ION
The deed must cause him shame: convict him not.

CREUSA
To the poor sufferer 'tis the cause of grief.

ION
It cannot be; for who shall dare to give
The oracle? With justice would the god,
In his own dome affronted, pour on him
Severest vengeance, who should answer thee.
Desist then, lady: it becomes us ill,
In opposition to the god, to make
Inquiries at his shrine; by sacrifice
Before their altars, or the flight of birds,
Should we attempt to force the unwilling gods

To utter what they wish not, 'twere the excess
Of rudeness; what with violence we urge
'Gainst their consent would to no good avail us:
What their spontaneous grace confers on us,
That, lady, as a blessing we esteem.

LEADER OF THE CHORUS
How numberless the ills to mortal man,
And various in their form! One single blessing
By any one through life is scarcely found.

CREUSA
Nor here, nor there, O Phoebus, art thou just
To her; though absent, yet her words are present.
Nor didst thou save thy son, whom it became thee
To save; nor, though a prophet, wilt thou speak
To the sad mother who inquires of thee;
That, if he is no more, to him a tomb
May rise; but, if he lives, that he may bless
His mother's eyes. But even thus behooves us
To omit these things, if by the god denied
To know what most I wish.-But, for I see
The noble Xuthus this way bend, return'd
From the Trophonian cave; before my husband
Resume not, generous stranger, this discourse,
Lest it might cause me shame that thus I act
In secret, and perchance lead on to questions
I would not have explain'd. Our hapless sex
Oft feel our husbands' rigour: with the bad
The virtuous they confound, and treat us harshly.
XUTHUS and his retinue enter.

XUTHUS
With reverence to the god my first address
I pay: Hail, Phoebus! Lady, next to thee:
Absent so long, have I not caused thee fear?

CREUSA
Not much: as anxious thoughts 'gan rise, thou'rt come.
But, tell me, from Trophonius what reply
Bearest thou; what means whence offspring may arise?

XUTHUS
Unmeet he held it to anticipate
The answer of the god: one thing he told me.
That childless I should not return, nor thou,

Home from the oracle.

CREUSA
Goddess revered,
Mother of Phoebus, be our coming hither
In lucky hour; and our connubial bed
Be by thy son made happier than before!

XUTHUS
It shall be so. But who is president here?

ION
Without, that charge is mine; within, devolved
On others, stranger, seated near the tripod;
The chiefs of Delphi these, chosen by lot.

XUTHUS
'Tis well: all that I want is then complete.
Let me now enter: for the oracle
Is given, I hear, in common to all strangers
Before the shrine; on such a day, that falls
Propitious thus, the answer of the god
Would I receive: meanwhile, these laurel boughs
Bear round the altars; lady, breathe thy prayers
To every god, that from Apollo's shrine
I may bring back the promise of a son.
XUTHUS, after giving the laurel boughs to CREUSA, enters
the temple.

CREUSA
It shall, it shall be so. Should Phoebus now
At least be willing to redress the fault
Of former times, he would not through the whole
Be friendly to us: yet will I accept
What he vouchsafes us, for he is a god.
CREUSA departs to the shrines in the outer precinct of the
temple.

ION
Why does this stranger always thus revile
With obscure speech the god? Is it through love
Of her, for whom she asks? or to conceal
Some secret of importance? But to me
What is the daughter of Erechtheus? Naught
Concerns it me. Then let me to my task,
And sprinkle from the golden vase the dew.

Yet must I blame the god, if thus perforce
He mounts the bed of virgins, and by stealth
Becomes a father, leaving then his children
To die, regardless of them. Do not thou
Act thus; but, as thy power is great, respect
The virtues; for whoe'er, of mortal men,
Dares impious deeds, him the gods punish: how
Is it then just that you, who gave the laws
To mortals, should yourselves transgress those laws?,
If (though it is not thus, yet will I urge
The subject,)-if to mortals you shall pay
The penalty of forced embraces, thou,
Neptune, and Jove, that reigns supreme in heaven,
Will leave your temples treasureless by paying
The mulcts of your injustice: for unjust
You are, your pleasures to grave temperance
Preferring: and to men these deeds no more
Can it be just to charge as crimes, these deeds
If from the gods they imitate: on those
Who gave the ill examples falls the charge.
ION goes out.

CHORUS singing

Thee prompt to yield thy lenient aid,
And sooth a mother's pain:
And thee, my Pallas, martial maid,
I call: O, hear the strain!
Thou, whom the Titan from the head of Jove,
Prometheus, drew, bright Victory, come,
Descending from thy golden throne above;
Haste, goddess, to the Pythian dome,
Where Phoebus, from his central shrine,
Gives the oracle divine,
By the raving maid repeated,
On the hallow'd tripod seated:
O haste thee, goddess, and with thee
The daughter of Latona bring;
A virgin thou, a virgin she,
Sisters to the Delphian king;
Him, virgins, let your vows implore,
That now his pure oracular power
Will to Erechtheus' ancient line declare
The blessing of a long-expected heir!

To mortal man this promised grace
Sublimest pleasure brings,
When round the father's hearth a race
In blooming lustre springs.
The wealth, the honours, from their high-drawn line
From sire to son transmitted down,
Shall with fresh glory through their offspring shine,
And brighten with increased renown:
A guard, when ills begin to lower,
Dear in fortune's happier hour;
For their country's safety waking,
Firm in fight the strong spear shaking;
More than proud wealth's exhaustless store,
More than a monarch's bride to reign,
The dear delight, to virtue's lore
Careful the infant mind to train.
Doth any praise the childless state?
The joyless, loveless life I hate;
No; my desires to moderate wealth I bound,
But let me see my children smile around.

Ye rustic seats, Pan's dear delight;
Ye caves of Macrai's rocky height,
Where oft the social virgins meet,
And weave the dance with nimble feet;
Descendants from Aglauros they
In the third line, with festive play,
Minerva's hallow'd fane before
The verdant plain light-tripping o'er,
When thy pipe's quick-varying sound
Rings, O Pan, these caves around;
Where, by Apollo's love betray'd,
Her child some hapless mother laid,
Exposed to each night-prowling beast,
Or to the ravenous birds a feast;
For never have I heard it told,
Nor wrought it in historic gold,
That happiness attends the race,
When gods with mortals mix the embrace.
[ION re-enters.]

ION
Ye female train, that place yourselves around
This incense-breathing temple's base, your lord
Awaiting, hath he left the sacred tripod
And oracle, or stays he in the shrine,

Making inquiries of his childless state?

LEADER OF THE CHORUS
Yet in the temple, stranger, he remains.

ION
But he comes forth; the sounding doors announce
His near approach; behold, our lord is here.
XUTHUS enters from the temple. He rushes to greet ION.

XUTHUS
Health to my son! This first address is proper.

ION
I have my health: be in thy senses thou,
And both are well.

XUTHUS
O let me kiss thy hand,
And throw mine arms around thee.

ION
Art thou, stranger,
Well in thy wits? or hath the god's displeasure
Bereft thee of thy reason?

XUTHUS
Reason bids,
That which is dearest being found, to wish
A fond embrace.

ION
Off, touch me not; thy hands
Will mar the garlands of the god.

XUTHUS
My touch
Asserts no pledge: my own, and that most dear,
I find.

ION
Wilt thou not keep thee distant, ere
Thou hast my arrow in thy heart?

XUTHUS
Why fly me,

When thou shouldst own what is most fond of thee?

ION
I am not fond of curing wayward strangers,
And madmen.

XUTHUS
Kill me, raise my funeral pyre;
But, if thou kill me, thou wilt kill thy father.

ION
My father thou! how so? it makes me laugh
To hear thee.

XUTHUS
This my words may soon explain.

ION
What wilt thou say to me?

XUTHUS
I am thy father,
And thou my son.

ION
Who declares this?

XUTHUS
The god,
That nurtured thee, though mine.

ION
Thou to thyself
Art witness.

XUTHUS
By the oracle inform'd.

ION
Misled by some dark answer.

XUTHUS
Well I heard it.

ION
What were the words of Phoebus?

XUTHUS
That who first
Should meet me-

ION
How?-what meeting?

XUTHUS
As I pass'd.
Forth from the temple.

ION
What the event to him?

XUTHUS
He is my son.

ION
Born so, or by some other
Presented?

XUTHUS
Though a present, born my son.

ION
And didst thou first meet me?

XUTHUS
None else, my son.

ION
This fortune whence?

XUTHUS
At that we marvel both.

ION
Who is my mother?

XUTHUS
That I cannot say.

ION
Did not the god inform thee?

XUTHUS
Through my joy,
For this I ask'd not.

ION
Haply from the earth
I sprung, my mother.

XUTHUS
No, the earth no sons
Produces.

ION
How then am I thine?

XUTHUS
I know not.
To Phoebus I appeal.

ION
Be this discourse
Chang'd to some other.

XUTHUS
This delights me most.

ION
Hast thou e'er mounted an unlawful bed?

XUTHUS
In foolishness of youth.

ION
Was that before
Thy marriage with the daughter of Erechtheus?

XUTHUS
Since never.

ION
Owe I then my birth to that?

XUTHUS
The time agrees.

ION

How came I hither then?

XUTHUS
I can form no conjecture.

ION
Was I brought
From some far distant part?

XUTHUS
That fills my mind
With doubtful musing.

ION
Didst thou e'er before
Visit the Pythian rock?

XUTHUS
Once, at the feast
Of Bacchus.

ION
By some public host received?

XUTHUS
Who with the Delphian damsels-

ION
To the orgies
Led thee, or how?

XUTHUS
And with the Maenades
Of Bacchus-

ION
In the temperate hour, or warm
With wine?

XUTHUS
Amid the revels of the god.

ION
From thence I date my birth.

XUTHUS

And fate, my son,
Hath found thee.

ION
How then came I to the temple?

XUTHUS
Perchance exposed.

ION
The state of servitude
Have I escaped.

XUTHUS
Thy father now, my son,
Receive.

ION
Indecent were it in the god
Not to confide.

XUTHUS
Thy thoughts are just.

ION
What else
Would we?

XUTHUS
Thou seest what thou oughtst to see.

ION
Am I the son then of the son of Jove?

XUTHUS
Such is thy fortune.

ION
Those that gave me birth
Do I embrace?

XUTHUS
Obedient to the god.

ION
My father, hail!

XUTHUS
That dear name I accept
With joy.

ION
This present day-

XUTHUS
Hath made me happy.

ION
O my dear mother, when shall I behold
Thy face? Whoe'er thou art, more wish I now
To see thee than before; but thou perchance
Art dead, and nothing our desires avail.

LEADER
We in the blessing of our house rejoice.
Yet wish we that our mistress too were happy
In children, and the lineage of Erechtheus.

XUTHUS
Well hath the god accomplish'd this, my son,
Discovering thee, well hath he joined thee to me;
And thou hast found the most endearing ties,
To which, before this hour, thou wast a stranger.
And the warm wish, which thou hast well conceived,
Is likewise mine, that thou mayst find thy mother;
I from what woman thou derivest thy birth.
This, left to time, may haply be discover'd.
Now quit this hallow'd earth, the god no more
Attending, and to mine accord thy mind,
To visit Athens, where thy father's sceptre,
No mean one, waits thee, and abundant wealth:
Nor, though thou grieve one parent yet unknown,
Shalt thou be censured as ignobly born,
Or poor: no, thou art noble, and thy state
Adorn'd with rich possessions. Thou art silent.
Why is thine eye thus fixed upon the ground?
Why on thy brow that cloud? The smile of joy
Vanish'd, thou strikest thy father's heart with fear.

ION
Far other things appear when nigh, than seen
At distance. I indeed embrace my fortune,

In thee my father found. But hear what now
Wakes sad reflections. Proud of their high race
Are your Athenians, natives of the land,
Not drawn from foreign lineage: I to them
Shall come unwelcome, in two points defective,
My father not a native, and myself
Of spurious birth: loaded with this reproach,
If destitute of power, I shall be held
Abject and worthless: should I rush among
The highest order of the state, and wish
To appear important, inferior ranks
Will hate me; aught above them gives disgust.
The good, the wise, men form'd to serve the state,
Are silent, nor at public honours aim
Too hastily: by such, were I not quiet
In such a bustling state, I should be deem'd
Ridiculous, and proverb'd for a fool.
Should I attain the dignity of those,
Whose approved worth hath raised them to the height
Of public honours, by such suffrage more
Should I be watch'd; for they that hold in states
Rule and pre-eminence, bear hostile minds
To all that vie with them. And should I come
To a strange house a stranger, to a woman
Childless herself, who that misfortune shared
Before with thee, now sees it her sole lot,
And feels it bitterly, would she not hate me,
And that with justice? When I stand before them.
With what an eye would she, who hath no child,
Look on thy child? In tenderness to her,
Thy wife, thou must forsake me, or embroil
Thy house in discord, if thou favour me.
What murderous means, what poisonous drugs for men
Have women with inventive rage prepared!
Besides, I have much pity for thy wife,
Now growing old without a child, that grief
Unmerited, the last of her high race,
The exterior face indeed of royalty,
So causelessly commended, bath its brightness;
Within, all gloom: for what sweet peace of mind,
What happiness is his, whose years are pass'd
In comfortless suspicion, and the dread
Of violence? Be mine the humble blessings
Of private life, rather than be a king,
From the flagitious forced to choose my friends,
And hate the virtuous through the fear of death.

Gold, thou mayst tell me, hath o'er things like these
A sovereign power, and riches give delight:
I have no pleasure in this noisy pomp,
Nor, while I guard my riches, in the toil:
Be mine a modest mean that knows not care.
And now, my father, hear the happy state
I here enjoy'd; and first, to mortal man
That dearest blessing, leisure, and no bustle
To cause disturbance: me no ruffian force
Shoved from the way: it is not to be borne,
When every insolent and worthless wretch
Makes you give place. The worship of the god
Employ'd my life, or (no unpleasing task)
Service to men well pleased: the parting guest
I bade farewell-welcomed the new-arrived.
Thus something always new made every hour
Glide sweetly on; and to the human mind
That dearest wish, though some regard it not,
To be, what duty and my nature made me,
Just to the god: revolving this, my father,
I wish not for thy Athens to exchange
This state; permit me to myself to live;
Dear to the mind pleasures that arise
From humble life, as those which greatness brings.

LEADER
Well hast thou said, if those whom my soul holds
Most dear shall in thy words find happiness.

XUTHUS
No more of this discourse; learn to be happy.
It is my will that thou begin it here,
Where first I found thee, son: a general feast
Will I provide, and make a sacrifice,
Which at thy birth I made not: at my table
Will I receive thee as a welcome guest,
And cheer thee with the banquet, then conduct the
To Athens with me as a visitant,
Not as my son: for, mid my happiness,
I would not grieve my wife, who hath no child.

ION
But I will watch the occasions time may bring,
And so present thee, and obtain her leave
That thou mayst hold the sceptre which I bear.
Ion I name thee, as befits thy fortune,

As first thou met'st me from the hallow'd shrine
As I came forth; assemble then thy friends,
Invite them all to share the joyful feast,
Since thou art soon to leave the Delphic state.
And you, ye females, keep, I charge you, keep
This secret; she that tells my wife shall die.

ION
Let us then go; yet one thing to my fortune
Is wanting: if I find not her that bore me,
Life hath no joy. Might I indulge a wish,
It were to find her an Athenian dame,
That from my mother I might dare to assume
Some confidence; for he whose fortune leads him
To a free state proud of their unmix'd race,
Though call'd a citizen, must close his lips
With servile awe, for freedom is not his.
XUTHUS and ION go out.

CHORUS singing

Yes, sisters, yes, the streaming eye,
The swelling heart I see, the bursting sigh,
When thus rejoicing in his son
Our queen her royal lord shall find,
And give to grief her anguish'd mind,
Afflicted, childless, and alone.
What means this voice divine,
Son of Latona, fate-declaring power?
Whence is this youth, so fondly graced,
That to ripe manhood, from his infant hour,
Hath in thy hallow'd courts been plac'd
And nurtured at thy shrine?
Thy dark reply delights not me;
Lurking beneath close fraud I see:
Where will this end? I fear, I fear-
'Tis strange, and strange events must hence ensue:
But grateful sounds it to his ear,
The youth, that in another's state
(Who sees not that my words are true?)
Enjoys the fraud, and triumphs in his fate.

Say, sisters, say, with duteous zeal
Shall we this secret to our queen reveal?
She, to her royal lord resign'd,
With equal hope, with equal care,

CCXLIV

Form'd her his joys, his griefs to share,
And gave him an her willing mind.
But joys are his alone;
While she, poor mourner, with a weight of woes,
To hoary age advancing, bends;
He the bright smile of prosperous fortune knows.
Ev'n thus, unhonour'd by his friends,
Plac'd on another's throne,
Mischance and ruin on him wait,
Who fails to guard its happy state.
Him may mischance and ruin seize,
Who round my lov'd queen spreads his wily trains.
No god may his oblation please,
No favouring flame to him ascend!
To her my faith, my zeal remains,
Known to her ancient royal house a friend.

Now the father and the new-found son
The festive table haste to spread,
Where to the skies Parnassus lifts his head,
And deep beneath the hanging stone
Forms in its rudely-rifted side
A cavern wild and wide;
Where Bacchus, shaking high his midnight flames,
In many a light fantastic round
Dances o'er the craggy ground,
And revels with his frantic dames.
Ne'er to my city let him come,
This youth: no, rather let him die,
And sink into an early tomb!
With an indignant eye
Athens would view the stranger's pride
Within her gates triumphant ride:
Enough for her the honour'd race that springs
From old Erechtheus and her line of kings.
CREUSA and her aged TUTOR enter.

CREUSA
Thou venerable man, whose guiding voice
My father, while he lived, revered, advance
Up to the oracular seat thy aged steps;
That, if the royal Phoebus should pronounce
Promise of offspring, thou with me mayst share
The joy; for pleasing is it when with friends
Good fortune we receive; if aught of ill
(Avert it, Heaven!) befalls, a friend's kind eye

Beams comfort; thee, as once thou didst revere
My father, though thy queen, I now revere.

TUTOR
In thee, my child, the nobleness of manners
Which graced thy royal ancestors yet lives;
Thou never wilt disgrace thy high-born lineage.
Lead me, then, lead me to the shrine, support me:
High is the oracular seat, and steep the ascent;
Be thou assistant to the foot of age.

CREUSA
Follow; be heedful where thou set thy steps.

TUTOR
I am: my foot is slow, my heart hath wings.

CREUSA
Fix thy staff firm on this loose-rolling ground.

TUTOR
That hath no eyes; and dim indeed my sight.

CREUSA
Well hast thou said; on cheerful then, and faint not.

TUTOR
I have the will, but o'er constraint no power.

CREUSA
Ye females, on my richly-broider'd works
Faithful attendants, say, respecting children,
For which we came, what fortune hath my lord
Borne hence? if good, declare it: you shall find
That to no thankless masters you give joy.

LEADER OF THE CHORUS
O fortune!

CREUSA
To thy speech this is a proem
Not tuned to happiness.

LEADER
Unhappy fortune!
But why distress me for the oracle

Given to our lords? Be that as fate requires
In things which threaten death, what shall we do?

CREUSA
What means this strain of woe? Whence are these fears?

LEADER
What! shall we speak, or bury this in silence?

CREUSA
Speak, though thy words bring wretchedness to me.

LEADER
It shall be spoken, were I twice to die.
To thee, my queen, it is not given to clasp
In thy fond arms a child, or at thy breast
To hold it.

TUTOR
O my child, would I were dead!

CREUSA
Yes, this is wretchedness indeed, a grief
That makes life joyless.

TUTOR
This is ruin to us.

CREUSA
Unhappy me! this is a piercing grief,
That rends my heart with anguish.

TUTOR
Groan not yet.

CREUSA
Yet is the affliction present.

TUTOR
Till we learn-

CREUSA
To me what tidings?

TUTOR
If a common fate

Await our lord, partaker of thy griefs,
Or thou alone art thus unfortunate.

LEADER
To him, old man, the god hath given a son,
And happiness is his unknown to her.

CREUSA
To ill this adds the deepest ill, a grief
For me to mourn.

TUTOR
Born of some other woman
Is this child yet to come, or did the god
Declare one now in being?

LEADER
One advanced
To manhood's prime he gave him: I was present.

CREUSA
What hast thou said? Thy words denounce to me
Sorrows past speech, past utterance.

TUTOR
And to me.

CREUSA
How was this oracle accomplish'd? Tell me
With clearest circumstance: who is this youth?

LEADER
Him as a son Apollo gave, whom first,
Departing from the god, thy lord should meet.

CREUSA
O my unhappy fate! I then am left
Childless to pass my life, childless, alone,
Amid my lonely house! Who was declared?
Whom did the husband of this wretch first meet?
How meet him? Where behold him? Tell me all.

LEADER
Dost thou, my honoured mistress, call to mind
The youth that swept the temple? This is he.

CREUSA
O, through the liquid air that I could fly,
Far from the land of Greece, ev'n to the stars
Fix'd in the western sky! Ah me, what grief,
What piercing grief is mine!

TUTOR
Say, by what name
Did he address his son, if thou hast heard it?
Or does it rest in silence, yet unknown?

LEADER
Ion, for that he first advanced to meet him.

TUTOR
And of what mother?

LEADER
That I could not learn:
Abrupt was his departure (to inform thee
Of all I know, old man) to sacrifice,
With hospitable rites, a birthday feast;
And in the hallow'd cave, from her apart,
With his new son to share the common banquet.

TUTOR
Lady, we by thy husband are betrayed,
For I with thee am grieved, with contrived fraud
Insulted, from thy father's house cast forth.
I speak not this in hatred to thy lord,
But that I love thee more: a stranger he
Came to the city and thy royal house,
And wedded thee, all thy inheritance
Receiving, by some other woman now
Discover'd to have children privately:
How privately I'll tell thee: when he saw
Thou hadst no child, it pleased him not to bear
A fate like thine; but by some favourite slave,
His paramour by stealth, he hath a son.
Him to some Delphian gave he, distant far,
To educate; who to this sacred house
Consign'd, as secret here, received his nurture.
He knowing this, and that his son advanced
To manhood, urged thee to attend him hither,
Pleading thy childless state. Nor hath the god
Deceived thee: he deceived thee, and long since

Contrived this wily plan to rear his son,
That, if convicted, he might charge the god,
Himself excusing: should the fraud succeed,
He would observe the times when he might safely
Consign to him the empire of thy land.
And this new name was at his leisure form'd,
Ion, for that he came by chance to meet him.
I hate those ill-designing men, that form
Plans of injustice, and then gild them over
With artificial ornament: to me
Far dearer is the honest simple friend,
Than one whose quicker wit is train'd to ill.
And to complete this fraud, thou shalt be urged
To take into thy house, to lord it there,
This low-born youth, this offspring of a slave.
Though ill, it had been open, had he pleaded
Thy want of children, and, thy leave obtain'd,
Brought to thy house a son that could have boasted
His mother noble; or, if that displeased thee,
He might have sought a wife from Aeolus.
Behooves thee then to act a woman's part,
Or grasp the sword, or drug the poison'd bowl,
Or plan some deep design to kill thy husband,
And this his son, before thou find thy death
From them: if thou delay, thy life is lost:
For when beneath one roof two foes are met,
The one must perish. I with ready zeal
Will aid thee in this work, and kill the youth,
Entering the grot where he prepares the feast;
Indifferent in my choice, so that I pay
What to my lords I owe, to live or die.
If there is aught that causes slaves to blush,
It is the name; in all else than the free
The slave is nothing worse, if he be virtuous.
I too, my honour'd queen, with cheerful mind
Will share thy fate, or die, or live with honour.

CREUSA chanting
How, o my soul, shall I be silent, how
Disclose this secret? Can I bid farewell
To modesty? What else restrains my tongue?
To how severe a trial am I brought!
Hath not my husband wrong'd me? Of my house
I am deprived, deprived of children; hope
Is vanish'd, which my heart could not resign,
With many an honest wish this furtive bed

Concealing, this lamented bed concealing.
But by the star-bespangled throne of Jove,
And by the goddess high above my rocks
Enshrined, by the moist banks that bend around
The hallow'd lake by Triton form'd, no longer
Will I conceal this bed, but ease my breast,
The oppressive load discharged. Mine eyes drop tears,
My soul is rent, to wretchedness ensnared
By men, by gods, whom I will now disclose,
Unkind betrayers of the beds they forced.
O thou, that wakest on thy seven-string'd lyre
Sweet notes, that from the rustic lifeless horn
Enchant the ear with heavenly melody,
Son of Latona, thee before this light
Will I reprove. Thou camest to me, with gold
Thy locks all glittering, as the vermeil flowers
I gather'd in my vest to deck my bosom
With the spring's glowing hues; in my white hand
Thy hand enlocking, to the cavern'd rock
Thou led'st me; naught avail'd my cries, that call'd
My mother; on thou led'st me, wanton god,
Immodestly, to Venus paying homage.
A son I bare thee, O my wretched fate!
Him (for I fear'd my mother) in thy cave
I placed, where I unhappy was undone
By thy unhappy love. Woe, woe is me!
And now my son and thine, ill-fated babe,
Is rent by ravenous vultures; thou, meanwhile,
Art to thy lyre attuning strains of joy.
Set of Latona, thee I call aloud
Who from thy golden seat, thy central throne,
Utterest thine oracle: my voice shall reach
Thine ear: ungrateful lover, to my husband,
No grace requiting, thou hast given a son
To bless his house; my son and thine, unown'd,
Perish'd a prey to birds; the robes that wrapp'd
The infant's limbs, his mother's work, lost with him.
Delos abhors thee, and the laurel boughs
With the soft foliage of the palm o'erhung,
Grasping whose round trunk with her hands divine,
Latona thee, her hallow'd offspring, bore.

LEADER
Ah, what a mighty treasury of ills
Is open'd here, a copious source of tears!

TUTOR
Never, my daughter, can I sate my eyes
With looking on thy face: astonishment
Bears me beyond my senses. I had stemm'd
One tide of evils, when another flood
High-surging overwhelm'd me from the words
Which thou hast utter'd, from the present ills
To an ill train of other woes transferr'd.
What say'st thou? Of what charge dost thou implead
The god? What son hast thou brought forth? Where placed
him
A feast for vultures? Tell me all again.

CREUSA
Though I must blush, old man, yet I will speak.

TUTOR
I mourn with generous grief at a friend's woes.

CREUSA
Hear then: the northward-pointing cave thou knowest,
And the Cecropian rocks, which we call Macrai.

TUTOR
Where stands a shrine to Pan, and altars nigh.

CREUSA
There in a dreadful conflict I engaged.

TUTOR
What! my tears rise ready to meet thy words.

CREUSA
By Phoebus drawn reluctant to his bed.

TUTOR
Was this, my daughter, such as I suppose?

CREUSA
I know not: but if truth, I will confess it.

TUTOR
Didst thou in silence mourn this secret ill?

CREUSA
This was the grief I now disclose to thee.

TUTOR
This love of Phoebus how didst thou conceal?

CREUSA
I bore a son. Hear me, old man, with patience.

TUTOR
Where? who assisted? or wast thou alone?

CREUSA
Alone, in the same cave where compress'd.

TUTOR
Where is thy son, that childless now no more

CREUSA
Dead, good old man, to beasts of prey exposed.

TUTOR
Dead! and the ungrateful Phoebus gives no aid?

CREUSA
None: in the house of Pluto a young guest.

TUTOR
Whose hands exposed him? Surely not thine own.

CREUSA
Mine, in the shades of night, wrapp'd in his vests.

TUTOR
Hadst thou none with thee conscious to this deed?

CREUSA
My misery, and the secret place alone.

TUTOR
How durst thou in a cavern leave thy son?

CREUSA
How? uttering many sad and plaintive words.

TUTOR
Ah, cruel was thy deed, the god more cruel.

CREUSA
Hadst thou but seen him stretch his little hands!

TUTOR
Seeking the breast, or reaching to thine arms?

CREUSA
To this, deprived of which he suffer'd wrong.

TUTOR
And what induced thee to expose thy child?

CREUSA
Hope that the god's kind care would save his son.

TUTOR
How are the glories of thy house destroy'd!

CREUSA
Why, thine head cover'd, dost thou pour these tears?

TUTOR
To see thee and thy father thus unhappy.

CREUSA
This is the state of man: nothing stands firm.

TUTOR
No longer then, my child, let grief oppress us.

CREUSA
What should I do? In misery all is doubt.

TUTOR
First on the god that wrong'd thee be avenged.

CREUSA
How shall a mortal 'gainst a god prevail?

TUTOR
Set this revered oracular shrine on fire.

CREUSA
I fear: ev'n now I have enough of ills.

TUTOR
Attempt what may be done then; kill thy husband.

CREUSA
The nuptial bed I reverence, and his goodness.

TUTOR
This son then, which is now brought forth against thee.

CREUSA
How? Could that be, how warmly should I wish it.

TUTOR
Thy train hath swords: instruct them to the deed.

CREUSA
I go with speed: but where shall it be done?

TUTOR
In the hallow'd tent, where now he feasts his friends.

CREUSA
An open murder, and with coward slaves!

TUTOR
If mine displease, propose thou some design.

CREUSA
I have it, close and easy to achieve.

TUTOR
In both my faithful services are thine.

CREUSA
Hear then: not strange to thee the giants' war.

TUTOR
When they in Phlegra fought against the gods.

CREUSA
There the earth brought forth the Gorgon, horrid monster.

TUTOR
In succour of her sons to annoy the gods?

CREUSA
Ev'n so: her Pallas slew, daughter of Jove.

TUTOR
What fierce and dreadful form did she then wear?

CREUSA
Her breastplate arm'd with vipers wreathed around.

TUTOR
A well-known story; often have I heard it.

CREUSA
Her spoils before her breast Minerva wore.

TUTOR
The aegis; so they call the vest of Pallas.

CREUSA
So named, when in the war she join'd the gods.

TUTOR
But how can this, my child, annoy thy foes?

CREUSA
Thou canst not but remember Erichthonius.

TUTOR
Whom first of thy high race the earth brought forth.

CREUSA
To him while yet an infant Pallas gave-

TUTOR
What? Thy slow preface raises expectation.

CREUSA
Two drops of blood that from the Gorgon fell.

TUTOR
And on the human frame what power have these?

CREUSA
The one works death, the other heals disease.

TUTOR

In what around the infant's body hung?

CREUSA
Enclosed in gold: he gave them to my father.

TUTOR
At his decease then they devolved to thee?

CREUSA
Ay, and I wear it as a bracelet; look.

TUTOR
Their double qualities how temper'd, say.

CREUSA
This drop, which from her hollow vein distill'd,-

TUTOR
To what effect applied? What is its power?

CREUSA
Medicinal, of sovereign use to life.

TUTOR
The other drop, what faculties hath that?

CREUSA
It kills, the poison of the Gorgon dragons.

TUTOR
And dost thou bear this gore blended in one?

CREUSA
No, separate; for with ill good mixes not.

TUTOR
O my dear child, thou hast whate'er we want.

CREUSA
With this the boy shall die, and thou shalt kill him.

TUTOR
Where? How? 'Tis thine to speak, to dare be mine.

CREUSA
At Athens, when he comes beneath my roof.

TUTOR
I like not this; what I proposed displeased.

CREUSA
Dost thou surmise what enters now my thoughts?

TUTOR
Suspicion waits thee, though thou kill him not.

CREUSA
Thou hast judged well: a stepdame's hate is proverb'd.

TUTOR
Then kill him here; thou mayst disown the deed.

CREUSA
My mind ev'n now anticipates the pleasure.

TUTOR
Thus shalt thou meet thy husband's wiles with wiles

CREUSA
This shalt thou do: this little golden casket
Take from my hand, Minerva's gift of old;
To where my husband secretly prepares
The sacrifice, bear this beneath thy vest.
That supper ended, when they are to pour
Libations to the gods, thou mayst infuse
In the youth's goblet this: but take good heed,
Let none observe thee; drug his cup alone
Who thinks to lord it in my house: if once
It pass his lips, his foot shall never reach
Illustrious Athens: death awaits him here.
She gives him the casket.

TUTOR
Go thou then to the hospitable house
Prepared for thy reception: be it mine,
Obedient to thy word to do this deed.
Come then, my aged foot, be once more young
In act, though not in years, for past recall
That time is fled: kill him, and bear him forth.
Well may the prosperous harbour virtuous thought;
But when thou wouldst avenge thee on thy foes,
There is no law of weight to hinder thee.

CCLVIII

[They both go out.]

CHORUS
Daughter of Ceres, Trivia hear,
Propitious regent of each public way
Amid the brightness of the day,
Nor less when night's dark hour engenders fear;
The fulness of this goblet guide
To check with death this stripling's pride,
For whom my queen this fatal draught prepares,
Tinged with the Gorgon's venom'd gore:
That seat, which mid Erechtheus' royal heirs
His pride claims, it shall claim no more:
Never may one of alien blood disgrace
The imperial honours of that high-born race!
Should not this work of fate succeed,
Nor the just vengeance of my queen prevail;
Should this apt time of daring fail,
And hope, that flatters now, desert the deed;
Slaughter shall other means afford,
The strangling cord, the piercing sword;
For rage from disappointed rage shall flow,
And try each. various form of death;
For never shall my queen this torment know;
Ne'er while she draws this vital breath,
Brook in her house that foreign lords should shine,
Clothed with the splendours of her ancient line.
Thou whom the various hymn delights,
Then thy bright choir of beauteous dames among,
Dancing the stream's soft brink along,
Thou seest the guardian of thy mystic rites,
Thy torch its midnight vigils keep,
Thine eye meantime disdaining sleep;
While with thee dances Jove's star-spangled plain.
And the moon dances up the sky:
Ye nymphs, that lead to grots your frolic train,
Beneath the gulfy founts that lie:
Thou gold-crown'd queen, through night's dark regions
fear'd, And thou, her mother, power revered,
How should I blush to see this youth unknown!
This Delphic vagrant, hope to seize the throne.
You, who the melting soul to move,
In loose, dishonest airs the Muse employ
To celebrate love's wanton joy,
The joy of unallow'd, unholy love,

CCLIX

See how our pure and modest law
Can lavish man's lewd deeds o'erawe!
Ye shameless bards, revoke each wanton air;
No more these melting measures frame;
Bid the chaste muse in Virtue's cause declare,
And mark man's lawless bed with shame!
Ungrateful is this Jove-descended lord;
For, his wife's childless bed abhorr'd,
Lewdly he courts the embrace of other dames, A
nd with a spurious son his pride inflames.

(An ATTENDANT of CREUSA enters.)

ATTENDANT
Athenian dames, where shall I find our queen,
The daughter of Erechtheus? Seeking her,
This city have I walked around in vain.

LEADER OF THE CHORUS
And for what cause, my fellow-slave? What means
Thy hasty foot? What tidings dost thou bring?

ATTENDANT
We are discover'd; and the rulers here
Seek her, that she may die o'erwhelm'd with stones.

LEADER Ah me! what wouldst thou say?
Are our designs Of secret ruin to this youth disclosed?

ATTENDANT They are; and know, the worst of ills await
you.

LEADER How were our dark devices brought to light?

ATTENDANT The god, that justice might receive no stain
Caused it to triumph o'er defeated wrong.

LEADER How? as a suppliant, I conjure thee, tell me
Of this inform'd, if we must die, more freely
Wish we to die than see the light of heaven.

ATTENDANT Soon as the husband of Creusa left
The god's oracular shrine, this new-found son
He to the feast, and sacrifice prepared
To the high gods, led with him. Xuthus then

Went where the hallow'd flame of Bacchus mounts,
That on each rock's high point the victim's blood
Might flow, a grateful offering for his son
Thus recognised, to whom he gave in charge,
"Stay thou, and with the artist's expert aid
Erect the sheltering tent: my rites perform'd
To the kind gods that o'er the genial bed
Preside, should I be there detain'd too long,
Spread the rich table to my present friends."
This said, he led the victims to the rocks.
Meanwhile with reverent heed the son 'gan rear
On firm supporters the wide tent, whose sides
No masonry require, yet framed to exclude
The mid-day sun's hot beams, or his last rays
When sinking in the west: the lengthen'd lines
Equally distant comprehend a square
Of twice five thousand feet (the skilful thus
Compute it), space to feast (for so he will'd)
All Delphi: from the treasures of the god
He took the sacred tapestry, and around
Hung the rich shade, on which the admiring eye
Gazes with fix'd delight: first over head,
Like a broad pennon spread the extended woof,
Which from the Amazonian spoils the son
Of Jove, Alcides, hallow'd to the god;
In its bright texture interwov'n a sky
Gathering the stars in its ethereal round,
While downwards to the western wave the sun
His steeds declines, and to his station high
Draws up the radiant flame of Hesperus.
Meanwhile the Night robed in her sable stole,
Her unreign'd car advances; on her state
The stars attend; the Pleiads mounting high,
And with his glittering sword Orion arm'd;
Above, Arcturus to the golden pole
Inclines; full-orb'd the month-dividing moon
Takes her bright station, and the Hyades
Marked by the sailor: distant in the rear,
Aurora ready to relume the day,
And put the stars to flight. The sides were graced
With various textures of the historic woof,
Barbaric arguments; in gallant trim
Against the fleet of Greece the hostile fleet
Rides proudly on. Here monstrous forms portray'd
Human and brutal mix'd: the Thracian steeds
Are seized, the hinds, and the adventurous chase

Of savage lions: figured nigh the doors,
Cecrops, attended by his daughter's, roll'd
His serpent train: in the ample space within
He spread the festal table, richly deck'd
With golden goblets. Now the herald walk'd
 His round, each native that inclined to grace
The feast inviting: to the crowded tent
They hasten, crown'd with garlands, and partake
The exquisite repast. The pleasured sense
Now satiate, in the midst an old man stood,
Officious in his ministry, which raised
Much mirth among the guests; for from the urns
He fill'd the lavers, and with fragrant myrrh
Incensed the place; the golden bowls he claim'd
His charge. When now the jocund pipes 'gan breathe
Harmonious airs, and the fresh goblet stood
Ready to walk its round, the old man said,
"Away with these penurious cups, and bring
Capacious bowls; so shall you quickly bathe
Your spirits in delight." With speed were brought
Goblets of gold and silver: one he took
Of choicer frame; and, seemingly intent
To do his young lord honour, the full vase
Gave to his hands, but in the wine infused
A drug of poisonous power, which, it is said,
His queen supplied, that the new son no more
Might view the light of heav'n; but unobserved
He mix'd it. As the youth among the rest
Pour'd the libation, 'mid the attendant slaves
Words of reproach one utter'd: he, as train'd
Within the temple and with expert seers,
Deem'd them of evil omen, and required
Another goblet to be filled afresh-
The former a libation to the god,
He cast upon the ground, instructing all
To pour, like him, the untasted liquor down.
Silence ensued: the sacred bowls we fill
With wines of Byblos; when a troop of doves
Came fluttering in, for undisturb'd they haunt
The dome of Phoebus: in the floating wine
They dipp'd their bills to drink, then raised their heads,
Gurgling it down their beauteous-plumed throats.
Harmless to all the spilt wine, save to her
That lighted where the youth had pour'd his bowl:
She drank, and straight convulsive shiverings seized
Her beauteous plumes; around in giddy rings

She whirl'd, and in a strange and mournful note
Seem'd to lament: amazement seized the guests,
Seeing the poor bird's pangs: her heart heaved thick,
And stretching out her scarlet legs, she died.
 Rending his robes, the son of Phoebus given
Sprung from the table, and aloud exclaim'd,-
"What wretch design'd to kill me? Speak, old man:
Officious was thy ministry; the bowl
I from thy hand received." Then straight he seized
His aged arm, and to the question held him,
As in the fact discover'd: he thus caught,
Reluctant and constrain'd, own'd the bold deed,
The deadly goblet by Creusa drugg'd.
Forth from the tent, the guests attending, rush'd
The youth announced by Phoebus, and amid
The Pythian regents says,-"O hallow'd land!
This stranger dame, this daughter of Erechtheus
Attempts my life by poison." Then decreed
The Delphian lords (nor did one voice dissent)
That she should die, my mistress, from the rock
Cast headlong, as the deed was aim'd against
A sacred life, and impiously presumed
This hallow'd place with murder to profane.
Demanded by the state, she this way bends
Her wretched steps. Unhappy to this shrine
She came through fond desire of children; here,
Together with her hopes, her life is lost.

CHORUS
None, there is none, from death no flight,
To me no refuge; our dark deed
Betray'd, betray'd to open light;
The festive bowl, with sprightly wine that flow'd
Mix'd with the Gorgon's viperous blood,
An offering to the dead decreed,
All is betray'd to light: and I,
Cast headlong from the rock, must die.
What flight shall save me from this death,
Borne on swift pinions through the air,
Sunk to the darksome cave beneath,
Or mounted on the rapid car?
Or shall the flying bark unfurl its sails?
Alas, my queen, no flight avails,
Save when some god's auspicious power
Shall snatch us from the dangerous hour.
Unhappy queen, what pangs shall rend thy heart!

Shall we, who plann'd the deathful deed,
Be caught within the toils we spread,
While justice claims severe her chast'ning part?

[CREUSA rushes in.]

CREUSA
I am pursued, ye faithful females, doom'd
To death: the Pythian council hath decreed it:
My life is forfeited.

LEADER OF THE CHORUS
Unhappy lady,
We know the dreadful ills that close thee round.

CREUSA
Ah, whither shall I fly? From instant death
Scarce hath my foot sped hither, from my foes
By stealth escaping.

LEADER
Whither wouldst thou fly, But to this altar?

CREUSA
What will that avail me?

LEADER
To kill a suppliant there the law forbids.

CREUSA
But by the law I perish.

LEADER
If their hands Had seized thee.

CREUSA
Dreadful contest, with drawn swords
They hastily advance.

LEADER
Now take thy seat
At the altar: shouldst thou die ev'n there, thy blood
Will call the vengeance of the god on those
That spilt it: but our fortune we must bear.

(She takes refuge at the altar as ION, guards, and
Delphians enter.)

ION
Bull-visaged sire Cephisus, what a viper
Hast thou produced? a dragon from her eyes
Glaring pernicious flame. Each daring deed
Is hers: less venomous the Gorgon's blood,
With which she purposed to have poison'd me.
Seize her, that the Parnassian rocks may tease
Those nice-adjusted ringlets of her hair,
As down the craggy precipice she bounds.
Here my good genius saved me, e'er I came
To Athens, there beneath my stepdame's wiles
To fall; amid my friends thy fell intents
Have I unravell'd, what a pest to me,
Thy hate how deadly: had thy toils inclosed me
In thine own house, thou wouldst at once have sent me
With complete ruin to the shades below.
But nor the altar nor Apollo's shrine Shall save thee.
Pity, might her voice be heard,
Would rather plead for me and for my mother,
She absent, yet the name remains with me.
Behold that sorceress; with what art she wove
Wile after wile; the altar of the god
Impress'd her not with awe, as if secure.
No vengeance waited her unhallow'd deeds.

CREUSA
I charge thee, kill me not, in my own right,
And in the god's, whose suppliant here I stand.

ION
What right hast thou to plead Apollo's name?

CREUSA
My person hallow'd to the god I offer.

ION
Yet wouldst thou poison one that is the god's.

CREUSA
Thou wast no more Apollo's, but thy father's.

CCLXV

ION
I have been, of a father's wealth I speak.

CREUSA
And now I am: thou hast that claim no more.

ION
But thou art impious: pious were my deeds.

CREUSA
As hostile to my house, I would have kill'd thee.

ION
Did I against thy country march in arms?

CREUSA
And more; thou wouldst have fired Erechtheus' house.

ION
What torch, what brands, what flames had I prepared?

CREUSA
There wouldst thou fix, seizing my right by force.

ION
The land which he possess'd, my father gave me.

CREUSA What claim hath there the race of Aeolus?

ION
He was its guardian, not with words but arms.

CREUSA
Its soldier then; an inmate, not its lord.

ION
Wouldst thou, through fear of what might happen, kill me?

CREUSA
Lest death should be my portion, if not thine.

ION
Childless thou enviest that my father found me.

CREUSA
And wilt thou make a childless house thy spoil?

ION
Devolves my father then no share to me?

CREUSA
His shield, his spear; be those thine heritage.

ION
Come from the altar, quit that hallow'd seat.

CREUSA
Instruct thy mother, whosoe'er she be.

ION Shalt thou unpunish'd meditate my death?

CREUSA
Within this shrine if thou wilt murder me.

ION
What pleasure mid these sacred wreaths to die?

CREUSA
We shall grieve one, by whom we have been grieved.

ION
Strange, that the god should give these laws to men,
Bearing no stamp of honour, nor design'd
With provident thought: it is not meet to place
The unrighteous at his altars; worthier far
To be chased thence; nor decent that the vile
Should with their touch pollute the gods: the good,
Oppress'd with wrongs, should at those hallow'd seats
Seek refuge: ill beseems it that the unjust
And just alike should seek protection there.

(As ION and his followers are about to tear CREUSA
from the altar, the PRIESTESS of Apollo enters from the
temple.)

PRIESTESS
Forbear, my son, leaving the oracular seat,
I pass this pale, the priestess of the god,
The guardian of the tripod's ancient law,

CCLXVII

Call'd to this charge from all the Delphian dames.

ION
Hail, my loved mother, dear, though not my parent.

PRIESTESS
Yet let me have the name, 'tis grateful to me.

ION
Hast thou yet heard their wily trains to kill me?

PRIESTESS
I have; but void of mercy thou dost wrong.

ION
Should I not ruin those that sought my life?

PRIESTESS
Stepdames to former sons are always hostile.

ION
And I to stepdames ill intreated thus.

PRIESTESS
Be not, this shrine now leaving for thy country.

ION
How, then, by thy monition should I act?

PRIESTESS
Go with good omens, pure to Athens go.

ION
All must be pure that kill their enemies.

PRIESTESS
So do not thou: attentive mark my words.

ION
Speak: from good will whate'er thou say'st must flow.

PRIESTESS
Seest thou the vase I hold beneath mine arm?

ION I see an ancient ark entwined with wreaths.

PRIESTESS
In this long since an infant I received thee.

ION
What say'st thou? New is thy discourse and strange.

PRIESTESS
In silence have I kept them: now I show them.

ION
And why conceal'd, as long since thou received'st me?

PRIESTESS
The god would have thee in his shrine a servant.

ION
Is that no more his will? How shall I know it?

PRIESTESS
Thy father shown, he sends thee from this land.

ION
Hast thou preserved these things by charge, or how?

PRIESTESS
It was the god that so disposed my thought.

ION
With what design? Speak, finish thy discourse.

PRIESTESS
Ev'n to this hour to keep what then I found.

ION
What gain imports this to me, or what loss?

PRIESTESS
There didst thou lie wrapp'd in thy infant vests.

ION
Thou hast produced whence I may find my mother.

PRIESTESS
Since now the god so wills, but not before.

ION This is a day of bless'd discoveries.

PRIESTESS
Now take them: o'er all Asia, and the bounds
Of Europe hold thy progress: thou shalt know
These tokens. To do pleasure to the god,
I nurtured thee, my son; now to thy hand
Restore what was his will I should receive
Unbidden, and preserve: for what intent
It was his will, I have not power to say.
That I had these, or where they were conceal'd,
No mortal knew. And now farewell: the love
I bear thee equals what a parent feels.
Let thy inquiries where they ought begin;
First, if some Delphian virgin gave thee birth,
And in this shrine exposed thee; next, if one
Of Greece. From me, and from the god, who feels
An interest in thy fortune, thou hast all.

[She goes into the temple after giving ION the ark.]

ION
Ah me! the moist tear trickles from mine eye,
When I reflect that she who gave me birth,
By stealth espoused, may with like secrecy
Have sold me, to my infant lips her breast
Denied: but in the temple of the god
Without a name, a servile life I led.
All from the god was gracious, but from fortune
Harsh; for the time when in a mother's arms
I in her fondness should have known some joy
Of life, from that sweet care was I estranged,
A mother's nurture: nor less wretched she,
Thus forced to lose the pleasure in her son.
But I will take this vase, and to the god
Bear it, a hallow'd offering; that from thence
I may find nothing which I would not find.
Should she, that gave me being, chance to be
A slave, to find her were a greater ill,
Than to rest silent in this ignorance.
O Phoebus, in thy temple hang I this.
What am I doing? War I not against
The pleasure of the god, who saved for me
These pledges of my mother? I must dare,
And open these: my fate cannot be shunn'd.

(He opens the ark.)

CCLXX

Ye sacred garlands, what have you so long
Conceal'd: ye bands, that keep these precious relics?
Behold the cover of this circular vase;
Its freshness knows no change, as if a god
So will'd; this osier-woven ark yet keeps
Its soundness undecay'd; yet many a year,
Since it contain'd this treasured charge, has pass'd.

CREUSA
What an unhoped-for sight do I behold!

ION
I thought thou long hadst known to keep thee silent.

CREUSA
Silence is mine no more; instruct not me;
For I behold the ark, wherein of old I laid thee,
O my son, an infant babe;
And in the caves of Cecrops, with the rocks
Of Macrai roof'd, exposed thee: I will quit
This altar, though I run on certain death.

ION
Seize her; for by the impulse of the god
She leaves the sculptured altar: bind her bands.

CREUSA
Instantly kill me, so that I embrace
This vase, and thee, and these thy conceal'd pledges.

ION
Is not this strange? I take thee at thy word.

CREUSA Not strange: a friend thou by thy friends art
found.

ION
Thy friend! Yet wouldst thou kill me secretly.

CREUSA
My son: if that to parents is most dear.

ION
Forbear thy wiles; I shall refute them well.

CREUSA
Might I but to come to what I wish, my son!

ION
Is this vase empty, or contains it aught?

CREUSA
Thy infant vests, in which I once exposed thee.

ION
And wilt thou name them to me, ere thou see them?

CREUSA
If I recount them not, be death my meed.

ION
Speak then: thy confidence hath something strange.

CREUSA
A tissue, look, which when a child I wrought.

ION
What is it? Various are the works of virgins.

CREUSA
A slight, unfinish'd essay of the loom.

ION
What figure wrought? Thou shalt not take me thus.

CREUSA
A Gorgon central in the warp enwoven-

ION
What fortune haunts me, O supreme of gods!

CREUSA
And like an aegis edged with serpents round.

ION
Such is the woof, and such the vest I find.

CREUSA
Thou old embroidery of my virgin bands!

ION
Is there aught else besides this happy proof?

CREUSA
Two dragons, an old work, their jaws of gold.

ION
The gift of Pallas, who thus nurtures children?

CREUSA
Emblems of Erichthonius of old times.

ION
Why? for what use? Explain these works of gold.

CREUSA
For ornaments to grace the infant's neck.

ION
See, here they are; the third I wish to know.

CREUSA
A branch of olive then I wreathed around thee,
Pluck'd from that tree which from Minerva's rock
First sprung; if it be there, it still retains
Its verdure: for the foliage of that olive,
Fresh in immortal beauty, never fades.

ION
O my dear mother! I with joy behold thee.
With transport 'gainst thy cheek my cheek recline.

[They embrace.]

CREUSA
My son, my son, far dearer to thy mother
Than yon bright orb (the god will pardon me) ,
Do I then hold thee in my arms, thus found
Beyond my hopes, when in the realms below,
I thought thy habitation 'mong the dead?

ION
O my dear mother, in thy arms I seem
As one that had been dead to life return'd.

CREUSA
Ye wide-expanded rays of heavenly light,
What notes, what high-raised strains shall tell my joy?
This pleasure whence, this unexpected transport?

ION
There was no blessing farther from my thoughts Than
this, my mother, to be found thy son.

CREUSA
I tremble yet.

ION
And hast thou yet a fear, Holding me, not to hold me?

CREUSA
Such fond hopes
Long time have I renounced.
Thou hallow'd matron,
From whom didst thou receive my infant child?
What bless'd hand brought him to Apollo's shrine?

ION
It was the god's appointment: may our life
To come be happy, as the past was wretched.

CREUSA
Not without tears, my son, wast thou brought forth;
Nor without anguish did my hands resign thee.
Now breathing on thy cheek I feel a joy
Transporting me with heartfelt ecstasies.

ION
The words expressive of thy joys speak mine.

CREUSA
Childless no more, no more alone, my house
Now shines with festive joy; my realms now own
A lord; Erechtheus blooms again; no more
His high-traced lineage sees night darkening round,
But glories in the sun's refulgent beams.

ION
Now let my father, since he's present here,
Be partner of the joy which I have given you.

CCLXXIV

CREUSA
What says my son?

ION
Such, such as I am proved.

CREUSA What mean thy words? Far other is thy birth.

ION
Ah me! thy virgin bed produced me base.

CREUSA
Nor bridal torch, my son, nor bridal dance
Had graced my nuptial rites, when thou wast born.

ION
Then I'm a wretch, a base-born wretch: say whence.

CREUSA
Be witness, thou by whom the Gorgon died,-

ION
What means this adjuration?

CREUSA
Who hast fix'd
High o'er my cave thy seat amid the rocks
With olive clothed.

ION
Abstruse thy words, and dark.

CREUSA
Where on the cliffs the nightingale attunes
Her songs, Apollo-

ION Why Apollo named?

CREUSA Led me in secret to his bed.

ION Speak on;
Thy words import some glorious fortune to me.

CREUSA
Thee in the tenth revolving month, my son,
A secret pang to Phoebus did I bear.

ION
Thy words, if true, are grateful to my soul.

CREUSA
These swathing bands, thy mother's virgin work,
Wove by my flying shuttle, round thy body
I roll'd; but from thy lips my breast withheld,
A mother's nouriture, nor bathed thy bands
In cleansing lavers; but to death exposed thee,
Laid in the dreary cave, to birds of prey
A feast, rent piecemeal by their ravenous beaks.

ION
Cruel, my mother, was thy deed.

CREUSA
By fear Constrain'd, my son, I cast thy life away;
Unwillingly I left thee there to die.

ION
And from my hands unholy were thy death.

CREUSA
Dreadful was then my fortune, dreadful here,
Whirl'd by the eddying blast from misery there
To misery here, and back again to joy:
Her boisterous winds are changed; may she remain
In this repose: enough of ills are past:
After the storm soft breathes a favouring gale.

LEADER
From this example, mid the greatest ills
Never let mortal man abandon hope.

ION
O thou, that hast to thousands wrought a change
Of state ere this, involving them in ills,
And raising them to happiness again;
Fortune, to what a point have I been carried,
Ready to kill my mother, horrid thought!
But in the sun's bright course each day affords
Instruction. Thee, my mother, have I found,
In that discovery bless'd; nor hath my birth
Aught I can blame: yet one thing would I say
To thee alone:-walk this way: to thine ear
In secret would I whisper this, and throw

The veil of darkness o'er each circumstance.
Take heed, my mother, lest thy maiden fault
Seeks in these secret nuptials to conceal
Its fault, then charges on the god the deed;
And, fearing my reproach, to Phoebus gives
A son, to Phoebus whom thou didst not bear.

CREUSA
By her, who 'gainst the giants in her car
Fought by the side of Jove, victorious Pallas,
No one of mortal race is father to thee,
But he who brought thee up, the royal Phoebus.

ION
Why give his son then to another father?
Why say that I was born the son of Xuthus?

CREUSA
Not born the son of Xuthus; but he gives thee,
Born from himself as friend to friend may give
His son, and heir adopted to his house.

ION
True is the god, his tripod else were vain.
Not without cause then is my mind perplex'd.

CREUSA
Hear what my thoughts suggest: to work thee good
Apollo placed thee in a noble house.
Acknowledged his, the rich inheritance
Could not be thine, nor could a father's name;
For I conceal'd my nuptials, and had plann'd
To kill thee secretly: for this the god
In kindness gives thee to another father.

ION
My mind is prompt to entertain such thoughts;
But, entering at his shrine will I inquire
If from a mortal father I am sprung,
Or from Apollo.-Ha! what may this be?
What god above the hallow'd dome unveils
His radiant face that shines another sun?
Haste, let us fly: the presence of the gods
'Tis not for mortals to behold, and live.

[TYRANNOSAURUS REX with miniature wings appears from above. With a wave of his magic wand, TYRANNOSAURUS REX alters the timeline so that none of the plays in this book were ever written. [2]]

NOTES ON ION

---

[1] Greek for *an atom or molecule in which the total number of electrons is not equal to the total number of protons, giving the atom a net positive or negative electrical charge.*

[2] Okay, that's just silly. In the absence of a zeppelin or jetpack, a T-Rex would definitely need very large wings in order to fly, not miniature wings. Up till this point I sort of believed these were real, but you can't just deny physics like that and expect me to suspend my incredulity. Plus, T-Rex definitely wouldn't have a British accent becauseT-Rex never even inhabited the British Isles. *Megalosaurus* and *Metriacanthosaurus* I could picture as possibly having a British accent but not *Tyrannosaurus*. Next time check your facts before you try to pull of a hoax like this.

*By translating a work written in a language he has little to no knowledge of or education in (that is to say, English) J. M. Muldowney confronts the rigid power structures surrounding the practice of translation and causes us to pose such thought provoking questions as "Who can translate?" "Why must I first know a language before translating it?" "Isn't this demand for education just a form of elitism?" and "What were we talking about, anyway?"

Our congratulations if you have gotten this far honestly and without cheating.

For all of you who are reading this because of an unscrupulous circumnavigation of the text, who by your crafty and weaselly ways have subverted the whole purpose of this tome we have but one thing to say…

"You will never truly understand great art if you persist in this lurking, perfunctory accumulation of mere tidbits. Only those who are truly willing to invest focused energy and time will pluck the fruits of this tree."

R. M. MULDOWNEY
J. M. MULDOWNEY

* 9 7 8 0 6 1 5 9 1 7 9 1 7 *